WORKING

WORKING FAITH

Faith-based Organizations and Urban Social Justice

Paul Cloke, Justin Beaumont
and Andrew Williams

First published 2013 by Paternoster
Paternoster is an imprint of Authentic Media Limited
52 Presley Way, Crownhill, Milton Keynes, MK8 0ES.
www.authenticmedia.co.uk

British Library Cataloguing in Publication Data

A catalogue record for this book is available from the British Library

ISBN 978-1-84227-743-0
978-1-78078-311-6 (e-book)

Cover Design by David McNeill (www.revocreative.co.uk)
Printed and bound by CPI Group (UK) Ltd., Croydon, CR0 4YY

Contents

Contents

Contributors

Editors

Paul Cloke, University of Exeter
Justin Beaumont, University of Groningen
Andrew Williams, University of Exeter

About the Contributors

Justin Beaumont is Assistant Professor in the Department of Spatial Planning and Environment at the University of Groningen, the Netherlands. He has developed new enquiries on postsecular cities, as well as faith-based organizations (FBOs) and social justice in urban areas. He is currently undertaking research on problems of the postsecular and ethical turn in urban theory. He is co-editor of *Exploring the Postsecular: The Religious, the Political and the Urban* (with Arie Molendijk and Christoph Jedan; Amsterdam, Brill: 2010), *Postsecular Cities: Space, Theory and Practice* (with Chris Baker; London: Continuum, 2011), *Spaces of Contention: Spatialities of Social Movements* (with Walter Nicholls and Byron Miller; Farnhem: Ashgate, 2013) and *Faith-based Organizations and Exclusion in European Cities* (with Paul Cloke; Bristol: Policy Press, 2012).

Paul Cloke is Professor of Human Geography at the University of Exeter, having previously held chairs in the University of Bristol and University of Wales. Over the last decade he has been involved in collaborative research into ethical geographies, focusing in particular on responses to homelessness, the new politics of ethical consumption and the growing significance of faith-based groups and theo-ethics in contemporary society. He is currently engaged in research on postsecularism and faith-based interventions in a range of welfare and justice arenas. His latest books include: *Swept Up Lives? Re-envisioning the Homeless City* (with Jon May and Sarah Johnsen; Chichester: Wiley-Blackwell, 2010), *Globalizing Responsibility: The Political Rationalities of Ethical Consumption* (with Clive Barnett, Nick Clarke and Alice Malpass; Chichester: Wiley-Blackwell, 2011) and *Faith-based Organisations and Exclusion in European Cities* (with Justin Beaumont; Bristol: Policy Press, 2012).

Maarten Davelaar is Researcher at the Verwey-Jonker Institute in Utrecht, The Netherlands. His background is in Political Science and his research focus includes work on governance issues, urban policies, strategies on homelessness, the participation of socially excluded people, the role of the voluntary sector and faith-based organizations. He was involved in cross-national research on urban social policy. Before joining the Verway–Jonker Institute he worked as a campaigner and project manager at the society for Diaconal Social Work (KSA) in Rotterdam (1993-2001).

Ingemar Elander is Professor of Politics at Örebro University, Sweden. His research interests cover urban governance in a broad sense as exemplified in publications on cities and climate change, environment and democracy, faith-based organizations and social exclusion in European cities, urban partnerships and public health. He is currently involved in a research project on Sustainable Development and Neighbourhood Renewal. He is co-editor of *Urban Governance in Europe* (F. Eckardt and I. Elander; Berlin: BWV Berliner-Wissenschaft, 2009), and co-author of *Faith-based Organisations and Social Exclusion in Sweden* (I. Elander and C. Fridolfsson; Leuven/Den Haag: Acco, 2011).

Charlotte Fridolfsson, PhD, is a Researcher and Lecturer at Linköping University, Sweden. She teaches graduate level and undergraduate courses in Political Science and Gender Studies.

Her research interests include political theory, new social movements, gender politics and cultural studies. She is presently involved in an interdisciplinary research project, Educational Pathways to Power, about the formal and informal education/ learning among Swedish politicians. 'Deconstructing Political Protest' (2006) was her PhD thesis.

Jennifer Klöckner studied Sociology, Psychology and Pedagogy at the University of Cologne, Germany, graduating with a Master of Arts. She was Junior Researcher at the Institute of Sociology at the University of Cologne in 2007, where she participated in the DFG (*Deutsche Forschungsgemeinschaft*) project on impoverished neighbourhoods. She is currently working on her PhD, which focuses on the differences between Islamic and Christian members of faith-based organizations in motivations for volunteering activities. In 2008, she was a Junior Researcher in the EU 7FP FACIT project.

Jon Langford is Associate Leader of St Paul's Church, Salisbury, UK. A qualified youth and community worker, Jon spent twenty-two years working with young people in a variety of settings, including St Paul's, before taking on this new role in 2011. He longs to see the church rise up and take on an active role in reaching the marginalized. Jon is married with two daughters and enjoys times with his family in the countryside, and at the seaside.

Herman Noordegraaf is professor and lecturer for Diaconate at the Protestant Theological University (Amsterdam and Groningen) in The Netherlands. He was one of the founding members and first chair of The Poor Side of The Netherlands anti-poverty movement and remains active in the network and ongoing struggle today. Herman has authored or co-authored a number of articles, books and reports on various social issues and is particularly well known for his biography of Bart der Ligt, the Dutch Christian socialist, anarcho-pacifist and anti-militarist. He has been active in the Dutch Labour Party (PvdA) for several years.

Mike Pears' involvement in urban ministry started in the north Peckham estates in the early 1980s where his understanding of the kingdom of God led him to a long-term involvement with justice issues, especially focusing on unemployment. Following a period in Vancouver, he now lives on a marginal white estate in Bristol, working both with mainline denominations and with new expressions of embedded Christian community. He is currently conducting PhD research on theologies of place and the locational relations of power.

Sam Thomas was a PhD student and Research Assistant in Geography at the University of Exeter, UK, and now works for Exeter YMCA. His PhD thesis is an ethnographic exploration of incarnational expressions of the Christian faith in socio-economically deprived neighbourhoods. Sam is happily married to Caz, and in his spare time can be found tending his allotment or surfing in north Devon.

Andrew Williams is Associate Research Fellow in Geography at the University of Exeter, UK. He is interested in the social and political geographies of the welfare state, homelessness and substance abuse, ethics and care, and the changing role of voluntary and faith-based organizations. His work uses an ethnographic approach to understand the neoliberal contextualization of welfare 'reform' in the UK and elsewhere, and the impacts these changes have had on different people and places.

CHAPTER 1

Faith in Action: Faith-based Organizations, Welfare and Politics in the Contemporary City

Paul Cloke, Sam Thomas, Andrew Williams

The Emerging Significance of FBOs[1]

Faith-based organizations (hereafter FBOs) are playing an increasingly important role in the provision of welfare and care, both locally and as part of wider networks of local global activity. The tensions and opportunities involved in faith-based social action has become an area of growing debate among academic, policy and theological/ecclesial circles. This book does not present a theological account of these debates. Rather, it introduces a series of case studies of FBOs as a means to better understand the practical outworking of faith at work, and to highlight the diverse ethics and politics of FBOs in the contemporary city. In this introductory chapter, we underline the importance of contextualizing the activity of these organizations within wider political-economic and state-society-religion processes.

Faith-in-action reflects a range of scales and spheres of activity. Take, for example, the homelessness 'scene' in a city such as Bristol, where on-street homelessness has over recent years become a visible reminder of the plight of people who have for various reasons fallen through the safety net of the welfare state. Exploration of the subterranean landscapes of homelessness in the city[2] reveals a wide range of non-statutory services that have been established to offer care, support and basic living – provision for homeless people for whom the care of the state was insufficient or inappropriate. Hostels, day centres, soup runs, drug rehab centres and a night shelter provide for the basic needs of marginalized people in times of trouble. Many of these facilities have been established by faith-based (mostly Christian) organizations as a response to an obvious social problem in the city – a response that involves a theological and ethical response to social need.

And it is not just about homelessness. Faith-based organizations (FBOs) have become involved in a wide range of welfare and caring services in the city – providing food banks, employment advice centres, support services for offenders and ex-offenders, youth support services, counselling and guidance centres, educational facilities, pastoral care on late-night city streets, and so on. As Jack Caputo[3] has written:

> If, on any given day, you go into the worst neighborhoods of the inner cities of most large urban centers, the people you will find there serving the poor and needy, expending their lives and considerable talents attending to the least among us, will almost certainly be religious people – evangelicals and penticostalists [sic], social workers with deeply held religious convictions, Christian, Jewish, and Islamic, men and women, priests and nuns, black and white. They are the better angels of our nature. They are down in the trenches, out on the streets, serving the widow, the orphan, and the stranger, while the critics of religion are sleeping in on Sunday mornings.

In one sense, it has always been thus – with some FBOs such as the Salvation Army exhibiting a long-term presence in the provision of social care alongside systems of state provision. However, over the last two or three decades, the FBO phenomenon has been assuming a growing significance, with new organizations and networks springing up to complement the work of more long-standing agencies. Within the broad context of post-Christendom[4] we had become used to the relegation of religion to a position that was subservient to the state, first in terms of a collectivist welfare state in which government took direct responsibility for many aspects of welfare, and then in a more individualist tide of neoliberalism as the state began to withdraw from direct welfare provision, contracting out some of its previous responsibilities and shifting others onto the shoulders of personal and collective citizenship culminating in the politics of the 'Big Society'. This age of neoliberal governance has, however, opened up opportunities for a resurgence of faith-based activity in the public sphere – activity that fills the gap left by the retreating welfare state. FBOs are once again becoming major players in the welfare landscape. Of course, some commentators will see this as simply providing 'public services on the cheap' as faith-motivated people become unwittingly *incorporated* into the political values of the neoliberal state. However, such an evaluation ignores several key factors in the equation, not least the stubborn adherence of many FBOs to their theologically inspired ethical positions involving the practice of *caritas* and *agape* rather than performing as dupes or puppets of government. We can therefore suggest that FBOs might legitimately be regarded (at least in part) as engaging in forms of *resistance* to the excesses and social evils of neoliberalism, bringing alternative 'theo-ethics'[5] into being in the performance of care in a society where government has increasingly lost touch with the practical and emotional needs of local communities.

This renewal of broad public legitimacy for FBO activities is in some ways surprising. Despite the constitutional position enjoyed by the Anglican Church, post-war Britain has witnessed persistent anxieties about the dangers of allowing religious morality and ethics to gain too great a political foothold in public life. Secular political interests have been active in keeping religious involvement in governance at arms' length – a tactic replicated in other spheres, notably that of academic and intellectual knowledge-making. Religion has been demonized by the Anti-God Squad[6] as the cause of the world's worst evils, and more generally it has been comfortably characterized as a relic of superstition whose role in society is steadily dwindling. Yet, religion has ultimately been difficult to hush up, and we can suggest four sets of factors in the UK context which have fanned the flame of religious involvement in social welfare.

First, the very significant traditional association between faith groups and social welfare has developed a long-standing faith presence in the provision of services. Whether it be the long history of church schools, the seemingly timeless presence of services run by organizations such as the Salvation Army and

Barnardo's, or the historic inflection of social politics in religious denominations such as Methodism, faith has never really disappeared from the political landscape. There has been a continuous strand of faith-motivated involvement in social welfare, from the nineteenth-century Christian reformers and philanthropists right up to the present day.

Secondly, the emergence of a 'Third Way' logic in politics in the 1990s[7] represented a turn towards an approach to social justice that sponsored both a philosophical realignment with some religious philosophy, and a series of practical opportunities for a new and more sympathetic involvement of faith groups in the mainstream of political life.[8]

Thirdly, faith groups themselves have actively campaigned for a greater role in social welfare. For example, the Faithworks campaign launched in 2001 called for an end to government discrimination against Christian churches and projects in areas of potential public funding and partnership. The campaign was well received by many prominent members of parliament who spoke in positive terms about the contribution made by all faiths to the well-being of local communities. As a result, new guidelines for funding and partnerships between local authorities and faith groups were introduced.

Fourthly, the impact of immigration on the changing demography of urban areas has led to local and national government enlisting FBOs to deliver services to 'hard-to-reach' communities.[9] More recently, the events of the 2000s have underlined the actual and potential ramifications of extremist religious activity in the politics of protest and resistance. As part of the governmental reaction to high-profile incidents of religious militancy, there has been a strong move to engage with, and to some extent incorporate, a range of faith-based and religious groups into the consultative workings of the state.

The rise of FBOs, then, is only partly attributable to the changing nature of the welfare state. Their positive history and long-standing engagement amongst needy people, their potential contribution to new political philosophies, their lobbying power, and their potentially moderate antidote to religious extremists, all added to the possibility that FBOs could make an effective contribution to tackling social exclusion, rather than just representing the voluntary sector dupes of the neoliberal state.

The Potential Contribution of FBOs

There are two main sets of arguments to suggest that FBOs can contribute in their own right to governance responses to social problems. The most obvious of these is that churches and other religious congregations and networks represent the last remaining vestiges of social capital in many communities. The availability of buildings, social leaders, a capacity for collective action, pools of voluntary labour, and a propensity for charitable giving, together offer very significant potential for social action at a time when other frameworks of communitarianism and voluntarism appear to be on the wane. This potential for social capital often remains unrealized. Sociologists of religion[10] remind us that many religious congregations become preoccupied with inward-looking concerns – maintaining buildings, employing paid workers, upholding traditional church-based organizations and rituals and so on – rather than using their social capital for the good of their community more generally. In such cases, bonding capital is not translated into bridging capital. However, elsewhere faith-based social capital does work centripetally; an outward-looking perspective is often associated with some kind of *spiritual* capital by which the outworking of religious philosophy is made dynamic through spiritual as well as social resources.[11]

The second line of argument is that FBOs can offer positive rationales[12] for inclusion into schemes of social welfare and civic renewal:

1. A *normative rationale* – faith groups have motivational linkages to their communities, bringing belief and persistent presence to bear on community values and identities. These normative values translate from religion to society in the form of ethical impulses – love, joy, peace, charity, justice, equality and so on – and can be harnessed in areas of welfare, community cohesion and ethical citizenship. It can be argued[13] that faith groups have been at the forefront of the development of ethical citizenship, not as an adjunct to the formation of neoliberal citizen subjects, but as a response to the shortcomings of neoliberal individuation. Faith groups, then, can sometimes be seen to offer a holistic commitment to communities, grounded in long-standing local

commitment and presence, and capable of validating and even celebrating diverse expressions of community identity.

2. A *resource rationale* – faith groups have a capacity for organization, mobilizing and training volunteers, and providing venues and funding, all of which present a suitable platform from which to engage with socially marginalized people. Such capacity enables faith groups to be enrolled into some of the top-down strategies of state governance, but is more likely to form the basis of local initiatives that fall outside of formal state-led or state-coordinated activities.

3. A *governance rationale* – faith groups will often have structures of leadership that operate at different scales. They are thus able to combine activities at the national level to represent particular ethical and political views and to promote particular understandings of social exclusion, with local level initiatives. Faith groups can thus offer a ready-made source of community representation, that can be utilized in consultation and partnership exercises that help to 'plug the governance deficit'[14] especially in hard-to-reach and disadvantaged communities.

To these three, we would add a fourth:

4. A *prophetic rationale* – religion is in the business of hope, whether in terms of eschatological promise, or in-the-present transformative theologies of social engagement. It has been argued[15] that the hope vested in the subversive power of spiritual belief is being accessed via three principal manoeuvres of the imagination.[16] First, faith groups are engaging in prophecy in order to nurture, nourish and evoke a consciousness and perception of the dominant culture, so as to energize the community to fresh forms of faithfulness, belief and vitality. Secondly, faith groups are engaging the spiritual interior of social issues as well as their material exterior, thereby introducing an analysis that recognizes that the heart of systems of oppression can be spiritual. It follows that to question the way things are with a vision for the way things should be means addressing and challenging the spiritual interiority of oppression and domina-

tion as well as their outer, more clearly politicized manifestations. Thirdly, faith groups are engaging in discernment, both politically and in terms of alternative spiritual consciousness, thereby sometimes permitting a rupturing of the seemingly hegemonic spaces of the current order, producing new spaces of hope, especially for those enduring oppression and domination.

When surveying the tensions that potentially arise as faith groups become more integrated into formal systems and structures of governance, this last prophetic rationale provides an important framework for understanding. As faith groups become integrated into secularized policy-making and service delivery, there can be significant mismatches in the objectives being pursued and the practices that represent the performance of those objectives. The fear of overt evangelizing and proselytizing is often a key aspect of mutual mistrust in these kinds of integrated partnerships, although there are clear signs that some faith-based groups are now embracing a strategy of postsecular *caritas* in which overt 'we serve you in order to convert you' evangelism is being replaced by a more undemanding form of relational service, with fewer strings attached. More often, tensions appear to arise over an apparent hijacking of the normative religious agenda, and over the incorporation of faith groups into a more professionalized and target-driven way of operating. That is, the practices and values of religious groups can be the first things to go as compromises are made in order to achieve partnership goals within formal governance.

The resources and governance potential of faith groups are, then, often compatible with Third Way politics of governance, but the normative faith values inherent in FBOs are often sources of conflict in such partnerships. We contend that the root of these conflicts may well be found in the prophetic rationale of faith groups. The normative values of faith practices within FBOs can often be tolerated within the partnerships of governance where such values relate to individual and group motivation, and are decoupled from the prophetic imperative. However, where faith values impart a prophetic discernment of the spiritual interiority of oppression and marginalization, there can often be both ideological and practical ruptures in the partnerships of governance as the state and its agents become included in, rather than immunized against, prophetic critique.

FBOs and Neoliberalism

The role of FBOs in welfare provision and political activism has been widely charted.[17] It is clear from these accounts that FBOs operate at national, regional and local scales, and cover a wide range of welfare arenas, including support for children and youth, the elderly, homeless people and asylum seekers and undocumented migrants, and welfare activities relating to housing, poverty and debt, disability and community regeneration.[18] Accounts of FBO activity, however, have tended to be contextualized in terms of one or other of two very significant debates in social science. The first is about neoliberalism – the championing of the free operation of market forces and of the freedom of the individual, packaged up as ideology and policy in the activities of successive governments.[19] Part of the neoliberal project has been to reduce the role of the state, by privatization, deregulation and shrinkage of welfare responsibilities, and the contemporary reorganization of the welfare state has typically been seen as a formative factor in the opening out of renewed opportunities for FBOs in the public realm. As neoliberal governance has led to shrinkage of public sector service provision, so FBOs have become tied into these wider political processes as agencies that can 'fill the gap' left by retreating government activity. As a result, FBOs are often represented as being co-opted into the policies, politics and ethics of market-led individualism – as a pragmatic device by which government can cut its direct costs and still claim that social problems are being dealt with.[20] According to this viewpoint, the enlistment of FBOs into broad partnerships with government merely represents a domestication, and perhaps secularization, of faith, and FBO activities can be assumed to be either entirely in keeping with, or subjugated to reflect, neoliberal values.[21]

This is an argument that needs careful scrutiny. It is certainly the case that FBOs have been caught up in the neoliberal incorporation of voluntary resources to occupy the vacuum of welfare space left behind by retreating central and local government activity. The rolling back of the welfare state in order to shrink the welfare safety net has been accompanied by a rolling out of new discourses of welfare and individual responsibility designed to contain or discipline marginalized and socially excluded people.[22] FBOs, by stepping in to address the needs of those who are caught out by the shrinking welfare safety net, inevitably become entangled in the new political discourses of welfare and responsible citizenship. As a result, FBOs can be represented as 'little platoons . . . in service of neoliberal goals',[23] as using their social capital and rationales for social action in a context where risk and responsibility for welfare is being delegated beyond government, but state control is being extended through regulatory mechanisms (especially performance targets and audits) to ensure that government objectives are being met.

In Britain, successive governments have followed this pathway. The Thatcher government's policy of decentralizing responsibility for welfare delivery onto the voluntary and private sectors coincided with a substantial incorporation of FBOs into the formal welfare system. Congregations and local faith-based groups, as well as more established FBOs (for example, the YMCA, English Churches Housing Group, NCH Action for Children and the Salvation Army) took the opportunity to expand their services in the community via delivery of public service contracts, albeit at the risk that their organizational autonomy would be eroded because of the strings attached to their contractual obligations.[24] The subsequent New Labour administrations continued this trend, although their 'compacts' with the Third Sector did involve a greater recognition both of the inherent strengths of non-statutory organizations in general, and more specifically of the contribution of faith groups in the public sphere.[25] FBOs benefited from their heightened status of 'fitness' for public service, but external and self-imposed regulation continued to suggest a realpolitik of compliance with neoliberal ideologies. The present Coalition government has used the idea of a 'Big Society' as a further prompt to the rolling back of welfare provision, and in so doing has marshalled FBO activities in support and legitimation of a conservative communitarian vision. In practical terms, the 'Big Society' idea seems paradoxical to many Third Sector organizations. On the one hand, the 'Big Society' appears to endorse their involvement in public service provision; on the other hand, the pursuit of 'smaller' government through accompanying austerity measures in public spending has resulted in the loss of previously available support funds for Third Sector activities. So while some FBOs understand the 'Big Society' as a significant recognition of what they are already doing in their social activism, others are concerned that its explicit urging of Christians to recolonize the secular public arena represents a suffocating and colluding return to the conditions of pseudo-Christendom, in which revolutionary Christian hope will be translated into some kind of passive acceptance of current political orthodoxies.[26]

FBOs and Resistance to Neoliberal Politics

Despite these indications of potential political collusion by FBOs with neoliberal politics, the idea of FBOs as 'little platoons' in the service of neoliberal governance has been strongly challenged on at least three grounds.[27] First, we need to understand neoliberalism as something other than a static endgame, or as a framework that is parachuted in a top-down manner onto particular spatial or temporal contexts. Rather neoliberalism is a much more dynamic and complex process; a precarious and messy fabrication of forms and practices that is open to contestation and resistance. In particular, it has been argued that neoliberalism has come about through particular combinations of the religious and the secular, and that the ways in which these different elements are co-constituted can just as easily lead to a contestation of the secular by the religious as to a co-option of the religious by the secular. So, the idea that FBOs are somehow inevitably captured by neoliberal goals tends towards a rather uncritical exaggeration of the ways in which governmental targets, objectives and organizational cultures are realized, normalized and internalized in the day-to-day workings of those FBOs. Rather, neoliberalism seems to rely on a series of everyday practices and performances that cannot be controlled by top-down ideology, and FBOs have at least the potential for day-to-day practices and performances that reflect the logics and emotions of faith-based ethics rather than ideological realpolitik. David Conradson's research on spaces of faith-based welfare[28] warns against any interpretation of FBOs solely as objects and subjects of governmental normalization and neoliberal subjectification. Rather, he calls for closer scrutiny of the organizational and ethical precepts that have helped to shape particular faith-based practice from charity to social and skills-based development. In this way, he argues, activities that for some analysts might resemble right-of-centre neoliberalism may actually turn out to be something rather different, associated instead with sets of theologically inspired ethics relating to wholeness, justice and human dignity:

> One might detect apparent echoes of right-of-centre arguments about service-induced dependency here, perhaps suggesting a degree of organisational capture by the wider neo-liberal social policy culture. However, interviews with staff instead suggested that this position was derived from a social work emphasis on client empowerment and various strains of liberation theology. This left-of-centre mix of thought was informing a particular evolution in the Mission's practice of voluntary welfare provision.[29]

The message from this research is clear; we need to be extremely careful not to assume that the locally contextualized practices of FBO welfare and caring activities merely mirror the neoliberal environment in which those contexts are set. Moreover, we need to be alert to the possibility that the top-down conditions of neoliberalism is being subverted by the agency of staff, volunteers and clients in services run by FBOs. Such agency reflects the ways in which policy can be interpreted and reinterpreted, common values can be negotiated, imposed identities can be resisted, and decisions on 'the right thing to do' can be taken on the spot rather than according to some previously consumed rule book.[30] In these simple ways, practitioners can bend official policy and practice towards different outcomes, develop alternative strategies in response to specific situations, or even disengage from official prescriptions of practice in order to develop new relationships with clients. These tactics of resistance may be invisible to the overarching neoliberal perspective, but they are capable of transforming subjectivities, identities and outcomes in the services concerned.

Secondly, it seems important to question any assumption that top-down neoliberal government will produce a *singular* set of logics and outcomes amongst FBOs.[31] Research into the scope of FBO activity in the UK[32] suggests that FBOs operate in complex roles that defy easy stereotyping as either 'insider' pseudo-governmental partners, plugging the gap caused by the retreat of the welfare state, or small 'outsider' charities lacking the resources to become part of joined-up welfare provision. Rather, FBOs represent a spectrum of different faith-based involvements in different domains of welfare. Moreover, different FBOs have responded differently to the tactical question of how to present themselves in the public sphere of service provision. At the national level, for example, some FBOs (such as Barnardo's) have presented themselves as professional and secularized organizations in order to avoid any accusation of being sectarian. Others, however, have maintained their religious character, albeit in different ways; thus Faithworks adopts an unreservedly Christian positioning in order to act as a faith-centred player in public debates on social policy and action, while the Salvation Army presents their staunchly Christian approach alongside more postsecular ideas of unconditional and non-proselytizing service.

Equally, FBOs such as the Salvation Army and the Church Urban Fund, who have been willing to use state funding for their activities, have at the same time been publicly active in contesting contemporary social conservatism. More generally, many campaigning FBOs have exhibited an obdurate streak of prophetic radicalism that has placed structural interpretations of poverty and debt onto the public agenda. Some of the most significant political and ethical protests of recent times have not only been organized in conjunction with FBOs such as Christian Aid, but have been focused on ethically inspired demands to Drop the Debt, Make Poverty History, Cut the Carbon and so on. In these ways and others, it seems inadequate to judge FBO activity simply in terms of co-option into neoliberal governance. There often seems to be a disconnection between the commentaries, beliefs and practices of FBOs that are responding to social issues and the extant neoliberal and neoconservative ideologies that supposedly shape the welfare environment, and the supposed dichotomy between 'insider' and 'outsider' organizations proves to be an inadequate model with which to reflect the complex relationships between FBOs and the policies of central and local government.

Overall, then, there are significant questions to be answered before FBOs can be universally tarred with the brush of neoliberalism. It is clear that the co-constitutive relationships between religion and neoliberal governance have been marked not by simple acquiescence, but by a series of challenges by FBOs to the political logic of how welfare has been conceived and discussed at government level. Whilst it is undeniable that FBO activities have blossomed under neoliberal conditions, recent research[33] has indicated that faith has embodied a resistance to neoliberalism in at least three ways:

1. *In the motivations that underpin much FBO involvement in welfare provision, and the types of need addressed therein.* Faith groups commonly become active in order to meet the needs of people from whom the state has chosen to withdraw its support (for example, homeless people and undocumented migrants). These welfare services represent a critique of the injustice of socio-economic and political policies of neoliberalism, and are motivated by and performed in the light of that critique. Furthermore, the ethical citizenship inspired in these spaces of care can run counter to the idealized neoliberal citizen-subject of consumer, entrepreneur and responsible individual.

2. *In the rejection of judgements about who deserves what.* FBOs often suspend the moralistic distinction between deserving and undeserving clients and recipients of care, choosing rather to affirm a more unconditional form of social welfare based on ethics of universality and sociality with the other. The unconditional performance of care by frontline FBO actors often serves to subvert rather than reinforce government discourses of neoliberal welfare.

3. *In the willingness to campaign and protest.* Counter to criticisms that prominent FBOs have eschewed structural political critique and become content with a reinforcement of neoliberal ideas of 'active citizenship',[34] the prophetic calling of faith-motivated actors to speak truth to power and to stand with the

poor, vulnerable and marginalized, seems alive and well. Part of what is distinctive about FBOs that challenge neoliberal politics is their reliance on foundational theo-ethics to map out new spaces of hope.

As Andrew Williams et al.[35] conclude:

> In these ways, the interconnections between faith, secularism and neoliberalism are much more fragmented and variegated than has been argued elsewhere. The ethical agency of organisations and individuals involved in the FBO sector cannot simply be circumscribed by the structures and ideologies of neoliberal government, and the connection of religion to contemporary capitalism defies straightforward characterisation as simply a legitimising force complicit in the powers that be . . . Even within the contractual arena of neoliberal governance, the frontline performance of care can often be understood as a site of subversion. In co-producing neoliberal structures of welfare governance, the ethical performance of staff and volunteers in FBOs rework and interpret the values and judgements supposedly normalised in the regulatory frameworks of government policy, bringing alternative philosophies of care into play.

FBOs, then, offer possibilities far beyond any perceived role as the little platoons of neoliberalism. Indeed, they may well represent one of the most significant sites within which neoliberal tendencies are subject to resistance and subversion.

FBOs and the Postsecular

The second context in which FBOs tend to be evaluated is that of postsecularism. A typical response to the activities of FBOs has often been to invoke a secular/religious divide in the evaluation of the role of religion in the public arena. By and large, from the secular side of that divide the work of FBOs has been treated with suspicion, based around the assumption that religious people will always be motivated primarily by an evangelistic urge to convert others to their beliefs and practices. Accordingly, from this perspective the analytical instinct has been to assume that FBOs are principally operating in order to proselytize. For this reason, the participation of FBOs in care and welfare issues has sometimes been interpreted as loaded and self-serving, with participants imagined as creating a particular kind of moral identity for themselves whilst attempting to capture marginalized people in the web of religious belief that pervades FBO activity.

It is worth noting that from the religious 'side' of this divide there have also been suspicions about socially active faith;[36] in Christian theology and practice, for example, 'evangelical' and 'liberal' positions have been adopted in order to express different, and sometimes mutually antagonistic, views about the significance of doing 'good works' in the world rather than more specifically 'spreading the gospel'. Of course, all such binaries obscure the detailed nuances involved in different forms of religious evangelism, which rarely conforms to simplistic stereotypes of Bible-bashing or being nice to people. Indeed there has been a gradual acceptance that biblical theology invokes, rather than being threatened by, the practice of justice, charity and love for neighbours. Nevertheless, there are important internal discussions within faith networks about the degree to which social action should be geared towards the narrating and performing of new spiritual hope as well as more material and practical care. These issues often revolve around the issue of whether serving marginalized people is performed in such a way as to make demands upon them (for example, by hearing faith messages, or participating in faith rituals) or whether such service can be without strings, as a simple demonstration of unconditional care.[37]

These polarized responses to the involvement of faith-motivated groups in social welfare and justice need to be carefully reviewed and revised in the light of increasingly significant ideas about post-secularism.[38] As Paul Cloke and Justin Beaumont have noted in their study of non-statutory welfare services in the city:

> Many of these services are organised by FBOs, with a specifically Christian ethos, yet most have opened out an opportunity for people who are not motivated by religious faith to join in with the wider praxis of providing care and support to socially marginalised people . . . The result is that there has been a coming-together of citizens who might previously have been divided by differences in theological, political or moral principles – a willingness to work

15

together to address crucial social issues in the city, and in so doing to put aside other frameworks of difference involving faith and secularism.[39]

This potential for 'postsecular rapprochement'[40] does not imply any notion of an epochal shift from the secular age to a postsecular age in which secular frameworks of public society have somehow been overthrown by a renewed set of religious influences. As has been make clear elsewhere,[41] religion has had a geographically varied but nevertheless consistent place within late modern capitalism, and so secularism has always involved some degree of domesticated or incorporated religion in society. Rather, these signs of postsecular rapprochement might usefully be understood as indicating some of the limitations of the secularization thesis rather than marking its demise, and the significance of ideas about postsecularism is more to do with tracing new interconnections between diverse religious, humanist and secularist positions and motivations in the dynamic geographies of the city. So what is being suggested in the postsecular context is that emergent spheres of social action over the past two or three decades have sometimes reflected a particular form of 'crossing-over' in the public arena between the religious and the secular. Previously assumed divides between the secular (=public) and the religious (=private) are being challenged and rendered permeable, and the current mix of neoliberal government and post-political public engagement is opening out new opportunities for both professional and voluntary social participation that transcends the secular/religious divide.

We should emphasize immediately here that recent research on FBOs in the UK[42] demonstrates that FBOs differ significantly in terms of ethos and approach as well as in the ways in which they respond to the dynamic environment of their activities. Clearly some FBOs function primarily to support their own faith networks, performing a duty of care to support or provide culturally relevant services for same-faith groups of people. Other FBOs, however, transcend these same-faith boundaries in different ways. For example, some FBOs have chosen to present themselves to the public using an explicitly *professional* image, even to the extent of reducing the emphasis on their faith ethos in order to present themselves to clients and funders as efficient and open to all in a particular sector. Faith ethos in such cases can variously be maintained as part of the public image (as in the rebranding of the Christian Nationwide Festival of Light as 'Care'), kept largely in the background (as in Barnardo's – a Christian FBO caring for children), or replaced by wider humanitarian principles that invite secular as well as faith-motivated support and participation (such as in the relaunching of the Grooms-Shaftesbury FBO, caring for people with disabilities, as 'Livability' in order to achieve a more all-embracing appeal). Elsewhere, FBOs have deliberately entered into partnerships with other secular and multifaith interests to form more avowedly *postsecular* liaisons, such as London Citizens – a broad-based alliance of faith-related as well as labour, educational and community-based organizations campaigning on a range of social justice issues.[43] Nor should it be forgotten that alongside these organizational perspectives, there is a significant role for individual professionals and volunteers in bringing together the religious and the secular in different settings. The embodiment of service and care for clients will be strongly influenced by individual performativity which may relate to faith motivation, but which due to differences in personality and circumstances is likely to emerge unevenly and cannot therefore be predicted by the ethos and the precepts of the organization concerned.

FBOs and Crossing Over the Secular/Religious Divide

The significance of these postsecular characteristics for an understanding of FBO activities is three-fold: they suggest some significant changes in current thinking about what previously has divided the secular and the religious; they open up real and important possibilities for more crossover (both discursive and practical) between the secular and the religious; and they point to a role in some potentially new and exciting geographies emerging in the city.

1. Changes in secular and faith-related thinking

The potency of ideas about postsecularism lies in recognizing important shifts in both secular and religious thinking that are mutually disposed towards greater degrees of rapprochement. These themes are detailed elsewhere[44] but can be summarized in terms of two waves of change. First there has been a critical debate about the achievements and outcomes of secularism as a result of which some secular opinion has been attracted into explorations of different forms of socio-political futures, including those inspired by theological ethics. Philip Blond,[45] for example, has identified key aspects of this critique. These include the tendency for secular society to exclude a public role for religious moderates, leading to a rise in religious fundamentalism; the debasing of democratic politics as market hegemony and individual self-interest have been permitted to envelop welfare and ethics; and the cynical pessimism and lack of hope that have accompanied a secular society that has become increasingly acquisitive, individualized, polarized and vulnerable to market failure. Each of these themes deserves detailed scrutiny, but in sum the overall claim is that secularism's emphasis on the visible / material, and the eschewing of the invisible / spiritual, has erased from the public consciousness the alternative imaginations that inform how individuals and their worlds can be transformed. It is significant that some leading contributors to intellectual debates around the future of materialist socialism (such as Derrida, Deleuze, Badiou and Žižek)[46] have as a consequence been attracted to ideas drawn from religion as prompts to the pursuit of justice and hope in contemporary society. These discourses have also found practical expression. In a recent report by Demos on 'faithful citizens',[47] it was concluded that 'in the UK, new movements of the left have sought to reconnect faith groups with mainstream politics by taking a more positive view of the role of religion in British society'. It is as though the search for hopeful futures beyond post-political pessimism is finding new crossover discourses from writings and events that reflect faith and belief, albeit in fragmented rather than overarching narratives.

It can therefore be argued that the philosophical and political critique of secularization has prompted a series of crossover discourses that potentially represent the common ground on which faith-based and non-faith activity can be allied. In the expansive work of FBOs, we can also begin to see a meeting place between the discursive and praxis arenas of postsecularism; a swirl of moving beyond the secular in the political and practical landscapes of the city, resulting in a positive engagement out of multicultural plural-ities of contemporary life, and reflecting a shift in the self-under-standing of secularist society. However, this shift has only occurred because of a second, collaborative, wave of change involving the increasing importance of faith praxis as a way of discovering faith ethics. In terms of Christian faith, many Christian groups are recog-nizing that biblical theology is inaccessible without a core horizon of practices that make sense of that theology, and the church more generally.[48] In other words, many faith-motivated people are being encouraged to discover the meaning of their faith *as they practise it* rather than as part of an enclosed and individualized relationship with God.

This emphasis on faith praxis has several dimensions: the increasing significance attributed to ethics (and especially virtue ethics) in the practice of faith;[49] an embrace of the need to bring prophetic discernment into the becoming-kingdom of the times, in a conjoining of the eschatological, the ethical and the political; a reduction in the demonization of the 'social gospel', along with an increasing embrace of social action by main-stream evangelical believers; and a greater willingness amongst some faith groups to work with people of other and no religion in order to *do something about* the social evils of the day. It is not suggested here that there has been some kind of totalizing transformation of Christian religion in the UK resulting in a homogeneous positioning of faith groups in urban landscapes of postsecularism. Far from it. It needs to be emphasized that not all faith groups are tuned into ethics of receptive generosity and unconditional service, and indeed that some groups will continue to reflect a pursuit of controlling power over margin-alized people. What can be suggested, though, is an emerging current of faith-motivated activity that is able to contribute to postsecular rapprochement, with an urgency about faith praxis that allows a broader coming together of ethical values and devices through which to serve that can to some extent blur the public/private boundaries of religion and secular action. Faith praxis has begun to move out into the mainstream in such a way as to be welcomed into what was previously assumed to be secular space.

Narratives of 'crossover'

The second aspect of the potency of postsecular ideas relates to the emergence of crossover narratives in society. Jurgen Habermas[50] has differentiated between 'secular' in the sense of an unbelieving person reacting agnostically to religious claims, and 'secularist' polemics expressing negative responses to religious doctrine and action, and seeing no public role for religion. In these terms, he sees the secular as being compatible with a postsecular balance between shared citizenship and respect for cultural difference, and as being open to the discovery, even in religious utterances, of various semantic meanings and personal intuitions that cross over into their secular discourses. We can equally discern within religion a similar mix of negativity and compatibility to the postsecular arena, with the practice of compatibility opening out the possibility of distinct crossover narratives between the secular and the religious. Postsecular rapprochement is therefore founded on the engagement of mutual tolerance across secular/religious boundaries. Habermas argues that the strength of democracy depends on the broad moral stances that emanate from pre-political sources such as religious ways of life; moral stances that do not form normative guidelines, but rather represent significant components in the background ether of political and ethical practices, and providing motivation for these practices. As Paul Cloke and Justin Beaumont have concluded:

> The postsecular, therefore, according to Habermas, acknowledges not only that modern societies should expect religions to persist, but also that society should enter into constructive dialogue with those religions in order to bring about a process of mutual translation in communication between the religious and the secular. Habermas' emphasis here is that the modern liberal state cannot flourish simply by ensuring the conformity of religious communities to a legally defined freedom of expression; rather the democratic state depends on a mode of legitimation that allows for convictions, and as such legitimation requires reasoning that can be accepted by religious citizens and secular citizens alike within a pluralist society.[51]

In other words, something is missing in society that can only be replaced by a complementary learning process in which the secular and the religious involve each other in a postsecular openness to the other.

This idea of postsecular crossover is both challenging and potentially rewarding for faith-motivated groups; challenging because of a fear that faith truths will be diluted as they are assimilated; rewarding because theological ethics can become instructive in the modernization of public consciousness. Habermas reflects these hopes and fears as he considers how theology can become translated into the general sphere and thereby made accessible to all citizens. Theology, he argues, can be impacted in two ways: either the religious canon be stripped of potentially significant concepts as part of the process of postsecularization, or religious concepts will be reconnected with their roots in wider society as new alliances are formed across the secular/religious divide. For FBOs, the challenge of the postsecular is clearly one of whether or not to be involved in this kind of assimilation, requiring crossover mutualities between religious and secular discourses that in turn equip broad-based alliances built on a willingness to focus on ethical sympathies and actions, even if that means setting aside potential moral differences. For some, such tendencies towards assimilation are too great a cross to bear, but for others they are a natural response to the social need that pervades contemporary society.

FBOs and postsecular geographies

The interpretation of faith-based expressions, organizations and practices has often in the past been shaped by the ideological assumptions of the universal secularization thesis. The deployment of postsecular perspectives opens up the possibility of a more sensitive analysis – theoretically, empirically and theologically – of the role of faith-based action within a more holistic view of the city. Geographies of postsecular rapprochement represent a radical departure in the understanding of the contemporary city, allowing access to the differences involving religious praxis that might otherwise be ignored. The potential of postsecular rapprochement is for a reterritorialization of engagement that embodies both an expression of resistance to neoliberal global capitalism, and new traces of energy and hope for social justice.

Such engagements are often likely to be reflected in the emergence of local spaces in which rapprochement occurs – spaces of care, tolerance, reconciliation, ethical agreement, protest and so on – and can be envisaged in a number of forms.

1. Spaces where the occurrence of obvious social need is met by an affective response from the collective ethical and political conscience. Regressive political-economic changes are resulting in deepening injustices, shrinkage of welfare and rising levels of impoverishment, indebtedness and exclusion. These needs in turn are capable of prompting new interventions and crossovers between faith motivated and other actors, creating spaces of intensity, energy and hope for just alternatives.

2. Spaces of direct resistance and subversion, where rapprochement across religious/secular divides focuses on coming together often in the poorest and most marginal spaces of the city to organize or join in with direct provision for the socially excluded. This involves both working inside government funding schemes, but in such a way as to undermine or deflect the neoliberal politics involved, or establishing alternative services using charitable and voluntary resources in ways that contravene the hegemonic ideology.

3. Spaces of voluntaristic or charitable cross-subsidy and solidarity. Ethical projects aimed at welfare, care and social justice often depend for financial backing and voluntary labour on people from other parts of the city, usually the more affluent suburbs where social need rarely presents itself. By providing flows of resource into spaces of care in the marginal areas of cities, these sources of suburban social and spiritual capital develop socio-spatial connectivities that unsettle not only perceived religious/secular boundaries, but also territorial ones.

4. Spaces of ethical identity, where campaigns around particular ethical tropes at a city level (fair trade, sanctuary, living wage and so on) reflect a range of religious and other interests that are brought together to express identities and values, at the heart of which lie significant points of ethical convergence

between theological, ideological and humanitarian concern. In such cases, the conventional neoliberal branding of the city can be challenged or even usurped by a postsecular repositioning of cultural-political identity.

5. Spaces of local reconciliation and tolerance, involving individuals and groups who are working across, or at least problematizing previous divides involving inter-religious, anti-religious or anti-secular tensions. These are everyday sites of embodied performance of identity – religious or otherwise – in which local lived spaces come to represent the potential for new formations of tolerance and assimilation in place of sectarian divides.

These categories are neither mutually exclusive nor exhaustive, but they illustrate both how the contemporary city *is* in places, and how the city *could be*, as postsecular spaces serve as liminal spaces in which citizens are able to journey from previous sectarian certainties into the unknown imagined and material spaces of rapprochement.[52] As Cloke and Beaumont conclude:

> Postsecular partnerships therefore could represent urban laboratories in which elements of self-interest and control are ceded to the greater aim of 'doing something about' social justice and caring for others, and in the process there are possibilities for transformations in ethical discourse and praxis.[53]

The Chapters of this Book

Having established this foundation for the study of FBOs, the remainder of this book is devoted to a series of case studies serving to illustrate the potential of FBOs in different contexts and at different scales. Each is designed to capture the essence and the detail of a particular project, reflecting both the potential and the challenges inherent in the practical outworking of faith at work. The case studies draw on examples from both the UK and from continental Europe, and they reflect a range of scales and spheres of activity.

Our intention here is not to present these case studies as ideal types or exemplars of particular impacts or achievements. Rather, and more modestly, we want these case study chapters to reflect the ordinary and everyday existence and workings of FBOs; some seeking to intervene at a national scale, and others representing a project inspired by and working within a much more local scene. In each case, the FBO concerned is working within a broad context of a neoliberal politics of welfare, and in each case its faith motivation and faith orientation responds to and works alongside the changing relationship between religion and society as suggested by postsecularism. In most cases there is evidence of rapprochement, although this takes different forms in different situations. Such case studies represent a wider invitation to take note of the activities of FBOs in wider society, and to recognize their achievements, and limitations, as part of a more holistic and all-embracing understanding of welfare and care in the city.

CHAPTER 2

Faith-based Action Against Poverty: Christians Against Poverty and Church Action on Poverty

Paul Cloke, Andrew Williams and Sam Thomas

Introduction

In this chapter we examine the faith at work in two rather different Christian organizations dedicated to counteracting poverty in the UK. The organizations share the same initials but represent significantly different approaches. The Christian gospel gives considerable emphasis to the poor. Jesus himself associated with a range of marginalized and excluded people who were otherwise held in low esteem in their society, and his invitation to bring good news to the poor has been an inspiration to those Christians seeking to merge the Jesus narrative with their own walk of faith. Bringing good news to the poor is not, however, simply about the marshalling of time, money and spiritual resources in order to help the least well off. Indeed it resonates ethically with the need to establish suitable interrelations between giver and receiver. Thus, faith-motivated action on poverty needs to be empowering rather than disempowering; it needs to be developed in such a way as to avoid placing donors at the heart of the process (for that risks a prime focus on moralizing the faith-based identity of donors) and it needs to bring hope in such a way that avoids any assumption that those being helped live in hopelessness or passivity. In this way the theological ethics of *agape* and *caritas* can be recaptured in a sense of unconditional love for other human beings, and a recognition that the image of God is in all of us, and that therefore the constraints of poverty constrain us all.[1] To echo the words of Christian Aid:

> Fundamentally, *poverty is disempowerment* – a lack of power to exert personal, economic, political and social freedoms. It follows then that *poverty is political* – not a momentary lack of income that a gift might solve, but a process that results from structural causes. By implication, our work must challenge these structures – and so our fight against poverty must also be political.[2]

This connection between disempowerment and the political has been problematic for some Christians who would prefer to keep political engagement or allegiance separate from their faith. Others with strong political views will at least implicitly often mould their faith through this particular political lens. In such circumstances it can be pragmatic to focus faith-based attention on contemporary situations of need, focusing on the provision of aid to the impoverished without being drawn into the more 'political' work of challenging structures. Such an approach plays well with supporters who want to feel that their money is contributing directly to the well-being of the poor; it also plays well with government who obviously will be much more likely to co-fund programmes of aid provision than political campaigns about the structural underpinnings of poverty. Such campaigns involve treacherous ground, for example the critiquing of welfare policy, or seeking to reform and regulate financial systems seen as integral to the national economy, but which are intimately wrapped up with the causes of indebtedness and economic hardship. There is therefore a very significant debate occurring within and between faith-based organizations about the balance between the strands of their work aimed towards aid provision and political protest. Some of the practical implications of this debate emerge in the following examples, in which two significant and very effective approaches to tackling disempowerment demonstrate rather different strategies for faith-motivated action against poverty.

Christians Against Poverty

Christians Against Poverty (hereafter CAP) is a debt counselling charity that operates over one hundred and fifty regional centres in the UK and envisages growing to some five hundred such centres by 2015. It also operates in Australia and New Zealand, and has plans to expand into other nations. The aim of the charity is to demonstrate the love of God in action by providing sustainable poverty relief to individuals and households suffering from crippling indebtedness. The work of CAP is characterized by two mutually reinforcing strands of activity. Firstly, clients are empowered to help themselves out of poverty by learning vital budgeting skills and by making use of a series of practical services; they are presented with professional debt management, financial education and face-to-face support and encouragement, either in designated centres, or via home visits for clients with restricted accessibility. A simplified payment system (termed a 'CAP Account') is used to develop a tailored budget for the client, and to negotiate on the client's behalf with creditors. Secondly, CAP operates an ethic of relationality, by providing support networks through local churches and thereby offering clients the opportunity to connect into what is expected to be a community of love and support. This relational ambition is central to the moral and ethical landscape developed by CAP: 'We celebrate in head office every time a client becomes debt free; however, greater satisfaction comes from the knowledge that people have been given friendship instead of loneliness, joy instead of depression, or a family meal instead of arguing.'[3]

It is this mix of financial expertise and unashamedly Christian support networks that has given CAP a distinctive modus operandi and ethos since its inception in 1996.

The development of the organization

As with many faith-based organizations, CAP was initiated because of the vision of one individual – in this case John Kirkby of Bradford. In his book *Nevertheless*,[4] John describes the circumstances in which his vision for CAP emerged. Having developed a successful seventeen-year career in the consumer finance industry,

27

he suffered the trauma of business failure, mounting debts and marital breakdown – becoming, in his own words, 'destitute':

> The word 'destitute' is often over used, but that is what I became, utterly devoid of any spirit, hurting, lonely and afraid. I now know that God used this and other desperate experiences in my life for good. It was through these traumatic times that a greater sense of his love, forgiveness and heart for me became more and more real. I also began to have an ever-increasing compassion for others who were in need.[5]

John's embrace of a Christian faith gradually led to a change of heart about the workings of financial services:

> The business of helping people to borrow money was making me feel more and more uneasy. I often dealt with people unable to pay back what they had borrowed and who were really struggling. My Christian heart was telling me to help them and I did what I could for them by reducing or stopping interest and accepting reduced payments.[6]

Accordingly in 1996 he started a registered charity called Christians Against Poverty, and with his new wife, Lizzie, set out on the long and difficult road to creating an international FBO.

Nevertheless provides a blow-by-blow of the practical difficulties of putting an ambitious vision into practice. Any expectation that cash and encouragement for the project would simply come flowing in quickly proved to be overly idealistic. Rather, the early years of CAP were marked by a continual treadmill of seeking funding to cover the costs of employees. The need for debt counselling was readily apparent in the stream of potential clients, but the resources with which to meet this need were hard to come by. Every conceivable network of donors, every Christian Trust and every other possible source of funding was repeatedly mined to keep the organization's financial head above water, and the early years were punctuated by successive crises necessitating a begging and borrowing from all possible sources just to maintain a limited local operation in Bradford. For example, John writes:

> Last week reached a new crisis. We needed £35,000 to clear our bills and wages and had nothing coming in. We had also reached the point

of real hardship being experienced by staff and their families. Some were almost begging and borrowing to maintain mortgages, food, bills etc. How could this be allowed to go on? I felt dreadful and sick inside. What had I led people into?[7]

There is also evidence that these financial hardships provoked dissonance in the wider group of devotees to the charity. Relationships with trustees were reported as becoming increasingly fractious as alternative (and less expensive) models of operation were proposed in order to reach a financially sustainable way of working. There is an irony here that the overriding vision to open more CAP centres and hire more staff in order to meet the needs of financially impoverished people was literally being held together through the financial impoverishment of the employees of the charity themselves. Nevertheless, four new centres outside Bradford were opened in 1998 and 1999, and in 2001 a new headquarters (Jubilee Mill) was opened in Bradford to provide central services for the various regional centres. The consolidation of CAP rested on the inflow of greater levels of resources, from a wider network of church-based donors, from generous gifts from a range of different businessmen, from funded participation in government schemes, and from a greater level of profile and acceptability in the Christian community, such that joint bids for resources could be mounted with influential partners such as Faithworks. By 2006 there were fifty UK centres, by 2009 there were ninety, and in 2010 the figure topped 150. In 2008, CAP launched a money management course – CAP Money – designed to teach budgeting, saving and debt prevention, and this course has subsequently been taken up by 800 different churches and more than ten thousand people have attended the course. By any reasonable evaluative criteria, the growth and impacts of CAP represent a formidable achievement, demonstrating that the drive and initiative with which John Kirkby's original vision has been put into practice has been capable of the eventual establishment of a highly valuable national-level service.

The impact of CAP services

It is clearly difficult to quantify the impact of CAP services. John Kirkby writes that in 2010, some 13,000 people per annum were

29

being helped by these services, and given the increase in the number of CAP centres since then, that number has presumably increased.[8] Any such figure needs to be set in context. The government's own Financial Inclusion Funding scheme for providing debt counselling in the UK's most deprived areas has claimed to help some 100,000 people per annum, of whom some two-thirds have been dealt with by Citizens Advice Bureaux. So CAP can therefore be regarded as a significant but not yet dominant provider in this field. What is more, with the recent reduction in local authority funding to Citizens Advice Bureaux as a by-product of public sector fiscal restraint, it seems likely that CAP could become proportionately more significant as a provider over the coming years.

Rather than relying on these kinds of figures alone, CAP has tended to reflect the successful impact of their services through the use of specific testimonies. Thus in his briefing to parliament, John Kirkby tells the story of Suzie:

> Suzie rang me whilst the bailiffs were at her door. Her cupboards were empty of food and she was about to lose the very little she and her daughter had. It was only the beginning. After spotting an open window upstairs, they came back with a ladder. Unsuccessful, they pinned a seizure notice to her neighbour's car. Poor budgeting and a low income had heavy consequences for this single mum.[9]

He then uses this story to illustrate the work of CAP in which people like Suzie are encountered on a daily basis. Debt affects the ability to feed and clothe children; it creates stress and leads to family break-up; it causes shame and stigma and drives people to do desperate things. CAP meets the short-term needs of clients, often through introducing them to local church-based support networks, and then tries to provide a longer-term sustainable solution to their underlying debt. The story of Suzie is repeated thousands of times over and is gradually producing a legacy of achievement and hope from the ground level interventions of the organization, 'transforming communities one at a time'.[10]

A recent CAP book, *Journeys of Hope*, underlines how financial advice goes hand in hand with evangelism in their work. Through detailed use of client testimonies, the book charts success in terms of lives being changed holistically – financially sorted and spirit-ually sorted. In one such testimony, Lyndsay and Mark describe their desperation because of indebtedness, culminating in the former's failed suicide attempt. Finally overcoming the shame of financial failure and suicidal response, they are visited by a CAP centre manager (Gemma) whose advice and help brings an imme-diate impact:

> That meeting was one of the most amazing experiences I've ever had
> . . . the greatest relief of all was to hear that Gemma would now be
> looking after our finances and helping us whilst we paid off the debt
> in manageable monthly payments . . . I could finally breathe again.[11]

However, this financial testimony soon became something more. Invited to an evening meeting arranged by Gemma for her CAP clients, Lyndsay has a Christian conversion experience:

> The following morning when I woke up, I still felt overwhelming
> joy and peace. It was like someone had reached into my brain and
> removed all the insecurities I felt and all the worry. When you have
> these insecurities it doesn't matter how happy you are in the moment,
> they're always there, at the back of your mind. The amazing thing
> was, they'd gone. Totally gone! I still struggle with them from time
> to time but now I know that I have the support and love of God to
> help me deal with them, he has turned my life around and I can't put
> into words how much of a help the love and support of CAP has been
> too.[12]

Mark and Lyndsey's story is therefore a powerful narrative of how a couple torn apart by debt and attempted suicide have now been reunited in hope, both practical and spiritual. CAP's work, then, is unashamedly faith-based and combines financial service with evangelism. This is not to say that entry into church-based support networks is a prerequisite for service, or that huge numbers of CAP clients are converted to a Christian faith. However, CAP is based on the idea that the power of God can change any situation, and in meeting people's needs with love, compassion and prac-tical help, CAP's employees and volunteers have no reluctance to introduce their clients to community-based church networks in which spiritual change can unfold. Indeed John Kirby notes that since the beginning of CAP in 1996, some two thousand clients have made a Christian commitment in the three countries of operation.

Controversies

Given such an unambiguous positioning of an organization representing faith at work, it is inevitable that some aspects of CAP's work have attracted controversy, and as part of the comparative analytical framework of this chapter, two significant points of conflict can be recognized. First, the avowedly Christian nature and practice of CAP and its staff has provoked some disquiet across the secular/religious divide in the UK. Regardless of other examples in which faith-motivated and other groups have been shown to be willing to work together for common goals relating to welfare and care,[13] in 2011 CAP was informed that its six-year membership of Advice UK – an umbrella group supporting community organizations who give free advice to members of the public – was now incompatible with the constitutional requirement that advice should be impartial and offered with no strings attached. The rift came after reports from other advice agencies, and from beneficiaries, that CAP staff had offered to pray with clients. The chief executive of Advice UK, Steve Johnson was quoted[14] as suggesting that the offer of prayer by CAP amounted to an emotional fee, and that clients were effectively being expected to pay for their advice by agreeing to pray with counsellors. CAP responded by emphasizing that it has never made prayer a condition of its free service, but that while it is committed to providing impartial help and advice to all members of society, the offer to pray with people does remain part of its broader expression of care for clients. The outcome was that CAP amicably agreed to relinquish its membership of Advice UK, but the incident illustrates both the wider distrust of any practice that could infer proselytization, and a more specific ignorance about different forms of evangelism, some of which rely on a simple performance of faith, and others of which represent a simple and unforced offer of the possibility of integration into local church-based networks of support.

Secondly, the relentless requirement to secure sustainable funds for an organization such as CAP often necessitates controversial decisions about what is, and is not an acceptable source of funding and support. In *Nevertheless*, for example, John Kirkby relates the dilemma of whether or not to apply for Lottery funding. There are, in Christian circles, many different views about the Lottery, with at least some arguing against being tainted by using the excess from what is effectively a form of gambling that is reckoned to be a factor in the further impoverishment of the most needy social groups in the country. In the end, CAP did apply for, and receive, Lottery funding. Along rather similar lines, disquiet has recently been expressed over CAP's alleged connections with Provident Financial – a UK personal loan agency reported by Murphy[15] to charge excessive interest rates to poor households who are not served by the regular banking system. In his book *A Just Church*, Chris Howson expresses surprise at these connections, noting that 'the Provident boasts on its website that it has been involved with CAP since its inception, and it has certainly been a generous sponsor' and that in turn CAP 'refuses to condemn the Provident's lending practices and on its website even gives advice on how best to pay back a loan from the "Provi"'. Howson's conclusion is that 'CAP do good work in helping those in debt, and have many excellent debt advisers, but they fail to see the dangers of being too close to one of the major sources of debt in the UK'.[16] Such allegations demonstrate just how difficult it is to tread a broadly acceptable ethical line between the practical desire to raise funds so as to meet the needs of impoverished people, and ensuring that association with particular sources of funding does not contradict the deeper-seated political message about how people become indebted in the first place. Equally faith-based organizations such as CAP are vulnerable to being situated into a particular political niche. Something as simple as accepting an award from the (Conservative) Centre for Social Justice (as CAP did in 2006) will for some suggest a broader implication within that centre's ideological framework, including the much-heralded 'Big Society' idea proposed by the current government. Such niching is often a matter of external perception. However, there does seem to be a more general risk when an organization has become successful in no small part because of the entrepreneurial DNA of its founder that this 'make it happen' entrepreneurship may involve connections (for example with government, or with financial institutions or individuals who have made their money through these institutions) that limit a faith-based organization's ability to speak out in the political and economic arena about the underlying causes of the indebtedness and poverty they are addressing.

Thirdly, this issue of the potential for political controversy in the work of an FBO extends to the relations between FBOs and wider government discourses. Some commentators[17] have suggested that the state is currently marshalling the activities of FBOs as a legitimation of its own particular conceptions of poverty. In this way, the activities of CAP, and the scale of their work in individual debt advice and emotional support, are ripe for enrolment in political discourse to emphasize people's own failure at money management rather than a basic lack of income. In this sense CAP can become unwillingly instrumentalized to propagate an ideological agenda of smaller government in an age of austerity in which it is efficacious to focus on ways of tackling poverty that do not involve public expenditure.

Church Action on Poverty

Church Action on Poverty (hereafter CAoP) is a national-level ecumenical charity committed to social justice generally, and specifically to tackling poverty in the UK. Founded in 1982 by John Battle, a devout Roman Catholic and Labour MP, CAoP was deliberately designed to be a cross-denominational, non-partisan organization aimed at educating and mobilizing the church in response to the increasing levels of unemployment and poverty during the 1980s. Its vision today remains largely unchanged: to mobilize grass roots activism in the church and beyond, and to give a voice to the poor to speak out against socio-economic injustice. CAoP partners with people and groups directly experiencing poverty, but also with churches, trade unions, anti-poverty campaigners and political organizations, over a number of key social issues such as income inequality, the destitution of asylum seekers, compulsory work for benefits, 'working poverty', living wages, and debt. CAoP has expanded over the past five years from around ten staff to nineteen staff and a further three associates.[18]

Theologically, CAoP implicitly draws upon a reformed strand of liberation theology that emphasizes the sinfulness of structures, not just of the individual. It is these structures – and those who use them to oppress the poor – that are to be opposed and overcome if the oppressed are to be liberated.[19] CAoP believes that all people have the right to share 'life in all its fullness'[20] and that poverty actively prevents this. Poverty is therefore understood as a reflection of a society that places a greater value on some than on others, and this understanding invites the conclusion that in a country rich in resources, poverty is an injustice that can and must be overcome. This theological basis for action emphasizes the articulation of God's bias for the poor – naming injustice as an act of faith and discipleship. Niall Cooper, the current national director, converses with government bodies and politicians to revise welfare policies impacting on the lives of the poorest.[21] Whilst he affirms the positive elements in government proposals, for instance, joining others to welcome – in principle – Universal Credit as a simpler more transparent system that 'makes work pay', he exposes the blind spots of such a policy, firmly placing on the public table alternatives which take a more structural interpretation of poverty. With the increasing tendency for politicians to present the problem of poverty at best as a matter of people's failure at money management rather than a basic lack of income, and at worst, as a result of some moral failure on the part of the poor – a problem of low aspirations, poor money management, poor work ethic, and dependency on drugs, alcohol or welfare[22] – CAoP has been an obstinate voice calling for the need to tackle systemic socio-economic inequalities that structure class dynamics in the UK. This has meant, for example, highlighting issues relating to job availability and job quality amid cripplingly low pay and rising job insecurity, and to the relationship between escalating levels of repossessions and indebtedness and the government programme of austerity which has led to significant increases in unemployment, particularly among public sector workers, and disproportionately squeezed the poorest 10 per cent of society through £18 billion cuts to welfare and housing benefits. Crucially, CAoP has attempted to move beyond what can be construed as sloganeering by deploying lobbying activities and participatory forums in which the voices of those experiencing poverty are used to present a powerful counter-narrative with which to challenge the dominant explanations of poverty by those in government. CAoP uses the theological principles developed, for example, in the work of Tony Campolo, Ron Sider and Jim Wallis in understanding austerity budgets as not just technocratic exercises, but as moral statements of what and who we value in society.[23] The unwavering commitment to God's preference for the poor leads to a stark critique of those in power whose degrees ensure an unjust system of wealth distribution stays in place.

The impact of CAoP

CAoP takes the view that the task of the Christian church is to make a difference in the world, not just to sit in moral judgement on that world. This theological position leads both to long-term involvement among the poor through programmes such as Changemakers and Participatory Budgeting, and to relentless campaigning on particular issues (such as the plight of asylum seekers) which tend to disappear from public consciousness in the ebb and flow of media coverage. In this section, we briefly discuss each of these aspects of CAoP's work.

1. Changemakers

As a campaigning body, CAoP has developed a number of community projects that aim to give a voice to the poor. One of their major programmes Changemakers, is a network of grass roots organizations in the UK working with local people to enable them to set the agenda in changing their communities, sometimes challenging the orthodoxy of state-directed programmes. The overall objective of the project is to develop the capacity and skills of the members of socially and economically disadvantaged communities, initially across Manchester but latterly also elsewhere in the UK, seeking to empower people to engage with powerful decision-makers. Drawing from a number of concepts from international development and from the work of liberation theologians and Latin American educators such a Gustavo Gutiérrez and Paulo Freire,[24] Changemakers reflects a process of 'conscientization', where individuals and communities become aware of their oppression and begin to seek ways to combat it through claiming their own political spaces where voices can be heard. Changemakers builds the ability of individual communities firstly to identify, and consequently to help meet their needs in participating more fully in local regeneration processes, the development of effective local and national urban policy, and society in general. This endeavour towards participatory democratic empowerment has heightened significance, given decades of community regeneration which has either bypassed local actors entirely (for example, as in the Thatcher government's flagship redevelopment programmes) or approached local involvement in a tokenistic manner through consultations wherein decisions had already been circumscribed by government experts (a problem associated with New Labour's New Deal for Communities).[25] In contrast, Changemakers represents an attempt to sponsor participatory forms of democratic activity alongside representative mechanisms – wherein the poorest and most marginalized communities are not conceived as powerless or indeed the 'problem' to be solved through government intervention, but rather as agents of change whose collective voice can begin to establish new political spaces capable of augmenting, challenging or even overturning the tables of power as currently structured.

2. Participatory Budgeting

As with many FBOs, CAoP has used effective initiatives to attract the gaze of government ministers. Since 1999, the organization has pioneered work on Participatory Budgeting (carried out with Community Pride, a project established with local partner churches in Manchester) in collaboration with Oxfam. Inspired by examples of participatory demography in Latin America, and in many ways acting as a precursor to the Changemakers programme, Participatory Budgeting has aimed to give individual communities more decision-making power in how new public investment should best be spent. The project involved developing a number of pilot projects around the country, events, publications and a national reference group involving key civil servants from a range of government departments. As a direct result of this work, Participatory Budgeting was adopted as a key priority by Hazel Blears when she became secretary of state for Communities and Local Government in the New Labour government. Her

Department of Communities and Local Government committed to ensuring Participatory Budgeting was taken up by every local authority in England by 2013, and worked with other government departments to introduce Participatory Budgeting within police and health authorities. CAoP's Participatory Budgeting Unit has become the lead agency in taking this work forward (with funding from DCLG), and the unit is now working directly with at least over fifty local authorities across England.[26]

3. Political protest and campaigning

CAoP represents an unwavering streak of prophetic critique within Christianity in the UK. Aspects of the church have too often been seen as domesticated into accepting the norms and parameters of public policy, forgetting there are alternative policy solutions to social problems than those enshrined in public debate. CAoP has provided the means by which alternatives can be explored. For example, Debt on our Doorstep (DOOD) is a campaign network co-founded by CAoP. Working with a wide range of organizations including the National Housing Federation, Oxfam, Citizens Advice Bureaux, and many local advice services, credit unions and community groups, the campaign aims to end extortionate lending and ensure universal access to affordable credit and other financial services. Whilst it is usually difficult to assess the impact of specific campaigns, DOOD has had some success at lobbying parliament, assemblies and other decision-makers to legislate for tighter regulation of extortionate lending, and promote models of affordable credit. Niall Cooper states:

> Through Debt on our Doorstep, we contributed directly to the Treasury's Child Poverty review proposals which led to the establishment of the Financial Inclusion Fund. In its first three years, £60 million was invested directly into expanding access to affordable credit via credit unions and the like: DOOD was the only organisation advocating this. Upwards of 60,000 people were directly given affordable loans in the first 3 years of operation. The Fund has now been extended for a further 3 year period.[27]

DOOD has also seen success in developing a code of practice amongst the 'predatory lenders' in the UK, including payday loan lenders and rent-to-own shops. The most recent action tackled the inflated prices of 'pay-as-you-go' utility firms (gas, electric, TV) whose clients, predominantly those on low incomes, pay considerably more than those with higher incomes who are able to pay monthly. In April 2010, hundreds of campaigners emailed and phoned the chief executive of Buy As You View, and persuaded him to listen to the concerns of his low-income customers. Since then, CAoP and Thrive, their local partner in Stockton-on-Tees, have been working closely with Buy As You View, other lending companies and the Office of Fair Trading to develop and implement a new code of practice designed to make these big companies behave more responsibly, and treat their low-income customers more fairly. Significantly, CAoP has engaged with one of the most prominent 'predatory lenders' – Provident Financial – on several occasions, in a hope of persuading them to join the campaign for a CAoP on national interest rates, yet with little success. Chris Howson was present in one such meeting alongside Alan Thornton from Church Action on Poverty. He writes:

> The [*Provident Financial*] management were more concerned about arguing that the 'Provi' was 'the true friend of the poor', lending where nobody else would and citing the company's extensive financial giving to Church-based organisations, especially the work of Christians Against Poverty. They said that they felt 'deeply hurt that a member of the clergy and a Church-based organisation were so actively campaigning against their business.'[28]

Liberation theology raises the uncomfortable question of structural sin, by which we refer to the conscious and unconscious acts of trespassing against one's neighbour, both proximate and distant, that are inherent in political and economic ways of working. Sometimes companies do project the image of social responsibility as a conscious act to deflect attention from the often immoral actions of their business,[29] to the extent that these are internalized by employees. However, the prophetic call of liberation theology is to expose the invisible lines of oppression, the structures – political-economic and spiritual – that reify a world in rebellion to God and disciple believers into 'conforming to the world as though its current state were inevitable, natural or divinely sanctioned'.[30] Indeed, Christians are thought to need a more radical perspective, a prophetic imagination not captured into thinking in terms of what the powers that be allow us to see, but an ethic rooted in the Jesus narrative and his reconciliation work on the cross which speaks a word of judgement upon our systems of violence and exclusion.[31]

To this end, CAoP has been prominent in mobilizing counter-hegemonic discourses of work and welfare in the UK, contextualizing and popularizing alternatives to New Labour's welfare-to-work and the Conservative workfare approach to unemployment. For example, in 2009, CAoP published grass roots research in association with OXFAM that helped to challenge the criminalization of 'welfare fraudsters' – an imaginary popularized by media campaigns of New Labour.[32] CAoP condemned New Labour's proposed policy which would have allowed people who inform on benefit 'cheats' to be given a share of the resulting savings. Contending the likely divisive effects this policy would have on communities and families, CAoP sought to remind policymakers that those who commit benefit fraud are largely dependent on working cash-in-hand to support their families because under the benefit system, and given the shortage of work, conventional employment is often not a viable route out of poverty. Furthermore, CAoP tried to show the implicit class bias in the government crackdown on welfare frauds. Through its Close the Gap, a campaign that called for government to address income inequality in the UK, CAoP highlights the impact of the 'Tax Gap' in the UK. 'Every pound avoided in tax is a pound less to spend on childcare, social care, health or education,' said Niall Cooper. 'At a time when spending cuts are having a real and damaging impact on the lives of some of the poorest and most vulnerable people in the country, it is morally indefensible for some of Britain's richest companies to be avoiding paying their fair share of UK taxes.'[33]

The Methodist Church and other denominations have followed CAoP, calling on the UK government and multinational businesses to end tax avoidance schemes. The Treasury admits to not collecting a record high of £42 billion in tax in the latest available figures. But independent analysts estimate the amount of lost tax to be much higher, at £120 billion. The poorest 10 per cent pay a much greater proportion of their income to the government in tax than the wealthiest tenth (46 per cent compared to 34 per cent). Paul Morrison, public issues policy adviser for the Methodist Church, states: 'Taxation shouldn't be a game of strategy where you win by paying the least. Paying tax is a moral obligation – it is unacceptable to engage in complex financial arrangements in order to wriggle out of paying your fair share.'[34]

In a similar vein, CAoP has been prominent in raising awareness of the treatment of asylum seekers. Through its Living Ghosts campaign (co-founded with Enabling Christians Serving Refugees, Churches Refugee Network, Churches Commission for Racial Justice and the National Catholic Refugee Forum), CAoP aims to mount pressure on the government to stop making refugees who are refused 'asylum' destitute by withdrawing welfare support. The campaign originated at a grass roots level as local churches mobilized the available resources to meet the basic needs of asylum seekers who had gone to the church for help. The fact that it was the church speaking out on the plight of asylum seekers immediately gave prominence to this campaign, implying that the church still has some cultural legitimacy in the public sphere. CAoP has been particularly active in mobilizing support against Section 55 of the Nationality, Immigration and Asylum Act 2002. To publicize their condemnation of asylum policy, they have launched a series of high-profile protests. One of these, for example, was a demonstration in the heart of Sheffield city centre in support of destitute asylum seekers in June 2006. Several hundred people joined in the demonstration at various times, and stewards handed out 1,300 leaflets to passing shoppers in an attempt to inform and mobilize public support. Many signed cards to the home secretary. Forty-five church leaders from different denominations also joined CAoP's protest by expressing outrage in an uncharacteristically political statement criticizing a policy that leaves refugees refused asylum totally destitute in the UK as a means to encourage applicants to return 'voluntarily' to the place from which they fled. In particular they emphasized many *refused* asylum seekers have often been rejected because of legal incompetence, and may not be able to be returned safely.

In September 2008, CAoP, working alongside other charitable organizations such as Oxfam and Save the Children, took a leading role in the launch and overseeing of the Get Fair campaign to mobilize and coordinate many organizations and networks already working on various aspects of the problem of poverty. The aim here was both to secure public support for action to tackle poverty in a difficult economic environment, and to enrol the commitment of all major political parties to deliver on existing commitments to end child poverty by 2020. The campaign drew on fundamental human rights principles of equality, dignity and respect for everyone living in the UK, at all life stages, to ensure that everyone has: a decent, adequate income; the right not to be marginalized or excluded from society; equal opportunities and fair access to services; and the right to live in neighbourhoods that secure health and wellbeing. CAoP has consistently acted as a founder member of anti-poverty coalitions and political protests.[35] Our final example of this political campaigning activity reflects what is often construed as the best example of interfaith and secular collaboration in political and social protests. The Living Wage campaign, in which broad-based organizations such as London Citizens collaborated with trade unions and national and local faith groups to campaign for the National Minimum Wage to be based on a scientific analysis of how much an adequate standard of living costs. The coalition staged highly visible protests outside a number of hotels in the City of London which paid their employees, many of them migrants, an insufficient wage. At the same time, CAoP called for all churches to set an example for other employers in paying their employees a living wage, and attacked the continuing excesses and hypocrisy in boardroom pay levels. In response, the Methodist Church, the Baptist Union and the United Reformed Church have all made commitments to pay a living wage to their employees. The Church of England's 'Faithful Cities' report, published in May 2006, called for the introduction of a 'Living Wage' in place of the inadequate National Minimum Wage, and in December 2007, a coalition of anti-poverty groups in Scotland launched their own Living Wage campaign.

The political promise of postsecular engagement

In this apparent 'post-political' age,[36] where the parameters of public policy are circumscribed to accept the inevitably of the technocratic governance of neoliberal capitalism, radical/alternative perspectives that challenge this 'consensus' are often reprimanded as illegitimate, unrealistic or insignificant in the public realm.[37] Ideological acquiescence seems to be a growing fault line by which secular *and* religious voices are equally included or excluded in public debates. However, CAoP's success in lobbying government and collaborating in broad-based campaigns which transcend hard and fast divisions between the religious (=private) and secular (=public) underlines the political power of faith-based, interfaith and postsecular protest movements. Indeed, postsecular alliances between religious and secular activists present an opportunity to re-politicize the 'consensus', not purely through the languages of ideology and counter-hegemony, but through the hopeful imaginations, and visceral politics,[38] derived from these beliefs-in-action which can provide a groundswell of alternative ethical citizenship.[39] The symbolic act of hospitality and solidarity with the poor can form a counter-narrative that cannot be dismissed or negated as sectarian or idiosyncratic, but rather invites all people to participate in the passions of caritas and *agape* working out in action: standing with the poor, vulnerable and marginalized, and enabling the oppressed to speak truth to power.

Conclusion

This chapter has discussed the work of two significant FBOs in bringing Christian perspective and action into the fight against poverty in the UK. The two organizations share many similarities. Each was founded due to the visionary and energetic efforts of a single individual, whose previous experience in the business and political realms led them to 'do something about something', acting on their Christian principles, and implementing their version of Christian ethical action in favour of the poor, the indebted and the marginalized. Both organizations have emphasized the centrality of empowerment as a core value and guiding principle in their work, and both have sought to enrol faith-based networks, albeit often at different scales, to enhance the scope and scale of their operation. In each case the FBOs have achieved a position of political influence, being granted access to key political spaces where relevant social issues are discussed and addressed. Together they reflect a faith response to poverty which is both innovative and effective, and each has provided a catalyst for wider faith-based acknowledgement of poverty as an issue in the UK, and a growing sense among churches and other faith networks that there are important mechanisms that can be used to practise faith in this poverty arena.

However, we should also acknowledge that Christians Against Poverty and Church Action on Poverty present very different strategies for faith-motivated action on poverty. CAP works on an individual basis, meeting people in their immediate need and helping release them from life-controlling financial burdens. Although much of the empowerment achieved is through personal support and training in financial matters, CAP has a clear commitment to evangelism, in that part of the 'answer' it offers its clients involves the potential for a life-changing personal relationship with Jesus Christ. This spiritual element is not made compulsory, but nevertheless lies at the heart of the motivation of staff and volunteers who serve indebted clients. Empowerment for Church Action on Poverty tends to work at a different scale, working principally at community-wide and structural levels to mobilize participatory democratic forms of community regeneration, and to challenge the unjust laws decreed by government.[40] These distinct strategies highlight both the diverse political theologies informing faith-motivated action in the contemporary city, and rather different relations between empowerment and politics. CAP prioritizes aid to the disenfranchised; CAoP embraces a clear goal of political engagement on behalf of the disenfranchised, at both national and local levels.

The activities of CAP and CAoP suggest to us the need to reframe the question of 'faith at work' beyond that of the balance between, on the one hand, providing immediate aid to the needy, and on the other hand, challenging the political-economic structures that underlie that need. Emphasizing this seemingly dichotomous pair of approaches can lead to somewhat fruitless discussions about whether a 'sticking plaster' or 'major surgery' is required. What this chapter has demonstrated is that *both* approaches are informed by specific political theologies and are contextualized by particular understandings of the structural roots of poverty. Providing aid to the poor and indebted essentially focuses on individual and household need, and can therefore inevitably become entwined with individualist political constructions that define what poverty is and what action should be taken in support of, or to incentivize, the poor. Political challenges to these constructions of poverty can themselves be drawn into discourses of opposition and resistance that can equally become bound into the political discourses of the day. The key requirement here is to present alternative, prophetic and hopeful re-imaginations of contemporary politics that will have direct relevance to those in need – based not on political opposition per se, but on a return to the politics embodied in the life and teachings of Jesus. To this end, aspects of CAoP's work with Changemakers represent an exciting example of faith-based action, moving away from colonial-tinged donor-receiver models of aid with their tendencies to speak on behalf of the other, and pursuing a more incarnational approach of 'conscientization' that empowers both the host and recipient to understand the processes and cycles of a person or community so that any flows might become 'unblocked'.[41]

Our sense, then, is that FBOs need to work together in a more seamless combination of sticking plaster and major surgery. The activities of CAP and CAoP present two clear openings for faith-based social action against poverty in the UK. Delivering these two strategies in isolation, however, risks the incorporation of local-level aid, in particular political constructions related to the supposed individual causes of poverty, and equally risks the incorporation of wider-scale protest into oppositional and counter-hegemonic discourses per se, that can easily be detached from the specificity of *theological* insights into the structural aspects of poverty. Isolated strategies are also susceptible to disconnected thinking on particular issues – an extreme example might be the contrast between CAoP's work to oppose and seek reform of the 'predatory' lending practices of particular financial companies, and CAP's alleged willingness to be sponsored by one of those self-same companies. Inevitably this 'joined-up' working faces key difficulties, especially in the areas of the tendency to cherish organizational autonomy and independence, the different organizational priorities involving evangelism, and the different political proclivities of leaders. Indeed, some of the contrasts revealed in this chapter mirror the observations of Joel Edwards, who draws clear distinctions between what he regards as the right-wing, middle-ground and left-wing shades of evangelical social action.[42] Whether these different elements can work together to combine structural and individual perspectives will say much about their capacity to draw radically on the undiluted gospel message and thereby to avoid incorporation and enrolment into contemporary political constructions. It will also be a litmus test of whether faith-based understandings are successfully crossing over into the political arenas rather than simply being co-opted into them.

CHAPTER 3

Practical Theology and Christian Responses to Drug Addiction

Andrew Williams

Introduction

This chapter examines the practical theologies[1] of two Christian organizations[2] responding to issues of drug addiction and substance abuse. Many books have been written about prominent ministries among drug users; for example, David Wilkerson's *The Cross and the Switchblade*,[3] Jackie Pullinger's *Chasing the Dragon*,[4] and Stewart and Marie Dinnen's *Rescue Shop within a Yard of Hell*.[5] Each book celebrates the testimonies of God working to deliver people from the bondage of addiction into a new life of freedom, hope and love. Outside the Christian subculture, these stories are shrouded by secular criticism that faith-based drug programmes represent a dangerous form of social control and religious indoctrination.[6] Indeed, some Christian residential programmes require clients to fully participate in prayer, worship and Bible study, and at best are often portrayed in the media as risky amateurs, or, at worst, as zealot fundamentalists preying on vulnerable people to win converts.[7]

The presence of such diametrically opposed views raises an interesting ethical question for practical theology; namely, how do Christians deal with 'otherness' in living out their faith? Ethical questions over 'self-other' relations in the praxis of mission and humanitarian assistance have become ever important as the Western church attempts to avoid forms of cultural imperialism that haunt its recent past. Recognizing the relationship between

caregiver and care receiver is far from self-evident, recent attention has been centred on the ethics of evangelism,[8] the moral
expectations and identities placed on 'the other' as conditions of
service, and the possibility of more unconditional forms of charity
that uphold the interrelations between giver and receiver.[9]

Through a comparison of two rather different Christian organizations serving drug users in the UK and The Netherlands, this
chapter highlights the diverse ethics and practices involved in
faith-based services for drug users. We first turn to Betel of Britain,
a semi-monastic Christian community for people with addictions,
before looking at the Pauluskerk in Rotterdam, a shelter and day
centre ministry best known for its controversial stance on permitting drug use on site. The aim of this comparison is not to present
one as superior to 'the other', but rather to provide context to
discuss different ways Christians deal with 'otherness' when
working with drug users.

Betel of Britain

Betel is a network of residential communities of ex-addicts based
in over eighty cities in twenty-one countries across Europe, Asia,
North America, Latin America and Australia. Betel is not a drug
rehabilitation programme in the traditional sense; rather, it aims to
be a church-planting organization among the outcasts of society,
discipling new converts in the context of community, and equip-
ping leaders to plant new churches. New residents first go through
a 'cold turkey' detoxification without any form of painkillers or
substitute opiates, such as methadone. During their withdrawal,
residents are closely supervised by an older resident and serve in
household duties such as cleaning, and preparation of food. Once
strong enough, residents help fund their own recovery and that of
others by working in the community business: usually gardening
and furniture restoration, although the type of social enterprise
varies according to the local opportunities in each city and country.
For this reason Betel residences usually occupy 'fringe' locations
in the countryside, near enough to business opportunities within
the city, but beyond the pressures of urban 'vices'.[10] Residents are
required to sign off all state benefits prior to joining the commu-

nity, and hand over bank cards for safe keeping as a means to physically remove the temptation of leaving the programme. Whilst there is no goal-based or counselling programme as such, the structured daily routine – encompassing work activities and participation in Bible study, prayer and singing – alongside mentoring and the peer-led example of older residents constitutes an overt Christian discipleship programme. The programme is designed to be around eighteen months, much longer than mainstream drug services.

Entry and exit in Betel residences is made entirely free and voluntary. This is in contrast to private rehabilitation providers and state sponsored programmes which entail eligibility assessments and short timed interventions, where increasingly clients are legally required to enter treatment after a drug-related offence.

This combination of evangelical church planting, semi-monastic community and social enterprise has given Betel a distinctive modus operandi and ethos since its inception in 1985.

Development of the organization

Betel (Spanish for Bethel, meaning House of God) was founded in 1985 on the streets of Madrid, when a small group of WEC[11] missionaries offered a bed to Rául Casto, a heroin addict who was awaiting a court hearing in two weeks' time and had nowhere to live. This act of hospitality led to the beginning of Betel's residential programme. Rául went through 'cold turkey' withdrawal as the missionaries cared for him, cooked for him, and tried to get him involved in their activities. After six days he became a Christian, and stayed in the flat for four months reading and discussing the Bible each morning and night with them. Eight other men came to live in the flat too, and followed this similar model of relational care and testimony. Since that first encounter on the streets of Madrid in 1985, Betel has helped tens of thousands of drug and alcohol dependent people across the world.

Betel came to Britain in 1995 when Kent and Mary Alice Martin, two Americans serving in the Betel church in Madrid, were asked to establish a Betel community in the UK. Kent already had links with Yeldall Manor, a Christian residential rehabilitation centre near Twyford, which helped set up a meeting with a cross-section of Christian leaders concerned about drug addiction and reha-bilitation. The original intention was to set up a centre in Liver-pool or Manchester where the need was considered greater, but a large country property outside Birmingham became available. The landlord of the property rented the building to Betel at the princely sum of £33 per month. The leader was advised to estab-lish a 'Christian community' rather than a rehabilitation centre, because as a faith community Betel would not have to meet the restrictions applied to licensed professionalized residential care programmes. Also operating under this guise, the organization would obtain a lower profile amongst local government and bypass potential NIMBY[12] activists. The reputation of WEC meant that Betel, a fledging unknown body, was acceptable in churches across the UK, and its profile grew to feature heavily in Christian conferences and festivals. Today, Betel has five centres in the UK, with plans for more centres in the coming years.

The impact of Betel

The countless lives changed through the work of Betel can be best appreciated in the individual testimonies of transformation documented in the several books written about the organiza-tion.[13]

In the UK, Betel's decision to eschew state funding to pursue its philosophy of free entry and free exit has given the organization options not open to rehabilitation services incorporated into the financial and regulatory frameworks of government, who often find their autonomy circumscribed by relevant funding and eligi-bility criteria. Betel's policy of free entry and exit makes it popular with those who cannot afford private treatment, or who have been denied access to public funded treatment. Despite operating on the outside of official funding and referral systems, Betel receives a large number of referrals from local probation officers and homeless hostels attracted to the community's little to no waiting list, as well as its reputation for transforming individuals whom mainstream agencies have given up on.

Internationally, Betel has become a model for many others to follow, in its methods of ministry to drug addicts, in coping with a large number of church members and workers living with

HIV and AIDS, and in effective discipling and training of former addicts to become pastors and missionaries.

Controversies

The men and women involved in Betel are receiving something many contemporary secular agencies do not provide: a community where they can belong.[14] The major problem of course is what happens to those who do not want to fit into Betel's religious framework? Are they simply cast out into the darkness? Or what of those residents who feel uncomfortable with the programme but stay because they have no alternative? What happens to those who leave the community after the eighteen-month period? In addressing each of these problems, we need to ask ethical questions of how 'the other' is conceived and treated in the Betel programme. Two distinctive points can be recognized. The first relates to a distinct evangelical ethos that places particular moral expectations and identities for residents to perform as conditions of receiving care. The second concerns the problems associated with pseudo-monastic programmes for drug users.

Evangelical caritas

Betel exemplifies an unashamedly evangelical ethos where the giving of care is driven by the desire to convert 'the other' into one's own faith. Residents are briefed prior to entry that Betel's programme is uniquely Christian and requires of them willingness to participate in prayer, communal worship and Bible teaching. Faith in Christ is seen as a positive replacement for addiction, and through prayer ministry and Christian teaching, residents are guided on 'proper' living and ways to avoid addictive behaviour. The underlying cause of addiction is talked about in terms of 'spiritual voids' to which conversion brings a 'lasting solution' to life-controlling problems.[15] Spiritual needs are elevated alongside more commonly recognized physical and emotional needs. Staff are explicit that the 'ultimate needs of residents is not simply to get clean, but to accept Jesus . . . [U]nless you are saved you will always be in danger of falling back into drugs because you will be trying to fill that [spiritual] void with something that will not satisfy'.[16] Critics of religion would warn against a talking-up of

51

conversion as a panacea for addiction, given cases of Christians continuing to relapse and struggle with drug use once they leave these programmes.

Whilst Betel is transparent about what it offers – an intense twenty-four hour a day, seven days a week Christian discipleship programme that may suit some, but welcomes all. This ethos places a particular set of moral expectations and identities on service users if they are to be helped. The programme offers residents to 'opt into' a 'tried and tested' structure based on Christian example and direction. For some this is seen as an attempt to convert 'the other' to a particular evangelical-informed sense of rationality, respectability and responsibility.

Service provision is not simply made conditional on the recipient adopting a sympathetic attitude towards Christian belief, but residents are strongly encouraged through mandatory participation in religious practices to work towards an idealized Christian identity. The goal of the programme is to encourage visible breaks with past lifestyle, and re-form the habits and desires of the individual on a religious-informed identity. Betel, and other rehabs like it, insists on particular dress codes, hair length, style, colour, no facial hair, dreadlocks. No tobacco. No secular music, books, TV or radio. The rules of the community seek to ensure an extended family atmosphere by prohibiting potentially divisive or unhelpful influences to the resident's recovery – for example, different tastes of music, euphoric music associated with past drug use, 'inappropriate' television content. The rationale underpinning this censorship is, for recovery to occur, there needs to be a clean break not only with drugs but also with all the cultural accompaniments of drug use. Instead, there is extensive instruction in the Bible and quiet times where residents are obliged to read Christian literature. Christian music can be understood by members to change the affective environment by repeatedly 'filling your minds with God's truth'.[17] Practices of confession, worship and sermons were understood to help re-equip residents with more healthy desires, and operate peer support and accountability for residents trying to remain free from sin.

In valorizing a particular mould of Christian belief to follow, little space is allowed for doubt, questioning the decisions of leaders, or different expressions and practices of the Christian faith other than the prescribed model. In this sense, the Betel ethos, particularly its understanding of addiction as a lack of acceptance of Christ, represents a non-recognition of alterity – an imposition of the Christian world-view onto residents. Religious conversion is not stipulated as a condition of staying in Betel residences, but individual progress is measured on one level by physical well-being, including their willingness to submit to the discipleship of others; and on the other, the individual's relationship with Jesus.

The underside of Betel's philosophy of 'free entry and free exit' is the choice facing residents: either 'opt in' to a relatively prescribed religious framework and submit to the authority of others as a means of re-aligning the self according to the values of the community, or leave. The inherent tension of Christian rehabs such as Betel, and other conservative evangelical groups like it, is that it is very successful in terms of long-term abstinence amongst graduates who complete the programme, and among that group, those who remain within the church network (Betel or otherwise) receive additional support. However, their retention rate over the first few months is low as new residents find the programme too intrusive or inappropriate. As one of the founders of Betel, Elliot Tepper, explains:

> The critic almost always assumes that there is a sectish agenda in our community living which robs the individual of his rights and freedoms and imposes unfair or outdated religious restraints upon his or her life. Often there is [the] insinuation that Betel has a design of entrapping vast numbers of weak and helpless people in its communal web. If that were so, our trap is like a sieve. Of the 33,000 individuals who have passed through Betel's residences over the last thirty years, only 1,200 live with us today, the rest leaving to return to their families or the street. Some choose to live drug free and some choose to return to drugs. (Our cure rate has ranged between 10% and 15% over the years.) All are free to select the church of their choice or a purely non-religious lifestyle. Of the 1,200 Betel residents only about 120 would be permanent or semi-permanent members who exercise some kind of full-time ministry either in the pastorate, as staff, or as monitors in our residences and shops. These are hardly the kind of statistics one would expect from a sect. In reality Betel is really more of a temporary rest shop where weary, broken people can piece back together their shattered lives before continuing on their journey.[18]

Betel's programme relies on the individual assimilating themselves to communal direction, 'if their attitude is right, and if they
are truly seeking God, they may find community to be a kind of
spiritual paradise'. However, Tepper concedes, 'fellowship and
calling cannot be forced'[19] and Betel does its best to refer unsatis-
fied residents to rehabs more to their liking.

Some would question the ethical basis of evangelism in closed rehab
environments where intense, repeated, and extremely programmatic
approaches are used to bring about conversions.[20] Indeed, organizations such as Betel need to tread carefully to avoid the possible
exploitation of power imbalances between the care host and the great
need of the care receiver. Even the declaration of 'free entry and exit'
entails a subtle material enticement to work the programme, given
the lack of alternative options to residents. Also, care must be given
to the lines of inclusion and exclusion that are drawn between Christian and non-Christian within these programmes to avoid favouritism and perceived 'social' incentives to conversion.

However, notwithstanding these concerns about compul-
sion and the 'tough love' ethos that characterizes the rules of
programmes such as Betel, it would be wrong to conclude that
this is all there is to the processes of recovery or, indeed, conversion. Alongside these rigid codes of behaviour one finds genuine
friendships among residents that instil a sense of belonging.
Inside Betel's organizational shell, residents carve out a therapeutic space for themselves as they participate in the programme,
and it would be wrong to assume their subjectivity is completely
circumscribed by the intentions and processes of the programme.
Many residents have told stories of how they came to faith not
with drip-fed indoctrination, but through a simple act of hospitality that transcends any desire or expectation of reciprocation.
One resident who is now a pastor of a Betel community recalls a
story that was instrumental in his faith:

One of the men ... [had] only been in Betel for a couple of weeks. His mum
had send him a pair of brand new, blue Nike trainers; I'll never forget
these trainers, the Lord really used [them] as a tool to reveal himself to
me. They came in the post, and he had them in the bedroom and he was
looking at them and he was like 'man these are well nice trainers'. And I
walked in and he looked at my grotty trainers; they were properly falling

apart – I had come from the streets and had been in Betel about twelve days. He handed them over, saying, 'I want you to have these.' I was like, 'So what's the catch?' You don't get anything for nothing, I was thinking from the street . . . no one gave me nothing, they always wanted something . . . That, I think was the turning point for me; it got me thinking, if this thing was for real . . . I had only just met the guy a couple of days ago, and for someone to just give that to me, I was like, man, you know! And this guy, he used to cut safes open, he was a bank robber, and he had only been in Betel for about six weeks and he was giving me a brand new pair of trainers, and I didn't understand it.[21]

It is through these ordinary experiences of friendship, unconditional acts of kindness, that prompt new residents to question the life of others, and the beliefs that drive them.

Semi-monastic community

Religious communities have been treated in recent times with a lot of suspicion. This is for good reason, many would argue, referring to historical abuses in extreme monasticism, the abandonment from the needs of others, and the religiosity institutionalized in fanatical sects.[22] Certainly, if a reified religious environment ceases to critique the values and practices of its own faith, then there is a possibility of sliding into an over-rigid fundamentalism, a position detriment to maturing faith in a pluralistic society.

In the eyes of some health professionals, semi-monastic communities such as Betel run counter to established best practice in the field of mental health. For some, Betel represents a bygone era of psychiatric institutionalization which were 'isolated, disempowering places where people very rapidly lose their sense of identity, where the focus is compliance, there are high levels of surveillance and where contact with people close to them is limited'.[23] The danger facing semi-monastic communities such as Betel is that limiting contact with their families or qualified medical and psychiatric care could exacerbate, rather than alleviate, mental health symptoms. Furthermore, some would argue that the lack of professionally qualified staff, safe facilities and regular reporting on the outcomes of those programmes represents an unnecessary high risk for clients. Given the health risks associated with non-medicated detoxification for alcoholism, there are serious questions concerning the ethics of cold turkey withdrawal. In the area of dual-diagnosis, mental health issues may go untreated given Betel's prohibition of all psychoactive drugs, including anti-depressants – or worse, remain undiagnosed or misunderstood by others as an unruly and rebellious spirit.

The biggest concern levelled at organizations such as Betel is that by discouraging individual autonomy and minimizing free time, residents become trapped within and dependent on the regimented structures of community. Life inside the community becomes an artificial and reified environment where residents become institutionalized into a habitual religious lifestyle. Some would argue that total detachment from the everyday challenges of the world reduces, rather than enhances, a person's ability to cope within the world. If, or when, a resident chooses to leave the community, they will experience difficulty readjusting to independent living. This underlines the importance of integrating aftercare in all stages of the programme in order to build resilience, motivation and relapse prevention when residents leave. Successful rehabilitation has to have intensive support and supervision in the early stages, but it has to move on from that. With more resources, Betel may be able to allow people to move on from peer supervision into independent accommodation or employment, whilst keeping some level of support with the Betel community.

In summary, Betel seems to work for a select number of individuals who thrive in a rigid abstinence-based religious community, yet the organization's statistics show the vast majority of drug users are not ready for the high demands of such a programme.

Let us now turn to a different way Christians have dealt with this problem in drug ministry. The problem is not simply one of retention, but a fundamentally new way of relating to the drug-using 'other'.

The Pauluskerk

Located in the heart of a deprived district of central Rotterdam,[24] the Pauluskerk (St Paul's Church) is a shelter and day centre for the homeless, drug users and illegal immigrants in the city. The church attracted controversy for its seemingly tolerant views on drug use. This pioneering harm-reduction service ranges from free advice and clean needle exchange to making supervised rooms available for heroin and cocaine users to take their drugs in a safe and sanitary environment.

The Pauluskerk runs voluntarily schemes to help people manage their addiction and contribute to society in a productive way. These include a scheme that gives people's benefits in regular allowances as to avoid destitution, voluntary placements and job opportunities in the creative arts, and regular activities that help stabilize the chaotic drug user's life. These activities are designed to be drug free. The church also provides temporary housing and financial support for immigrants who have been denied refugee status or an immigrant permit. Attached to this service-provider role, the Pauluskerk is involved in political advocacy and demonstrations to raise awareness on the plight of undocumented migrants and drug users in the city. The Pauluskerk is not simply another social service agency, but its vision is to be a worshipping community that serves the outcasts of society.

Development of the organization

In 1979, the Dutch Reformed Church gave Reverend Hans Visser a carte blanche to develop his vision of an inclusive church amongst the homeless, addicted and socially excluded population in Rotterdam. Visser was returning to his native Holland from being a missionary in Indonesia for ten years. His vision was driven by Jesus' parable of the sheep and the goats in Matthew 25: how we love the 'least of these', which he read to be the homeless, drug users and illegal immigrants, is a reflection of how to love Jesus.

In 1980, the Pauluskerk opened its doors as a place where people could meet and find comfort in the form of a bed, a meal, a conversation, or even a drug, in a safe and nurturing environment. Its liberal drug policy was on one hand intended to reduce blood-borne infections and overdose-related deaths associated with intravenous drug use in risky environments, whilst on the other it was driven by Visser's vision to build a church amongst the addicted that accepted the person in their particular circumstance and did not demand they should change their behaviour or identity in order to come and experience a loving community. It is careful to ensure standards of conduct are loving and respect the dignity of all persons, so that the ethos of acceptance does not become a way to justify inappropriate or hurtful behaviour. To this end, violence, intimidation and discrimination are not permitted under any circumstance, and individuals who cross these boundaries are asked to leave the centre.

One of the first activities of Pauluskerk was to set up a drop-in service next to Central Station where chaotic drug users could meet friends and social workers to have a meal, coffee, and through pre-existing contacts, obtain access to hard and soft drugs. Local businesses complained that the 'dumping' of drug users in the surrounding area, dubbed 'Platform Zero', had increased incidents of pick-pocketing and robbery. This led to the forceful removal by the police of suspected drug users and homeless people from the area. One famous incident occurred on the 22 June 1992 when a group of off-duty marines ran through the area, beating people and breaking things in the day centre. The Dutch public sided with the marines and there was little public sympathy towards the Pauluskerk. Visser began to consider other solutions, and developed new schemes in the Pauluskerk to help drug users after the closure of Platform Zero in December 1994.

Despite these confrontations with police in 1992, the Pauluskerk developed good working relationships with public health and social services, which provide a doctor and three mental health nurses, as well as medication and supplies such as needles and condoms. Access to consultation and medical care is essential for people without insurance. There are weekly meetings between the Pauluskerk and local officials and police where concerns can be aired, but the Pauluskerk is not an extension of the government and therefore never cooperates in, for example, investigations.

In 2007, shortly after Visser's retirement, the Pauluskerk scaled back its activities as a new purpose-built centre was erected on the site of the Pauluskerk. This followed some years of often grim negotiation between municipality and the church. (For more information on the political and organizational context, see Davelaar, Williams and Beaumont, this volume.)

During this time, minister Dick Couveé continued the vision of the Pauluskerk in a small day centre adjacent to the church,

working with twelve paid employees and about a hundred volunteers, where in previous years this was closer to fifty and more
than one hundred and fifty respectively. The new centre has five
floors; two for the open house, one for religious worship and two
floors where twenty rooms are built for temporary shelter. Also in
the new building there is a café, an alternative bank and a store
with fair trade products.

Impact

The Pauluskerk seems to divide many inside and outside the
church and Dutch society. Some assert the policy of tolerance
breaks Dutch law and suggest Visser's unorthodox views on drug
use and prostitution are immoral, un-Christian and counter-productive to encouraging abstinence. Yet the majority in the Dutch
church are attracted to Visser's radical ethos of engagement, and
whilst the very nature of the Pauluskerk approach does not enable
us to make any direct statistical comparisons in the success of the
organization, I wish to outline at least three distinctive points
concerning the significance of the acceptance ethos, or what some
scholars have termed postsecular *caritas*.[25]

Postsecular caritas

The Pauluskerk's ethos of acceptance derives from Christ's incarnation into a sinful world, listening and striving to understand
our processes to become fully engaged in them. In welcoming
'the other', the Pauluskerk counters the prejudice and injustice
of how people are treated in Dutch society, particularly the belief
that drug users who fall through the welfare safety net have themselves to blame and do not deserve help: that it is better for them
to hit 'rock bottom' sooner to recognize the need to change their
ways. Similar 'tough love' attitudes are levelled at soup runs in
the UK, suggesting food handouts artificially support harmful
lifestyles.

However, the Pauluskerk's radical understanding of Christian
caritas and God's unconditional love for *all* people leads to an act
of hospitality that challenges moral notions of (un)deservingness.
Visser's pragmatic acceptance of drug users using their drugs on

church premises does not imply a passive endorsement of long-term substance abuse, nor is it exclusively concerned with public health and the safety of the user; rather, it is an attempt to resist the dehumanizing process of 'othering' that works to stigmatize drug users as untrustworthy deviants. People suffering from drug addictions, Visser believed, have been punished enough through drug-related biopsychosocial vulnerability, so further punishment in the form of criminalization, exclusion from public spaces, and withdrawing basic assistance in the hope that drug users will suddenly enter treatment, was seen as counter-productive and contradictory. More likely, such a policy potentially pushes addicts further from support agencies that can help them manage their addiction. Visser believed this carrot and 'baseball bat' approach was inconsistent with Jesus' own ministry of drawing alongside and befriending the déclassé of Palestinian society. Faced with social-spatial isolation that conspires to strip individuals of their God-given worth and dignity as created beings,[26] the Pauluskerk sought to create an inclusive, undemanding space where persons of all backgrounds or circumstances could gather to find physical, social, and spiritual sustenance as required.

What marks out the Pauluskerk as different from other forms of charity is the sense of community and sociality between the volunteers/staff and service users. Its practices of hospitality and solidarity with 'the other' build relationships of trust, openness and belonging where those who have very little freely choose to give a lot. These spaces of sociality create a distinct non-hierarchical atmosphere, not always found in top-down and detached processes of giving. Furthermore, the acceptance ethos creates an environment where individuals feel comfortable and safe to acknowledge their behaviour and identity in a deep way. This has helped facilitate more honest relationships between service users and mainstream social workers, and connect 'hardest to reach' individuals with health and social services.

The Pauluskerk affirms the unconditional gesture of 'come as you are', but discourages the hopelessness that implies entrenched drug users cannot change. Its activity programme directs drug users in the possibility of drug-free lives. Yet drug use is not immediately singled out as the exclusive problem, and the centre helps people deal with problems often associated with drug use:

homelessness, violence, crime, mental health problems, relationship breakdown, poor self-worth, and financial exclusion.

It is argued that the undemanding ethos of the service is essential in meeting the chaotic drug user at their point of need, ensuring their safety, and helping them manage their addiction; yet the Pauluskerk's relational ethic of hospitality goes beyond this to express an openness to 'otherness' that reaffirms the equality and dignity of all human beings in their differences.

In this sense, the Pauluskerk's ethos embodies a postsecular *caritas* that places very little to no expectation on services users to change or conceal aspects of their identity as a condition of service. No demands are made in terms of mandatory participation in religious practice, nor are participants required to work towards an idealized notion of personhood. Visser argued that demanding someone to change their behaviour is not only counter-productive, in that it is potentially alienating, but it also suggests that the person is only of value if he or she is willing or able to change who they are. This is a stance towards hospitality that refuses to obscure the alterity of 'the other'.[27] Rather than convert 'the other' into their own norms of acceptability, an act that risks imperialism, staff and volunteers enter the world of 'the other', seeking to understand what makes sense for them in their particular context. This stance is more than person-centred care that populates healthcare provision; rather, it is a therapeutic relationship between giver and receiver that brings about an understanding of commonality and interdependency of human life. Through this, a much more invitational and dialogical relationship develops between different Christian and non-Christian perspectives coming together in creative ways. While some groups would eschew this opportunity as a threat to the purity of theological belief, and would prefer to remain sheltered inside a common doctrinal set of beliefs, Davelaar et al. (this volume) point to the Pauluskerk becoming a space of rapprochement between different humanist, secular and religious motivations.[28]

There are two further lenses I would suggest we can see the Pauluskerk through. Firstly, the Pauluskerk can be understood as a 'temporary autonomous zone'[29] amid hostile city space, a place free from the confines of law and social norms, creating a space *able* to re-imagine social relations and identity. It injects hope in overpowering situations, giving people quick glimpses of what a new world might look like; inviting participation in a counter-cultural vision of a different order: one that makes a spectacle of moral notions of 'deservedness'.

Secondly, these symbolic spectacles pronounce the subversive ethics of the gospel in a society stripped of grace and coming together, and through these acts the Pauluskerk illustrates the opportunity for the church to truly become an incarnational community whose ethics of inclusion and sociality with 'the other' prophetically discern and challenge the ways – direct and indirect – people come to live highly precarious lives.[30]

Differences

One of the striking differences between Betel and the Pauluskerk are the spaces occupied by these FBOs. Betel residences are usually located in or on the edge of the urban-rural fringe, and are prem-ised on the need to take people out of the supposed territories of socially excluded groups to minimize distraction. In contrast, the Pauluskerk uses a church in the centre of a deprived district of Rotterdam to form not just an appropriate centre to 'reach out' from or 'drop into', but to build resilience among people trying to gain control over their addiction in the environment they would likely to return to if they entered/completed residential treatment. Also the Pauluskerk's central location in the city challenges the scripting of public space and the rights to the city more directly. The Pauluskerk represents the potential of FBOs to paint prophet-ically alternative pictures of the city (and the church), through the denouncement of the socially excluding practices of contain-ment and 'othering' that work to stigmatize those struggling with addictions.

Lastly, the Pauluskerk differs from Betel in that it gladly works with volunteers who do not share the same beliefs structure. To this end Couveé says, 'The Pauluskerk is a church in the strictest sense of the word',[31] a worshipping community that has porous walls between 'believer' and 'non-believer', and welcomes people who are passionate about making a difference to partic-ipate in the Jesus narrative even if they are deeply ambivalent towards elements of Christian doctrine. In order to stay clear from missional drift and to promote the mixing of beliefs, Couveé tries to strike a balance within the volunteer work teams, and encourages teams to comprise of religious and non-religious individuals. The church has created 'reflective spaces' to stimulate dialogue and spiritual development. These are not forcefully evangelical; instead, they take a more postmodern approach that attracts those with humanist and other motivations to participate in a shared hope in the present.[32] This open attitude to volunteering is in contrast to Betel's more guarded boundaries of difference between the Christian faith and others, which does not risk threatening the purity of the organization by working with believers who do not share their own theological practice.

One of the challenges identified by Couveé is how the Pauluskerk maintains this model of church premised not on the doctrinal unity but on the blurred encounters of religious insiders and outsiders. This echoes wider questions of how Christians remain faithful to living a life that showcases Jesus in a pluralist church context. Here it seems there is an opportunity to embrace a more postmodern style of mission that brings religious and non-religious people to practice theo-ethics of hope, faith, and love,[33] which I would argue is not only a part of discipleship and belonging, but integral to the establishment of God's pursuit in redeeming this world. In these spaces of rapprochement, more visceral understandings of God as love matter more than identity or doctrinal distinctions; and in engaging 'the other' within the self, God, and neighbour, we cultivate the kinds of selves required to live in harmony with each other in a pluralistic world.[34]

Conclusion

This chapter has discussed the work of two significant FBOs bringing about transformation in the lives of people struggling with addictions and exclusion. Both organizations show us the passions, perseverance and risks involved in acting on the Christian principles of *caritas* and hope in working with drug users. Each organization reflects a prophetic and subversive community of believers whose beliefs in action seek to redeem the indifferent stasis of postmodern nihilism. In the context of neoliberal urban governance, these organizations increasingly provide essential services for those excluded from, or falling through, the shrinking welfare safety net.

Despite these similarities, there are stark differences in the ethos and methods pursued by Betel and the Pauluskerk. Betel works on an individual basis, bringing people into a semi-monastic environment geared towards Christian discipleship and long-term abstinence. In contrast, the Pauluskerk emphasizes the need for harm-reduction services in the spaces inhabited by drug users, and to open up church spaces to become a community of acceptance amongst the socially excluded. There is more to these differences than a debate about the merits and perils of abstinence and harm-reduction interventions. Rather, this chapter has reflected on the criticisms each organization has faced – for Betel, this is largely the suspicion of social control and religious indoctrination, and for the Pauluskerk, the view that its services act as a disincentive for abstinence. These problems were explored through the lens of practical theology to ask questions about how Christians deal with 'otherness' in drug ministry.

To this end, we can present two provisional conclusions. The first relates to the ethics of evangelism. Betel's evangelical ethos exemplifies a common attitude amongst Christian groups dealing with drug users, which demand 'the other' to assimilate to the norms of the host through mandatory participation in prayer, worship and Bible teaching. Christian discipleship is the programme, not simply a condition service users must consent to. To this end, care is strictly given on the terms of the host, without taking into account the specific position of 'the other'. In contrast, the Pauluskerk follows a dialogical stance to 'otherness' that stresses the interrelations between caregiver and receiver. There is little to no expectation on clients to adopt and perform religious identities if they are to receive assistance. In doing so, the Pauluskerk remains open and accessible to all people at different stages of addiction, and can therefore reach a wider group of people, not just the select few.

Evangelical outreach ventures into the world of 'the other' with the intention to bring them in line to the host's norm of respectability, whereas Pauluskerk's postsecular ethos enters the world of 'the other' but takes up residence there, learning what has meaning in their context and empowering the care receiver to dialogically set the terms of engagement. This reduces the stark asymmetrical power relations between host and guest. These ethics of dealing with difference have their correlative in the types of spaces inhabited by these organizations.

The second conclusion refers to the tension between (semi-) monastic and more open-styled organization. The clear strength of semi-monastic community is the intensive support available and worldly detachment that can sometimes bring about spiritual renewal. However, this strength can also be considered a weakness as those leaving the community find it hard to adjust to the challenges of daily life outside regimented monastic life. Furthermore, whilst a large number of residents benefit from the religious programme, Betel certainly does not suit all, and many find the discipleship programme either too intrusive or unhelpful when taken alongside previously held beliefs and circumstances.

The strength of the Pauluskerk's non-monastic and undemanding ethos enables relationships and a sense of belonging to be built amongst those who are not 'ready' for treatment, or those for whom an abstinence-based programme is simply inappropriate and unrealistic. In its incarnational presence and long-term engagement with drug users, the Pauluskerk could address the deeper issues underlying drug addiction. As a result, drug users may be better equipped to reduce and eventually stop substance use because they have done so amid the ready availability of drugs rather than the physical removal from it.

These two organizations reflect two very different approaches in faith-based responses to drug use and treatment. Through the lens of practical theology, these case studies have raised interesting questions about how Christians relate to 'the other' and the different ethics of evangelism practised in drug ministries. In spite of these differences, both organizations meet the needs of people who live highly precarious lives, and do so in a way that communicates hope and God's love in his created, but hurting, world.

CHAPTER 4

Re-engaging With the Margins: The Salvation Army 614UK Network and Incarnational Praxis

Sam Thomas

(Names have been changed in this chapter to preserve anonymity)

Introduction

In contemporary Christianity, many evangelical Christians are currently coming to terms with how they might best couple together practice and theology. At the heart of this challenge is an attempt to authentically interconnect sharing the good news of Jesus Christ, his life and resurrection, with the task of displaying this good news through progressive practice in local communities.[1] This is provoking many Christians to question how they might best live in relation to a myriad network of known and unknown others.

How do I live out just and positive relationships with others? How might we, the church, best get involved in our own local cities, towns and villages? Trying to answer these questions has led many Christians to engage in different expressions of social justice, both local and international in scope. Underpinning this is an attitude of doing something rather than nothing; a move to see faith-through-praxis held hand-in-hand with faith-through-dogma.[2] And enlivened by a generosity of spirit, these Christians are driven by a passion to seek to live a lifestyle that immanently reflects the full character of God.

One significant expression of this turn to action in the UK has been moulded around the reflexive and continual questioning of how the church should re-engage with marginal and under-resourced neighbourhoods. What should the posture and the practice of the church be in these circumstances? These attempts to re-engage have brought a colourful collection of people to the place where they are convicted by the practical application of the Christian faith, and this conviction has led them to live out radical and meaningful expressions of what it means to be a Christian *within* these communities, serving from the inside as local neighbours. This chapter focuses on these attempts to re-engage with society's margins in an incarnational manner, and it is structured into three sections.

Firstly I draw upon the example of the Salvation Army 614UK network to present a case study of what it might mean to be an incarnational expression of church among marginal, socially excluded people. This case study example paints a tangible expression of how a local church can find its roots in local community, embedding itself in the local social landscape to work towards social justice and transformation. Secondly, with the aim of giving greater context to this specific example I step back from the 614UK Salvation Army case study and outline how particular reflexive critiques have shaped portions of the Christian church to consider how it should re-engage and reconnect with socio-economically deprived geographic communities. Thirdly, and with the aim of providing some theological and discursive backbone to this chapter, I give an overview of the type of Christian theology that has shaped these re-engagements. Here I focus on the Christian theology of Christ's incarnation and I outline the key driving elements that shape incarnational praxis in deprived areas. This outlines how the attempts to share and serve as fellow neighbours in socially and economically deprived areas are grounded in attempts to try to pursue radical Christian discipleship; following the example of Christ and the way he encountered the outcast, the marginalized and the oppressed, without judgement and with unconditional love.

The Salvation Army 614UK Network

The Salvation Army 614UK network is a network and strategy for planting Salvation Army teams in some of the most deprived neighbourhoods within the United Kingdom and Ireland. The 614UK network identifies areas of high multiple deprivation, what it termed the 'forgotten 5 per cent',[3] and recruits teams of people who will move into the area to live and work. The 614UK network iterates that it does not believe the answer to be to import service programmes, rather it is about a commitment to a certain way of living out God's story, which is all about favouring the poor, living in the neighbourhood, experiencing transformation and building community.[4]

For these teams, being a part of a SA 614UK community is not only about living in these areas because of God's compassion for these places, but it is because they believe the Bible re-imagines something different for these neighbourhoods.[5] At present the SA 614UK network is based in eight different communities across the UK. One particular SA 614UK project is based in Oldham, Greater Manchester.[6] Oldham SA 614UK runs in partnership with the Eden-Network.[7]

Historically Oldham was a thriving mill town, but by the mid-twentieth century it was severely affected by industrial decline. Today Oldham suffers from high rates of unemployment and has been subject to a serious lack of economic reinvestment due to the town's historical over-reliance on the cotton industry. In recent years, Oldham has become known in the media for the race riots that took place in 2001.[8] These riots evoked several independent enquiries reportedly claiming that the riots erupted out of a number of bedrock issues: a reliance upon one single industry, segregated patterns of settlement and education, a lack of social and cultural mixing, and perceived cultural differences and ethnic clustering.[9] Before receiving significant amounts of regeneration funding under Labour's New Deals for Communities scheme, the specific neighbourhood in which Oldham 614UK is based was quantified as being in the top 2 per cent of the most deprived neighbourhoods in the country.[10] In the most recent government statistical analysis, this neighbourhood was still ranked in the top 500 most deprived neighbourhoods in the country.[11]

Oldham SA 614UK was established in 2003 on the back of the Christian summer festival, Festival Manchester.[12] Oldham SA 614UK has several paid staff workers and over a dozen volunteers; all of them live in the immediate neighbourhood. Weekly ongoing projects included drop-in youth clubs, football clubs, a multimedia project that aims to build positive stories and depictions of the neighbourhood, a school cookery club, a school's learning and support project and a school educational project linking two different local schools, one local comprehensive and one fee-paying former grammar school. Once a week, Oldham SA 614UK runs a Christian youth club and a mentoring programme. Both these activities give a signposted space where young people can find out more about the Christian faith and journey with it for themselves.

Oldham SA 614UK describes itself as a Christian community who express their faith by 'working to improve their community through commitment, friendship, action, care, compassion, love and neighbourliness'.[13] Oldham SA 614UK is transparent and open to the fact that as a faith community they are committed to a personal faith in Jesus Christ and that this is expressed both 'through prayer and worship but also through personal relationships, [and] how they represent their community and fight for justice'.[14] As a community of faith, Oldham SA 614UK collectively gathers in several homes for prayer, worship and teaching, and it meets corporately as a 'church' in a local primary school hall for worship, teaching and a shared lunch.

Oldham SA 614UK and incarnational living

For Oldham SA 614UK to become incarnationally embedded in the local community involved the choice of a number of volunteers and staff to purposefully relocate into the immediate area. For many of these volunteers it has meant sacrificing other opportunities: turning down job prospects or places at high-profile universities to embrace the commitments of being a part of the Oldham SA 614UK, and embracing becoming a local neighbour in the community.

As volunteers and staff move into the local area, a certain *exposure* takes place.[15] The lack of facilities, resources and diminished standards of living often forms the seedbed for action. Many individual members of Oldham SA 614UK are *affected* by the stories of relative hardship and deprivation that they witness. In effect, these encounters empathetically draw volunteers closer to the wider community, binding them to individuals and consolidating a concern for their wellbeing. Similar to the accounts of the *Pastoraat Oude Wijken* in the Netherlands, just 'being there' creates a people-centred approach rather than solely a problem-solving culture.[16] This people-focused approach means it is commonplace for volunteers and staff of Oldham SA 614UK to be deeply affected by the testimonials, narratives and daily witnessed lived-accounts of people living in the area.

One example of this exposure is in the account of a young Christian mum and volunteer named Claire. Having spent a lot of her spare time on the estate tutoring one young person, she felt urgently challenged by the way the educational system seemed to fail some students caught up in a host of other social issues:

> . . . it was just something that I was really annoyed about, particularly Sharon, who was completely off the rails . . . I taught her A-level biology for a bit . . . she did not do very well in her GCSEs, and then I was, like . . . 'Well, I will teach you some biology, then we will see how we go' . . . then she would turn up every week . . . We would talk about it for forty minutes, she would go away and she would do no work all week and she would just reproduce it, like, half-stoned, it was just incredible . . . The whole system does not really work for those kids . . . I did not know what to do . . .'[17]

Claire's sentiments were also affected when she was deeply troubled by the inadequacy of healthcare in the local neighbourhood. This drove her to acknowledge a deep-seated personal anger about this, and the complacent and apathetical acceptance of substandard access to care, as she explains:

> I was really angry about the healthcare my neighbours and the people I knew were getting . . . and everybody knew that the doctors were [rubbish] and they gave prescriptions for ridiculous things, and [people] were referred on . . . nobody could do anything about it.

Her anger with the structural injustice embedded in the provision of both local educational and healthcare provision finally led her to sacrificially stall completing her own medical degree to set up a health company. She set aside her personal ambitions to pursue the wellbeing of the wider neighbourhood in order to actively provide better healthcare for her neighbours. Claire saw this as part and parcel of practising a sense of incarnation, developing a gracious self-giving sense of selfhood that prioritized the well-being of others before her own career success.

For Susan, another volunteer, embracing this incarnational theo-ethical prompt to be Christ-like led her to intentionally work in the local secondary school. This opened her up to develop an attitude of concern and discontent against a school system that repeatedly labelled certain 'sink students' devoid of making it through, and consequently of less value; somehow deserving less attention in the school community.

Oldham SA 614UK and community

The partnership with the Eden Network, which has its roots in working with young people, has meant that much of the practical application of the Christian faith in this local context has worked its way out in faithfully engaging with young people. This has been emphasized by the fact that some of the volunteers drafted in through the Salvation Army have been able to draw upon their church-based experience of working informally with young people, while others put to use their professional skills as trained youth workers.

Through being deeply affected by the structural injustices that persist in both the neighbourhood and among the local public services, Claire and Susan went on to develop various inclusionary initiatives. For Claire this developed into an initiative that partners young people in the local comprehensive school with local pupils from the privately paid school in the same area. This initiative has snowballed into both a social responsibility initiative and a tutoring programme to widen the chances of their participation in tertiary education. In turn this initiative aims to begin to redeem the ghettoized nature of the estate through bridging young people of different economic backgrounds.

In contrast to Claire, Susan responded to her feelings of disaffection and disapproval by wanting to change the school system from within. Susan worked alongside the full-time Eden youth worker, Phil, to imbue hope into situations that can at times be awash with target-based league tables and tokenistic qualifications. With the help of Phil, Susan started responding to this malaise of concern by delivering a targeted curriculum and investing extra time in and out of school in the lives of these young people. Using Phil's previous occupational skills as a chef, they delivered a cookery class to encourage and engage with these individuals and matched this with a school timetabled set of lessons.

Matching these two responses with the examples of how both Susan and Claire became aware of the level of need, having both been repeatedly exposed to people's stories and lives, hints towards how many of these initiatives are set up as a direct result of the relational encounters and experiences with individual young people in the neighbourhood. What is particularly interesting is that the lines of flight that each and every one of these initiatives take is only made possible because of the volunteer's incarnational presence in the community. This incarnational presence enables them to feel and hear quite clearly what is needed. The physical body becomes a direct and discerning way of knowing what are the problematic social issues, and being physically close to socio-economically deprived others becomes a key tool through which compassion is enlivened and turned into a sentiment to act on behalf of, and with, others. In the case example of Oldham SA 614UK, however, sometimes it is also clear that social initiatives simply arise as a response to *plug a gap* in provision. For Oldham SA 614UK this took the form of catering for an underrepresented age range or a night of the week when there was no statutory provision.

What is significant about these particular responses to plug gaps in provision is the way that these spaces are made up of the ongoing attempts of volunteers and staff to faithfully live out good and godly Christian virtues. These performances of faith, as something notably expressed in behaviour, create a certain 'feel to the place' and encourage a particular culture. Displays of good character and friendship are generated and enacted during the intermingling of volunteers, staff and local young people and, in effect, these moments of laughter, conversation, support and guidance have the ability to transform particular micro-geographies of the estate into more positive environments, translated as open, friendly, welcoming and peaceful localized spaces of hospitality.[18]

In the case of Oldham SA 614UK, this is clearly seen in the account of a local Police Community Support Officer (PCSO), Amanda, describing a youth drop-in that Oldham SA 614UK provides:

It is always very welcoming when you come in . . . Frank really makes me laugh . . . and I get on well with Dave as well, and even though they are a faith-based group, in that the Eden project is run by the Salvation Army, they don't throw the church in your face or anything like that, they don't try and change you; you are what you are . . . and I do believe that the kids have more respect here and stuff like that. When you are in the youth club [statutory provision], you are dealing with issues, and when I come here I can relax and I can play pool, there is just no issues . . . it's dead chilled. I [can] sit on the couch and the kids [will] come round me; you see, if I sat in there [statutory provision], [I] would not have any kids round [me]; you gotta go to the kids. Here the kids will come to you, speak to you; it is kinda a lot more chilled atmosphere, it is a lot more like family . . .[19]

Amanda's testimony speaks of what she feels when she visits the Christian-run youth drop-in club. It makes her feel a welcomed visitor, at ease about being a PSCO in this amicable setting. The way she describes it as lacking any signs of 'church in your face' speaks of the way in which the Christian faith is not overtly pushed. Yet at the same time, it is clear that she is recounting something of how the Christian faith is outwardly performed in these youth-orientated spaces. She testifies of something that she experiences about the drop-in club that feels different. While she describes that no one is out to obviously try to change her, her encounters within this chilled and family atmosphere testify to something different. Overall what is clear is that these spaces become known for their welcoming nature, and the staff and volunteers who weekly make them a reality become renowned for their hospitality and their kindness.

Alongside creating spaces of hospitality, through which youth and other statutory workers can harmoniously interact together, Oldham SA 614UK has put in place many measures to effectively build spaces of partnership. This has been done through building imaginative resonance of what the estate could become. Practically this has involved organizing 'visioning days' to collaboratively bring together different local activists, Third Sector organizations and statutory organizations to collectively re-imagine the estate. Deliberately, this has involved attempting to re-narrate the estate through a media project venture with the young people. Here the intention is to collectively give space to the hopeful and positive stories already emerging from within the neighbourhood, countering the effect of wider negative media discourses.

Pragmatic in nature, these partnerships are often created with the impetus of building the capacity for action by increasing access to financial and social capital. This has often been built on the back of a common rationale and a good relationship. In the case of the youth sector involvement, the Oldham SA 614UK partnerships have officially and unofficially developed with other organizations that seek to positively impact the lives of young people. These range from partnerships with police, the youth inclusion programme and local schools. Most of the time these are not set up as a means to an end (e.g. to reduce antisocial behaviour), but to give more space to developing greater relationships with both the young people and the partnering staff members of other organizations. In turn, this has fed back into the ability for Oldham SA 614UK to collaboratively build spaces and practices of hospitality and mutability on the estate.

Just as the example of the youth worker, Phil, highlights how some members of the church might draw upon their professional youth work skills to make a difference through provision and partnership, other members, like Claire, have become embedded in building the 'kingdom of God' through the healthcare sector. Drawing upon a combination of her discontent with the inadequacy of healthcare provision, and her own interest in health and medical care, Claire tirelessly put every effort into renewing local healthcare so that it would have a focus on excellence and justice. With a group of committed Christian general practitioners Claire set up a healthcare community interest company and social enterprise called Hope Citadel.[20] This gave those involved a chance to do medical care differently, battling against the bureaucracies of a target-based culture that sees results, figures and statistics put before the locally contextualized lives of patients. Moving beyond these mandatory targets has meant that Hope Citadel can prioritize effective change and increased wellbeing in the local neighbourhood community over healthcare that is driven by free market ideology.

In this first section I have used the case study account of the partnership between the Salvation Army 614UK network and the Eden Network to illustrate how Christians are radically re-engaging with marginal, socio-economically deprived areas. This case study and the denomination and networks by which it is supported is certainly not the only example of marginal re-engagement in the UK, but it presents an interesting example of the practical outworking of what is in fact a broader set of faith-inspired projects within Christian praxis. Aiming to contextualize this specific example within a wider framework I now want to step back and enter into a broader discussion of the critical and theological foundations that motivate similar expressions of the Christian faith more generally across the UK.

Critiquing Church Praxis

Many critical questions have been asked of how the Christian faith should be practised in the light of socio-economical and political needs of surrounding communities, and a good number of these criticisms have been from outside of Christian faith networks. On the one hand, these criticisms[21] have questioned the right Christians have to ardently proselytize and, on the other hand, they have queried[22] whether Christian acts of intervention and charity are only the displays and constructions 'do-gooders' seeking to better themselves. Recently, however, a reflexive resurgent critique from within Christian networks has prompted the Western church to question how it relates to 'the poor',[23] and this critique has motivated many cases similar to the Salvation Army 614UK network to question the theology of how we engage with today's poor. Particular Christian faith-practitioners have questioned how urban Christian faith communities and FBOs should be structured,[24] where they should be placed, and what values should be central.[25] Here, however, I just want to focus on the specific set of criticisms that have motivated Christians to relocate to marginal, socio-economically deprived parts of the UK. I will do this by drawing on the critical contribution of Gary Bishop, a faith-based practitioner previously working for the Salvation Army who is now the managing director of Justlife,[26] a community interest company that tackles drug addiction in east Manchester.

The critique by Gary Bishop, in his book *Darkest England and the Way Back In*,[27] suggests a two-fold contradiction in what the Christian faith so often upholds as its central narratives. In the context of his own denominational movement, the Salvation Army, he writes that what has emerged is both a physical distance between churches and the marginalized, and a particular way of engaging with the marginalized; one that is temporary, and one that is often solely mediated through run-from-a-distance organizational and project-based contexts. Gary Bishop explains that the physical distance between the Western church and 'the poor' has been exacerbated by the increasing wealth of those who practice Christianity. He highlights how the Salvation Army has grown from a nineteenth-century movement to a twenty-first century respectable organization, broadly being subject to an upward shift in socio-economic terms. The practical implications of these changes have meant that Christian congregations enter into areas of deprivation in a breeze-in breeze-out fashion, and this has directly shaped the way in which Christians relate to marginal others. As a result, Christians only briefly stand side by side with those they are seeking to serve, and this has huge consequences on the way in which relationships lack both real permanence and solidarity.

Bishop is certain that in contrast to these distant and delocalized expressions of the Christian faith what would be most effective is to *journey back in*, consciously choosing to live within these areas of socio-economic deprivation. This, he believes, would result in 'becoming part of these communities, making real friendships with people that may seem very different to us at the onset but allowing them to shape and change us so that we can become at home in their native territory'.[28] He hopes that this would result in an asymmetrical relationship with others, opening up 'a level of relationship with local people that is difficult to achieve when you only do things *for* the community'.[29]

The challenges of Gary Bishop have been echoed by Shane Claiborne,[30] another prominent Christian activist. As an American Christian author and activist, Shane Claiborne has repeatedly suggested – and here he honestly and admittedly includes himself – that the hypocrisy and complacent indifference with which Christians treat Jesus' teachings on the marginalized has both depersonalized poverty and has created a relational, and in some cases spatial and emotional distance, from the marginalized. Shane's critique of the church is that it is often too safe and too comfortable, and that this needs to change if we do not want to continue to mirror wider society in excluding those Jesus himself would have embraced and loved.

Both of these critiques mirror a wider discontentment among many Christians. While the teachings and life of Christ reflect how close he was to the lives of the poor, many Christians are frustrated with how far removed the church is from the lives of the poor today. In a heartfelt and sincere form, many of these Christians have felt convicted that God's mission is not something that we just take to the poor, but something that we live out *with* and *among* them. As in the case of the Salvation Army 614UK network, this critique has been a key driver in motivating Christian men and women to relocate and make their home in deprived neighbourhoods across the UK. Beyond the individual example of the Salvation Army 614UK network, a number of other organizational and denominational networks exist whose purpose is to redistribute resources – particularly volunteers, time and money – to support other Christians who have been in these deprived areas all along.

A broad survey across the UK uncovers that these *incarnational* expressions of Christian witness in deprived areas take many different forms. They differ according to the level of organizational and denominational backing, and whether an initiative is part and parcel of an attempt to grow or plant churches in what are statistically under-churched areas. The shape and nature of what actually happens is also rather dependent on the capacity of each individual initiative. Spanning the UK, the shape of these incarnational expressions of Christian witness in deprived areas might be the result of Christian individuals willing to relocate; or, contrastingly, in another form, be the collective ambition of a group of friends or university leavers wishing to carve out a collective semi-monastic rhythm to life in a deprived neighbourhood. More obviously formed as a result of the endeavours of a Christian church denomination or Christian charity, expressions of incarnational witness in deprived neighbourhoods can also emerge out of a Christian organizational network's facilitation of a creative partnership with small local churches already present in the area.[31] Some, like the example of the Salvation Army 614UK network, are simply new attempts to church plant into one of these statistically deprived areas of the country, and sometimes these are backed by wider denominations.[32]

Underneath the way that they all differ in size, shape or denominational culture, there does appear to be core theological and discursive themes that structure the nature of praxis across this emerging landscape. These attempts at tackling issues of social justice are theologically influenced by a sincere deep grappling with the narrative of Christ's incarnation, and a careful and discerned questioning of the way in which the church and Christians should participate in these disadvantaged communities.

Being Incarnational: Embracing Proximity and Developing Virtue

A resounding conversation is building across contemporary Western Christianity, and it is one that is focusing on how the Western church, as an embodiment of Christ, should look and act after Christendom.[33] Whether the church has in part, or in full, fallen from being a major institutional stakeholder of power in contemporary Western society, Christians are deeply questioning what appropriate stance the church and its members must take in today's admittedly multi-vocal, multifaith and seemingly relativistic cultural setting. At the centre of this conversation is a turn to consider the life and death of Jesus Christ in ways that re-centre the importance of Christ's incarnational witness.[34] These considerations are focusing in again on the habits and virtues that Christ both exhibited, and extolled, the way that he treated and spoke of others, and the way in which he became flesh and dwelt among us. Comparing the contemporary practices of the church and therefore themselves to those of Christ, this is very clearly shaping the actions of Christians involved in incarnational expressions of the Christian faith in deprived neighbourhoods.

Considering that the church is supposed to be theologically representative of Christ's body, many involved in incarnational expressions of the Christian faith in deprived areas have come to question the discrepancies between the biblical narratives of Christ and the practices of the church. As biblical narrative portrays the embodied life of Christ as often dwelling among and with the marginalized in society,[35] Christians involved in these forms of praxis are reflexively asking how they can emulate such a life-style when it is at times not reflected in the contemporary church. Drawing a comparison between the church and the narratives of the incarnation has therefore provided the main motivation for relocation efforts into areas of socio-economical deprivation. Initiatives such as the Eden Network[36] have sought to follow the example of how Christ dwelt with, and among, the marginalized, as they turned to question how they may be shaped by how Christ lived, as well as by what he said. Matt Wilson explains this in his book, *Eden: Called to the Streets:*

> We've spent a lot time looking at the way Eden is influenced by the physical reflection of who God is, represented in the arrival of Jesus in human history. It's also right for us to offer ourselves to be shaped by what Jesus said in his brief time here.[37]

For many of those who are incarnationally embedded in deprived parts of the country, Christ's incarnation does not only present them with a question of where they should live, it also challenges how they might live. In recent years, Western Christianity has begun to return to questions of virtue and character,[38] and questions of virtuous living have been central to those who have chosen to relocate into marginalized areas. This is clearly illustrated in how Chris Neilson, leader of a 614UK Salvation Army church, draws upon the letter of St Paul to the Philippians to express how his Christian faith has led him to try to be more Christ-like in the context in which he finds himself in Oldham, Greater Manchester:

> What I see differently about faith is this downward mobility, which you see in an example like Jesus; take the Bible passage: Philippians 2:5: 'Let your mind be like Jesus, though he had equality with God he did not consider equality with God but made himself of no reputation,

taking on the form of a servant and became obedient even to the point of death, therefore he was highly exalted' [sic]. I quote that because I think that is absolutely central to what we do. In a society that says upward mobility is right, it is our neighbourhood that exists because of this. It is the people who have lost in that game.[39]

For Chris, it is the narrative of the sacrificed and humble incarnate Christ that shapes the way he seeks to actively embody his Christian faith as he lives and shares life with others in one particular neighbourhood of Oldham. Chris is convinced the reason behind why marginal neighbourhoods – like the one he has moved into – exist is because society upholds and encourages a different set of virtues or values. In light of this upward mobility, Chris seeks to follow the example of Christ as portrayed in the narrative of the incarnation, something he words as 'downward mobility'. Chris's faithful following of the discourse of the incarnation could be seen as a countercultural ethic,[40] opposed to the widely hegemonic perusal of wealth, individualism, gain and pleasure.[41] In this way the incarnational discourse is a narrative that presents a certain confrontation in its theo-ethical call to go beyond the self, embracing what Savoj Žižek accounts to be the very 'subversive core' of Christianity.[42]

For other Christians in these contexts, the narrative of the incarnation of Christ motivates them to daily try to *identify* with marginalized others. In the same way that the Gospel presentations[43] of Christ portray him as identifying with the socially outcast, vulnerable and neglected, many of those involved in incarnational initiatives in deprived areas try to emulate this as best they can, seeking to live out a life that relationally identifies with the 'poor'.

Working towards this virtue of identification sometimes means practically moving away from a lifestyle that emulates contemporary fixations with materialism, so often the cause of instilling division and exclusion. It also means moving beyond the politically espoused virtue of liberal tolerance towards difference,[44] instead seeking to adventure towards a transformational journey of practically attempting to work out how these cultural norms are best replaced with theo-ethically derived attitudes and acts that are grounded in more radical attempts to embrace[45] and be hospitable[46] to the differences that present themselves in these marginal contexts. This might take the form of learning to create cultures of hospitality and generosity at home, inviting in strangers to share in a meal or a feast,[47] or, at the local youth drop-in club, learning to become comfortable with differences that present themselves in the use of profane language or attitudes towards sex without immediately imposing a preconceived rule-based code of conduct.

Out on the street, at the school gate, or in a partnership meeting with other organizations, these theo-ethical incarnational values might find their form in the shape of intentional attempts to create spaces of encounter;[48] temporary moments when the chance is given to shape out more time and space to cultivate habits of listening[49] to others' stories, desires and issues, rather than jumping to speak and testify of our own. Practising all these habits and strengths of character while living in socio-economically deprived areas has the potential to forge a relational closeness between the immediate Christian incarnational 'community' and the wider geographic community. It also forcefully unpicks and breaks cultural virtues that stem from materialism, consumerism and individualism, virtues that so easily can act as barriers to authentic living with and alongside others in community.[50]

Living in and creating community: Searching for transformative practice and partnership

Embedding themselves in the wider geographic community, those that are involved in incarnational expressions of the Christian faith in deprived neighbourhoods are constantly searching for how they can best become interwoven into practices and partnerships that already exist in the area. In some cases, this might lead to collective attempts with others of goodwill to bring about a common good through an involvement in community organizing,[51] while in other cases, using what vocational skills each individual Christian has, the capacity for a common good to increase in community is also envisaged and worked out through Christians actively seeking jobs in local services and using their skills to increase the welfare and wellbeing of the area.

When services and vocational participation are not available, others incarnationally living in these deprived areas often create a range of community-centred projects themselves. Very often these soon become projects collaboratively run with others who are not directly involved in the community of faith. This forms an action-based postsecular rapprochement[52] between those of faith and those of no faith, forged together by both sides wanting to locally make a difference.

Alongside efforts to become embedded into the neighbourhood community, incarnational expressions of the Christian faith in deprived areas can also be seen as creating a sense of community in, and of, their own right. Many incarnational initiatives involve some level of creating community through shared living arrangements, sharing meals and, in some cases, a shared economic purse. They also often have clear rhythms of collective Christian worship and discipleship, gathering together to read scripture and sharing in common faithful fellowship. These community arrangements are intentionally 'present for others', and they seek to have intentionally permeable boundaries between themselves and others in the neighbourhood. This two-fold approach to community means that Christians faithfully living in these marginal contexts search for ways to participate and to engage with others beyond the community of faith and, in holding onto what makes them distinctive, these Christians continue to hold to the conviction that they are also called to follow Christ Jesus, model his ways and testify of his work in their lives. This involves a continual questioning of what it means by being in the world, but not of it. This aims not to divide and cast judgement – that is only the work of the one who made us – but to live as active witnesses of our Redeemer.

Conclusion

What is so exciting about these re-engagements with the social and economic margins of British society is that they are transforming the church at the same moment that marginal, socio-economically deprived areas are being physically, socially and spiritually transformed. The margins appear to be speaking back to the church, and the church is learning and reflecting. Christians in these settings are intrinsically embedded in social change, and radical expressions of social justice are emerging in the micro and the macro, both in individual friendships and in the structural renegotiation of power and resources. Being incarnationally present in these areas brings a new level of understanding, and reshapes the church in ways that prompt reflective practice that sees Christians tackling what church might look like and how it might respond when situated once again in and amongst areas of severe social and economic deprivation.

In contrast to church being something that might look comfortably middle class and geographically removed from peripheral 'sink estates' and inner-city social housing estates, this move to 'live amongst' presents a challenging example of what radical discipleship might look like.

As Christians and others of goodwill turn to consider not only *what is* in these areas, but also *what could be*, new landscapes of hope are emerging. These assemblages of hope give space for Christians to gently and respectfully give an account of the Christian hope that is in them.[53] In these dialogical moments, Christians displaying and faithfully pursuing theo-ethical virtues are working towards what it means to be both fully human and 'born into community'. Living incarnationally in marginal neighbourhoods provides a wonderful opportunity to theo-ethically embrace the otherness of those that the unchecked spirit of capitalism drives us to dispel and write off[54] as undeserved of God's love. Instead of being obsessed with self-enrichment and self-fulfilment, where the oasis of self-gratification calls on all fronts, these faithful Christians seem to be journeying into the wilderness in search of making the impossible possible,[55] prophetically praying that dry riverbeds will run with crystal waters; a prayer that they are asking of themselves as well as of others in these disadvantaged communities. Returning to the preliminary claim that the evangelical church is once again searching how it might best move towards a return to couple together both theology and action, practice and preaching, perhaps these self-exiled journeys into the heart of unfamiliar forgotten places might be one of the radical ways in which this is happening. Perhaps expressing the Christian faith incarnationally in marginal and disadvantaged neighbourhoods is one of the ways that Christians can participate in the kingdom of Christ; a kingdom that may appear to be something more attuned with the Mad Hatter's tea party[56] than with the convenience that loving only our chosen nearest neighbour presents. God's redemptive love is certainly making its mark in these nearly forgotten places,[57] and it is very inspiring to see these communities of Christians continually asking what it means to act justly, to love mercy, and to walk humbly[58] in areas where others might choose to cross the road rather than walk through them.

CHAPTER 5

Urban Expression: Convictional Communities and Urban Social Justice

Mike Pears

Introduction

There is no doubt that over the last three decades or so, there has been a significant shift of understanding in Christian circles in the UK about the nature of the church's engagement with the multicultural inner city communities and marginal white estates. Of course, adaptation and change is nothing new for the urban church, but the early 1980s marked a significant point of departure for a number of reasons. The picture is complex, and experience varies from city to city so a short introduction inevitably runs the risk of misrepresentation or oversimplification. However, with this qualification in mind, I will seek to describe briefly some of the factors involved in shaping the nature of the church's urban engagement, before focusing on one particular organization, namely Urban Expression, and its values-based approach to this task.

The plight of many inner city communities through the 1970s is well documented, with the desolate conditions experienced in many areas being a cause for acute political concern.[1] The policies of the Thatcher government implemented around the mid 1980s really marked the beginning of major physical, social and political transformation of urban landscapes. The sheer scale of change through this period can be exemplified by considering just one of Thatcher's policies, that of the sale of council housing, which, along with sharply rising house prices, seriously impacted the lives of the urban working class, in many cases undermining long-standing community roots.[2]

At the same time, the early 1980s saw a renewed interest amongst many Christian denominations to engage in the issues of social injustice present in deprived urban communities. This interest was fuelled significantly in 1985 by the release of the Church of England report 'Faith in the City' which took a very critical stance towards government policy on urban regeneration. This report, along with the subsequent setting up of the Church Urban Fund, proved a seminal moment for the urban church of all denominations and informed its involvement in urban life for at least the following two decades.

Other important trends were developing amongst urban congregations through this period. In broad terms, these included a growing emphasis on the local church as 'community' (rather than solely a formal place of worship), which perhaps allowed for a stronger relational ethos and more authentic involvement with the everyday practical challenges faced in urban neighbourhoods. Also significant was the participation of faith communities in areas of serious and chronic deprivation in inner city communities. Whilst some denominations (such as Methodists and Salvation Army) had a long history of involvement with marginalized and disadvantaged communities, the notable shift from the 1980s onwards was the growing engagement of evangelicals and Pentecostals in these areas.[3] Alongside these developments was the rapid and, in places, explosive growth of black and ethnic minority churches – so many churches being planted in some areas of inner London that it was almost impossible to find any public buildings that were not rented out for the whole of Sunday for church services!

As a practical consequence of these developing patterns within British inner cities, local churches became increasingly involved in running projects which sought to address issues of deprivation and injustice. These were encouraged through a variety of major funding streams including the creation of Urban Priority Areas (UPAs) by the Thatcher government, the Church Urban Fund and availability of European funding. Despite secularizing pressures inherent within some funding streams (notably through the formation of the National Lottery), as organized communities of local people with a sense of social responsibility, churches often found themselves in a strong position to gain funding.[4]

This very brief sketch of Christian faith and life of the church within the rapidly transforming urban situation belies, however, the complexity and tensions that surrounded those within faith projects. One aspect of this complexity was the tension between spiritual and sacramental expressions of Christian faith on the one hand, and the practical work in addressing specific issues of social injustice and deprivation on the other – questions abounded as to how these two aspects worked together. For churches, the difficulty was, in part, related to the place of social involvement within mission; or more specifically the need to reconcile somehow the conviction that simply to serve a person's physical and practical needs was not adequate; the real issue was the need for conversion. The growing sense of secularization within cities fuelled a genuine sense of conflict within many churches and church projects over this issue. At the same time, non-faith bodies such as local authorities and funding organizations exhibited a deep suspicion that the real motivation for the church's engagement was for 'proselytization'. In a hardening secular environment it became increasingly difficult, if not impossible, for Christian faith-based projects to maintain any substantial expression of Christian spirituality.

Within this diverse mix of urban life and faith, a progressive expression of Christian life has gradually emerged, which I will refer to here as 'convictional communities'. These communities are typically small, experimental and not well networked – many, in fact, are not aware that similar groups exist at all. The critical characteristic of these communities is the intentional embodiment of values within the community itself; where 'values' are not simply a list of desirable lifestyle choices, but are precisely the virtues that the Christian community understands as descriptive of Jesus himself.[5] This is not to say that doctrine or theology are not of significance (of course they are), but that if theology is to be taken seriously then it must be embodied within the very character of the community. In short, the community might suggest that theology is something they enact rather than simply talk about.

The actual form that such communities take is varied and often somewhat fluid and lacking definition, and it remains an open question as to whether they constitute 'church' or not –many of them do not have formal church services and would be shy of identifying themselves as a church. There are, however, important elements that give them particular shape: eating and sharing meals (sometimes with liturgy) is common to most, with relationship and hospitality being frequently held values; they tend to be deeply connected with their immediate local area, and many are intentionally located in areas of urban deprivation; rhythms of prayer, reflection and Bible reading inspired by monastic and Celtic traditions are often a feature.

Importantly for the wider discussion of this book is that convictional communities tend to be adverse to the faith-based project approach described above. They tend to emphasize an 'incarnational' approach which understands the importance of actually living in and being deeply involved with a particular neighbourhood, especially living alongside and caring for the marginalized. Convictional communities come as listeners and learners; they are open to being changed through their encounters with others; their convictions will lead them towards participative approaches to work in the community by joining with individuals and organizations irrespective of their faith convictions or none; their inclination is to be a peaceful and peacemaking presence in a community.

Thus faith 'works' within the poorest sections of society because the community of 'embodied conviction' offers a completely different paradigm to that of the traditional 'service provider' (which sometimes includes provision offered by many Christian projects that have been shaped by secular agendas as much as by faith agendas). In particular it invites a completely different kind of engagement – one in which relationship and community are at the heart. Rather than the distanced professional relationship of a service provider with targets and outcomes set from 'above', incarnational communities call for a costly engagement in long-term relationships of mutual respect. New imagination about what is possible arises from within the community, motivating and empowering it to take responsibility for itself rather than submitting to schemes that are devised by distant policymakers. For the convictional community, faith is at the heart of this stance – they believe that Jesus is not only a model for this kind of engagement, but the one who is uniquely present in, and empowering of, the lives and daily encounters of the community itself.

The rest of this chapter focuses on the stories of four such convictional communities all of which come under the auspices of a small Christian organization called Urban Expression (UE).[6] The stories of the four small teams of people who moved into challenging urban environments to live within specific neighbourhoods are recounted here as a way of exploring how faith in Jesus was central for determining what eventually unfolded in their experience. As I write, each of the stories is still ongoing. I have tried to capture some of the essence and vibrancy of the accounts which most impressed me, but am aware that I have only touched the surface. Each team will have a rich store of other stories from which, I'm sure, much could be learned.

Whilst each story speaks for itself, their impact is considerably enhanced when we hear them together. Thus I have sought to listen to the connections and resonances between the stories and present them in a way that I hope invites the reader to do the same and perhaps draw their own insights. I intentionally present the stories as a sequence with very little comment and then, in the second part of the chapter, draw out six observations that emerge from the resonances between the narratives.

This chapter might be regarded as a modest exercise in doing 'theology from story'. The starting point of this approach is the real situation or experience of a person or group. This is followed by a process of interdisciplinary investigation and theological reflection which leads eventually to freshly informed practice.[7] This is, I suggest, a particularly appropriate way of 'doing theology' amongst marginalized communities, as it tends to make space for voices that are not often heard. In this instance it brings to our attention the characteristic richness and creativity of urban communities, as well as the gritty realism and struggle encountered by those who live in these areas. I have tried to communicate this feel by including, as far as possible, the voices of the actual people whose stories these are.

The Glamis Adventure Playground

In 1997 a group of eight people moved, as part of an UE team, into Shadwell, East London, led by Jim and Juliet. Jim describes the housing scheme which had become their new home – it was dominated by a number of large tower blocks, in the middle of which was a derelict and rubbish-filled fenced-in piece of land. In the seventies and eighties this land had been a thriving adventure playground, until in the late eighties, council funding was removed and the playground fell into disrepair and decay. It is the story of the restoration of this playground and the part it played in community transformation that I want to explore here.

The team's initial focus was to learn about the community and be attentive to what was going on. Guided by their UE values, they started to participate in community activity, especially youth work, walking the streets and spending regular time in prayer and reflection. They quickly began to connect with some of the young people in the area, and learn about the challenges they faced. Juliet explains that a remarkable statistic for the estate at the time was that 75 per cent of the population was under 24 years of age, and there were pressing problems with what were known locally as 'feral kids'.

Through their conversations and growing relationships, the team's attention was gradually drawn towards the abandoned adventure playground, realizing that it held important representational and practical significance in the community. Through a compilation of comments and shared memories, an image emerged of a previously thriving playground that contrasted sharply to the current eyesore. Jim comments that for the team, 'It gave us a very real picture of how people thought about the place they lived – the decay of the playground echoed people's view of the whole of the estate . . . being right at the centre of the estate, it was quite symbolic.'

It was during a time of prayer that experience of the preceding years came into sharp focus. As they prayed, someone saw in their mind's eye an image of the playground awash with colour and vibrancy – for the team this conveyed a sense that God was somehow leading them to help develop this area of waste land so that it might be transformed into a place of life.

Things still moved slowly with respect to the playground, but now the team was journeying with a new sense of understanding. Their deep involvement in local community, with a combined sense of the decaying playground as an important local place and a glimpse of God's heart for renewed vibrancy, meant that when the opportunity came along to work on the redevelopment of the playground, the team were ready. Jim hastens to add that although the project was being initiated by the UE team, their desire was not to label it as a 'church project'. This valuing of partnership and shared ownership was strongly and practically expressed, for example, in that three or four others from the mainly Bangladeshi community joined the team to begin rebuilding the adventure playground; indeed, the person eventually appointed play-leader presented himself as an atheist.

The 'icing on the cake' came for the community in 2007 when, to their delight, the playground was awarded Best Adventure Playground in London Award for 2007. This kind of achievement by the local community was considerable; it demonstrates an ongoing and powerful process of community transformation with all the contingent implications for social justice.

Possilpark and the Claypits

The second story is centred on Possilpark, one of Glasgow's large estates just a mile north of the city centre. Through 2008, an UE team of eight adults and two children was formed as the families moved into the estate and started to explore what an incarnational church presence might look like.

Paul, the UE team leader and former tour guide, who had moved to Possilpark the previous autumn with his wife, describes how the main focus for the first year was about getting to know the community and the place. Time was invested in listening to people, making friends and developing contacts with estate activists.

A particularly noticeable feature of the estate itself were the very large derelict brown-field sites which seemed to embody Possil's own struggles and decay; especially depressing were two large 'gap sites' where buildings had been demolished. Paul comments, 'There was lots of concern about these areas . . . lots of drug dealing happened around them.'

By the winter of 2008, intriguing connections were beginning to emerge for Paul and the UE team. To the surprise of all, the

91

Green Party candidate was elected councillor for Possil and one of her first moves was to establish the Friends of Possilpark Greenspace (FOPP), which four of the UE team joined. By this time, Paul and the team had invested a lot of time walking around the area exploring every nook and cranny, trying to understand what Possil was about. In his travels, Paul discovered an almost forgotten area right on the doorstep of the estate – an old overgrown clay pit covering about thirty acres. Here was a very wild, obscure and infrequently visited location with great views over the whole city centre and the west end of Glasgow. Paul really liked the site, and his tour-guide eyes quickly saw the potential of the unique blend of natural creation and urban heritage right next to, and standing in contrast to, the depressed environment of Possilpark.

Through the work of UE and FOPP, plans to develop the Claypits into a green heritage space for the community began to emerge. The work drew together a remarkable array of organizations and people, ranging from large companies such as British Waterways to small projects working with children and young people and others related to conservation, archaeology, beekeeping and even pigeon fanciers.

At the heart of the UE team's engagement in the community was their commitment to a values-centred approach to ministry, with an emphasis on incarnational presence and open-hearted partnership. These convictions were concretely expressed in the way that the team intentionally facilitated partnership and shared ownership with the estate community and other organizations. This included the team laying down ideas about labelling this as a Christian project; Paul himself sought to personally express this stance by coming as a local resident rather than a local church leader. As Paul tells the Claypits story, this open posture of authentic partnership emerges as a defining ethos that governs the whole feel of what has subsequently developed.

This stance, however, directly challenges the mindset that to achieve desired goals and be successful, any developing project must work actively to hold certain strings of power. Not least of the challenges were the interactions with the 'big players' in terms of land ownership – especially British Waterways and the City Council. Aware of the land's potential for commercial development, the first thing the UE team did was to walk and pray around the site as an early step of faith and vision. Soon after this, the potential for housing development was ruled out by the council in 2009 when it legislated against the burying of power cables in the area. This move was critical both for the future of the land itself and the nature of relationships between community groups and the 'big players'. In Paul's words, 'BW are now a massive supporter of the Claypits development' – it seems to them as a very encouraging answer to prayer.

The uncompromising commitment to partnership and shared ownership also challenged relationship with other Christian organizations. Part of the developing story for Paul was about negotiating with Christians who wanted to maintain control in particular ways and to label the project 'Christian'. But for the UE team, such a move would be to revert to a Christendom mindset where the church exercised power as the senior or central player. Critical for an incarnational approach was not to gain the strings of power or be in control, but to stand in solidarity with those whose experience is one of disempowerment.

The Claypits regeneration is still in its early days, but the aim of transforming a neglected space into a community place is already bearing fruit. An exciting milestone is a weekend of community celebration called Bats, Beasties and Buried Treasure which will have a strong emphasis on storytelling. The planning team understand that 'stories engage people and give people a sense of belonging and ownership . . . the idea is to be able to tell stories to one another about our experiences [of] the big story of the history of Possil from the perspective of the clay pit." Stories will be told of the wildlife and flora, and the story of the buildings and industrial remains. People will recount their own memories of the site from childhood and more recently, and also create new stories of fun and adventure through an activity programme.[8]

The richness of the project lies not only with the physical development of the site itself, but with a broad sense of ownership from a wide variety of groups and people. It conveys the sense that social transformation is not related primarily to improving the physical environment, but rather to a sense of the overall inner wellbeing of the whole community. This wellbeing is relational at heart, and might well be described in spiritual terms; it certainly evokes the theological sense of 'shalom' which describes an all-embracing sense of peace and wellbeing that arises as a gift to the community as a whole.

The Ocean Estate

The Ocean Estate in London's East End is the setting for our third story. Although just a few miles from Canary Wharf and the City of London, it is amongst the most deprived estates in the country. Its claim to fame is that it was once the cheapest place to buy heroin in Europe.

It was here in 2003 that Salvation Army officers Nick and Kerry moved with their family. Their experience of ministry in similar estates in south London had already begun to form a sense of the values they felt were important for working in urban communities. The commitment of the Salvation Army to be located amongst the most marginalized of society was very significant, but in addition to this was the importance of what Nick describes as being 'incarnational' in their approach to the area. For them this meant 'identifying with the community . . . not about being the answer to everybody's issues, but to come alongside people and be as much a part of the community as everybody else'. Incarnational community is 'about throwing yourself entirely into it; it's a lifestyle, not a 9 to 5 but 24/7 commitment'.

These convictions profoundly shaped their approach to ministry with important practical consequences – notably taking a key decision in their early days in Stepney to turn down the opportunity to renovate the existing Salvation Army building. They knew that to justify the financial investment necessary to renovate the site they would need to run and maintain a raft of programmes. Rather, they wanted to be free to focus on being good neighbours to those that they now lived amongst. It was whilst exploring this approach that they developed a relationship to UE.

Incarnational convictions were decisive in informing direction in a number of other significant ways. They realized that the name 'Salvation Army' had fairly strong Jihadist overtones for the predominantly Bengali Muslim population. This was clearly unhelpful and contrary to the vision that the church was here as a 'neighbour' to the whole community, not just a one people group.

In response a new name was chosen: 'Hope-Asha: the Salvation Army in Stepney' (*asha* being Bengali for hope); this was a public expression of openness and belonging to the whole community.

One of the most pressing issues for the Ocean Estate, where it seemed hope was most noticeably lacking, was the overwhelming heroin culture on the estate. Nick and Kerry talk powerfully about the blatant and 'in your face' nature of the drug culture – drug dealing would not be an uncommon sight if you were with your children at the playground in the centre of the estate; it seemed that dealers took no measures to hide their trade.

Kerry talks about how her own children could point to bushes where drugs were stashed, and the places where drug deals took place. She saw the massive impact on people whose friends or family members were drug takers, and the daily disruption caused to those who lived next door to drug dealers. She describes the very obvious financial results of trading drugs: 'It was clear to all [that] every Bengali family would have had enhanced income from the drug dealing . . . which [was evident] in the new sofas and TVs.'

Perhaps the most disturbing aspect of this situation was that despite the terrible destructiveness of this pervasive drug culture, there were no public expressions of protest or outrage. It seemed that the community was corporately turning a blind eye to the problem. Particularly noticeable was the sense of denial within the Bangladeshi community and the lack of response to the problem by community elders. As Nick and Kerry began to make efforts to find other local people who were concerned about the issue, they discovered a loosely networked group of fathers who also shared their concern about drug dealing. Many of the fathers were in some way associated to the local mosque which for Nick and Kerry meant that their concern for drug dealing became a natural point of contact with some local Muslim groups. The clear need to take a stand, and the growing relationships, were a catalyst in bringing together a group known as the Stepney Fathers. The group were very keen to start working together, and arranged the first public meeting on the estate to ask, 'What is going on and what can we do to respond?'

Deal With It Day was one of the main initiatives to come out of this first conversation. The idea was a festival to be run both *by*

and *for* the local community in the very park that had been dominated by dealers. This was, explains Nick, about raising a different
voice in the community, acknowledging their own responsibility
for the drug culture and the problems it caused, and reclaiming
the physical ground in the middle of the estate – the park. This
clearly wasn't a complete answer, but has proved to be a very
important step for the community, with a broad range of significant outcomes.

An innovative element of the day was a seminar organized
and presented by local people as a way of explaining the estate's
drug problems to council officers and police, and asking them for
a response. This was a significant shift from previous initiatives,
which were always organized by outside authorities and took
the form of a typical community consultation or listening exercise which, explains Nick, you would attend and then never hear
from again. Now the tables were turned, and the community were
making demands of local authorities and seeking to hold them
to account. As a direct result of these actions, the police set arrest
targets for drug dealing – the first time that such a policy had been
adopted in the borough. Under the banner 'a dealer a day', the aim
was to arrest 365 dealers in a year. An unanticipated outcome of
this action was that other forms of crime such as domestic robbery
and car theft also declined quite dramatically.

The ongoing story is far from easy; it is one of continuing
struggle, with its triumphs and setbacks. The festival, however,
has become an annual event, and Hope-Asha has become a vibrant
community with deep relationships, richly embedded in the life
of the Ocean Estate. The significance of the part played by Hope-
Asha was underlined when Nick was presented the London Citizens 2007 Leader of the Year award in 2007 for his work.

The Geoff Ashcroft Community (GAC)

Of the four stories related here, that of the Geoff Ashcroft Community is perhaps the most complex to relate. It tells of the formation of a small urban Christian community, and how and why
this community became involved with people who were being
marginalized because of mental illness. In doing so, it draws

together our central themes of faith and urban justice, and relates them together around the core idea of community – specifically, community that comprises those who are arguably the most vulnerable and marginalized of all in our society.

In order to engage well with this story, one needs to understand the picture or narrative that was foundational for forming and guiding the community. Karen, one of the group's early founders, explains it in the following way: the picture is of a banquet, a table where Christ is host, all are welcome and none are excluded. In this story of radical inclusion, *all* are honoured as guests, whether they feel confident to gather around the top table or for some reason still stand far off – the welcome and status of honoured guest is extended to all.

The GAC story starts with a small group of praying people in Wapping, led by Karen, who was at the time a trainee Baptist minister. Karen's own background played a particular role in founding the community and shaping its character. In the late nineties, Karen was partway through a ministerial training course and student minister at a large evangelical church in the London-Kent suburbs. Her experience of church and college was, however, 'driving her mad'. This deep frustration was in part rooted in personal experience; both her brother and mother were suffering from long-term mental health problems, and had through their time of illness started attending the church. The church, though, seemed very disconnected with what was going on in the family and, instead of being embraced by a loving community, Karen witnessed a process of misunderstanding and marginalization, not only with her own family members, but also with others in similar situations.

A deep struggle emerged in Karen, knowing that church should be different – somehow radically inclusive – but not knowing what this looked like. Connections with UE and the Mennonite Centre led her eventually to move to Wapping and become part of a small group of praying people there. Along with Karen and a friend who moved to join them this team of just five people was the beginning of an UE church plant which over the next seven years was to journey to become the Geoff Ashcroft Community.[9]

Also informative for shaping the group was the seeming dispro-portionate number of encounters with local people living very disturbed and chaotic lives due to mental health problems. Relationships developed in part through Karen's work as chaplain in the local psychiatric hospital, and the growing realization that many with mental health problems were isolated and exceptionally lonely.

From these and other influences they wanted to make their small expression of community something that was both flexible and very safe, somewhere which was strongly welcoming and where people felt invited.

The first step was a Sunday afternoon meeting (people could not get up in time for the morning), always with a meal, a simple liturgy, Bible reading and prayer. For Karen, the main thing she noticed was that people just wanted to talk, and their main problem was getting people to leave at the end.

In reality, there were some very difficult people. Karen admits that even as a core team they were 'a bit odd', and as others joined them their social interaction would have looked a 'total disaster to most people'. She talks about some of those who began to connect with the community. There was H, who often turned up drunk, was very smelly and frequently disruptive. Then there was P, who had autistic tendencies, would stand much too close to people and talk *at* them about his latest favourite subject. And there was M, one of the older women and a compulsive liar. It seemed that the welcoming environment of the group brought out the oddities in people. 'In fact,' says Karen, 'we gave up trying to normalize things . . . we just let people be as they are. The joy of it was that people could be themselves.'

At this stage, the core team realized that the community as it stood was vulnerable and unsustainable. They needed somewhere that could provide a point of contact every day and could be served by people with time and professional expertise to keep the ethos of welcome and safety. To help them move forward, an open meeting was organized and invites extended, especially to those who had started to attend the community, as well as patients from the hospital. The result was the formation of a charitable trust, The Geoff Ashcroft Community, which would aim to be strongly welcoming and inclusive of those with mental health problems, seeking to be available every day of the week.

The main debate in setting up the community was about inclusiveness. For Karen personally, this reflected her own family's experience of prejudice associated with mental illness: 'We didn't want any of that . . . We really didn't want anything to stop anyone feeling they could belong.' That determination for connection between people means that the GAC is not an easy community to be part of; to belong is to participate in vulnerability and struggle.

Karen describes its meetings as unpredictable and most of the group as socially dysfunctional. 'Most people,' she says, 'wouldn't want to touch us with a barge pole.' Yet the community aspires to, and to some extent achieves, an inclusiveness that seems unattainable to most.

The spiritual essence of the GAC was shaped primarily by its vision of the banqueting table; this was a rich expression of communion embodying both connectivity with God, and connectivity with each other. 'For me,' says Karen, 'my longing is for connection.' It is clear that the community moves beyond being a service provider and offers a place of stability and open friendship. Even in its smallness it stands as a challenging and somewhat provocative sign for justice and community in the heart of a prosperous city.

Incarnational Expressions

Having heard these four stories, our task is to engage them in some form of theological conversation. Rather than reflecting on each story in turn, we will listen to them together with the aim of hearing the resonances between them. My intention in doing this is to explore how and why small groups of Christians have achieved a seemingly disproportionate transforming effect in tough urban settings, especially in relation to issues of social justice.

'Incarnational' was often used in conversation with UE team leaders as a way of articulating their approach to ministry, and it is this that I want to take as a starting point. Whilst the sense of what incarnational means is, without exception, richly exemplified in their own lives and also clearly demonstrated through the lives and the stories of the UE communities, the actual articulation of that meaning was often less clear. The impression gained was that 'incarnational' functioned as a kind of 'catch-all' or shorthand for a number of related concepts that cluster together. So, whilst

I will not attempt pursue a theological discussion about incarnational ministry as such, I will seek to tease out what is meant by the use of this language. I will focus on six aspects of the meaning that I see as emerging from the above accounts.

1. First, and perhaps rather obviously, incarnational ministry is to live within the host community. This 'living within' includes both the geographical sense which for UE teams often entails moving into an estate, as well as a relational sense of participating fully in the life of the local community. In each one of the four stories, the events which have unfolded have done so *precisely because* they have been from within the community. The apparent simplicity of this point should not cause us to overlook its importance – it is, I believe, profoundly impactful for community formation and life. Every team leader talked about moving into and living in the community for at least a few years as an essential contributing factor for what eventually emerged. In Shadwell, for example, it was only after a considerable time that the adventure playground initiative began to form, and as Jim comments, 'It was really because we had been there for five years that something could happen . . . it was because we were already involved in the community in this way.' Moving into and living within a community that suffers from long-term marginalization is not, however, for everyone, and requires considerable openness and resilience to do so effectively. It entails, for example, that those moving in seek to face up to and confess their own prejudice and fear as an essential part of building authentic relationships.

It should be noted in particular that 'living within' represents a challenge to the city's traditional power map where 'help' and 'resources' flow from the city's centres of power to its 'needy' areas. It is this unequal and unjust distribution of power that in part defines marginalization and, ironically, the so-called 'help' that is offered often reinforces this status quo. In contrast, learning to 'live within' the community, to appreciate it and celebrate it is perhaps a modest step towards inspiring a sense of hope and dignity within the community itself.

This was demonstrated powerfully in the Hope-Asha story, where the councillors and police were held to account for their actions by local residents who had begun to take responsibility for their own community's problems. Nick comments:

> The council and police did not like this approach . . . it was at times a very tense relationship, because we were telling them what to do. We were a community voice on this issue; more than that, we were going to take responsibility for this . . . we were saying that we didn't think that police or council had the answers on this, and we did not want to devolve all our responsibility to them, though we would happily do it in partnership with them. We would always get these police events saying 'Come along and share your views', and then nothing would happen. But this time we *invited them to our event* and held them to account for doing these things . . . They were not used to working like this. In fact, there was one meeting where they were incredibly rude to us, saying, 'We are not accountable to you!'

This challenge to the established landscape of power by 'living within' seems to strike at the heart of the issues which cause and sustain the marginalization of whole communities within our cities, and the associated multiple injustices which are embedded within them.

2. Secondly, a strong emphasis of each team was to come as listeners and learners. Indeed, this is an important part of the UE values which state: 'We believe in doing things with and not just for communities, sharing our lives with others and learning from others who share their lives with us.'

To come as a listener and learner is an intentional stance or spiritual discipline which contrasts to the perspective that sees people or communities as having 'problems' that need 'fixing', and Christian teams as those who have the answers and tools to help. Rather, the conviction carried by UE teams is that to be a listener opens the way for joining in with what Jesus is already doing in and through people in the community. Jim comments on this when he talks about how the ideas for restoring the adventure playground began to take shape: 'For the first time we realized that it wasn't just us coming with something, but that this stuff was two-way.'

For those moving into these kinds of small incarnational communities, there is often a sense of surprise, one which is somewhat double-edged: on the one hand, the surprise as to the richness of the learning experience as we listen to those we previously considered as 'marginalized'; on the other hand, the revelation of our own inadequacy as people who thought we had 'answers' for this community's 'problems'.

After many years of involvement in the Geoff Ashcroft Community, Phil tells of how the importance of listening was brought home to them with fresh force. A large church had been planted right on their doorstep, and the small team were feeling rather overwhelmed by the sheer size and 'success' of a congregation which was able to offer a wide range of services to the community and, says Phil, 'They do everything better than we do!' The heart searching that followed led them back to a core value of the Geoff Ashcroft Community: 'To be a multi-voice church ... knowing that God can speak through *all* people present (including those with mental illness), so we need to listen carefully to what everyone is saying.' For the Geoff Ashcroft Community, this 'listening to' and 'learning from' others, especially the chronically mentally ill, was not simply a mechanism whereby good strategies for mission could be developed – that is a means to an end – rather listening to each other was an essential expression of godly presence.

3. Thirdly, implicit within the experience of all four teams is an appreciation of the 'sense of place'. This is more than the awareness of physical geography alone; it is a recognition that the community itself is rooted or 'placed' in a defined location, and that the 'sense of place' arises out of this interplay between location and community so that the physical environment somehow embodies the characteristics and stories of the community that have played out over many years.

The discovery and regeneration of the Claypits in Possilpark is an impressive account of how places might experience transformation by being 're-storied'; by coming together to care for the land the community develops a rich variety of new stories about overcoming adversity, discovering hope and finding reconciliation. Furthermore, these stories are evident within the physical make-up of the place itself – or in other words, the physical landscape embodies the memories of these stories. Paul recounts one touching illustration of this. He tells of a long-running difficult relationship with one of his own neighbours; the man was part of an extended family in the estate and was 'hated in Possil'. He is, however, an enthusiastic pigeon fancier and, along with his family, now owns four of the six pigeon lofts in the Claypits. As a result, they have become involved in the community effort to renew the site, discovering as they do so that bridges are being built where relationships had previously been antagonistic or even hostile. For local people and those involved in the Claypits story, pigeon lofts stand as a physical testimony to reconciliation and peacemaking within the community.

Similar sentiments were expressed by Jim about their estate in Shadwell: the physical decay of the adventure playground mirrored for local people the decay of the community as a whole: 'Nothing ever happens here . . . this is a rubbish place.' By contrast, the regenerated playground stands as a physical testimony to the community's own ability to achieve change together; it is a place of gathering, fun and, according to Juliet, has a deep sense of spirituality about it – it is the place that people gravitate to, just to talk.

4. Participation is another valuable aspect of incarnational ministry which emerges from these four case studies. In one sense, participation is understood as a joining in with what the Spirit of God is already doing. Although this aspect of participation in the context of mission is of fundamental importance and a central expression of the UE values, I don't intend to explore it here; rather I want to explore what is, I believe, an outworking of this essential essence of participation. The particular challenge that has emerged is that in each context, this spirit of participation is not exclusively the privilege of Christians, in the sense that Christians alone can participate in the activity of God. Rather, participation is more like joining a dance where all are invited to the dance floor; it suggests that we learn the steps with others and thus *together* learn to participate in what God is doing.

Participation, thus understood, is deeply challenging to some expressions of evangelical faith which have emphasized an 'us and them' or 'insider and outsider' approach to the practice of faith. However, all of the stories told here have intentionally embraced a participatory approach and, I would argue, have experienced a level of transformation within communities precisely because they have gone down this path. I hesitate to use the word 'radical', but of all the aspects of incarnational ministry discussed here, I suggest that in our current culture participation is the most radical expression of this kind of ministry.

The rich expression of participation that became evident might be summed up simply as 'doing things *with* people rather than *to* people' where the 'doing with' is always with the marginalized 'other'; where otherness includes expressions of ethnicity, disability, religion, culture, sexuality or class. Thus participation for the UE team in Shadwell meant that the group that developed the playground included a number of Bangladeshi Muslims, and the playground itself was eventually managed by someone who described himself as an atheist. Whilst not publicly identified as a church project, the participation of the community together allowed a very interesting ethos to develop; Juliet describes the playground as 'a very spiritual place . . . in the sense that it was accessible to all different kinds of people and they felt comfortable there . . . they were on a level pegging, and felt free to ask spiritual questions'. Quite symbolically for the UE team, the 'atheist' manager of the playground found a one-way street sign which he fixed to the highest point of the playground pointing in an upwards direction. When asked about it, he said it was a 'nod to the Maker'; what's more, he added, 'I'm not a Christian, but if I was . . . I would become one like you.'

The story of the Glamis Adventure Playground graphically illustrates how the spirit of participation stands in contrast to the need to control something either by explicitly naming it as Christian, maintaining ownership, or occupying management positions. Juliet echoes the words of other UE team leaders when she says that 'Lots of churches wanted their names stamped on it [the adventure playground]'. In Possil, Paul experienced similar pressure from Christian leaders in developing the Claypits; the conviction that if it were going to be an 'effective Christian project' then it should be named and managed as such.

The sense of participation embodied by the UE teams specifically relinquishes such naming and control. It understands that the way of Jesus, or shalom, is not achieved through the manipulation of power, even if the 'ends' are laudable. Rather, the essence of participation is to join in with Jesus in what he is doing, and underlying this is the conviction that Jesus associates first with the powerless and marginalized.

To participate in this way is a faithful acknowledgement that he is Lord, and a practical recognition that *all* are invited to join in his activity of peacemaking or shalom, not just the powerful.

Significantly, such participation challenges the unjust distribution of power which is so characteristic of contemporary urban life. By relinquishing positions of management, ownership and the right to name, we contest the established power map of the city. Conversely, if participation is on *our terms or not at all*, then we simply reflect the way things are routinely done in wider society – the way that keeps the powerful in power and the marginalized in poverty.

The often repeated sentiment of UE leaders is that these kinds of partnerships are precisely the place where their faith comes alive. Nick, for example, describes his relationship with the Bangladeshi Muslims as they work together for justice on the Ocean Estate:

Some of [the] concerns we had before [working together] have not really materialized. For example, I think we are not pushing a pluralist idea here – we are not saying our faith doesn't matter that much, but we are finding a core partnership where we hold different views on theology but we share a humanity . . . sharing theological views come out as we are working [*sic*].

The opportunities for evangelism are far greater in working this way. We are also more honest – we are not trying to get our message in wherever possible . . . We are very confident in who we are; we do not compromise our beliefs about Jesus because of the Muslim in the room – we don't say he is not the Son of God, for example. We actually get more respect because they see [us] as caring for the other. But this goes both ways; if I hadn't got involved in this work and got to know people better through it, I might have been easily swayed by [negative portrayals of other faiths]. But it is only in a genuine, real relationship that you can actually talk with authority on anything in the world, and I am very grateful for real relationships with a number of Muslims where I can find out what they really think and are like.

5. Implicit within the notions of participation and incarnation is the bringing of one's unique self to the community or situation. If incarnation is to be more than a mission methodology, then it will fully embrace the personhood of those involved; their frailties and vulnerabilities, their interests and passions.

In conversation with UE team members, for example, it is not uncommon to hear confessions of how they have struggled with their own sense of middle class-ness when coming to an urban area. Those who are brave enough to admit it will say that they went through a phase of speaking differently – trying to sound less middle class and more 'urban'. These challenges are often talked about in a slightly light-hearted way, but when engaged with more reflectively, they demonstrate how challenging it is to truly be ourselves when encountering others in different cultural contexts; there is considerable anxiety about encountering people of difference and the potential for rejection by them.

This sense, I believe, often makes us slow to bring interests, passions or even hobbies to the situation. Yet incarnation implies the immersion of the whole person, all that we are, to a situation. It suggests that somehow as we follow Jesus – the Incarnate One – we begin to understand how to bring our whole selves, including our vulnerabilities, anxieties and weaknesses; things which on the surface might seem to detract from mission, rather than add to it.

It is inspiring to see how the skills, interests and vulnerabilities of UE leaders have had a creative impact on the shape of their involvement in their communities. Paul, for example, moved to the Possil estate as a tour guide whose training had included 'How to interpret Scotland'. Paul had found inspiration during his training from reading Patrick Geddes, a botanist and one of the fathers of modern town planning. It is not surprising, then, that Paul saw Possil and the Claypits from this tour guide perspective. Perhaps more unexpected is that this very perspective became a significant factor in shaping ministry on the estate – restoring the Claypits seems an unlikely strategy for church planting or urban mission. However, even in the relatively early days of the work it seems that there was a sense of deep transformation at work, not only in the landscape itself but in the community of the Possil estate adjacent to it.

Karen also exemplifies this sense of incarnational ministry in moving to Wapping with a personal faith journey that is deeply affected by the mental illness within her own family. It seemed entirely fitting, then, that her involvement in urban ministry be strongly shaped around the lives of those who were struggling to cope with mental illness and its consequences, particularly that of loneliness. Karen's vision of Jesus as an all-inclusive and welcoming host and the resulting Christian community that grew out of this vision has its source, it seems, in Karen's own family's struggles.

In both these stories, communities are appreciably shaped by the unique personalities and personal interests of the UE team members. Those involved in incarnational ministry do not leave the 'less desirable' personality traits or personal interests at the door – they come as they are and learn truly to 'be themselves' in their new host community. They learn humility in discovering that they cannot fully understand this community, but are conscious that they can only see it through their own eyes; they are reflexive in their interactions; they learn to be self-aware in bringing their own interpretations and passions. It is precisely as they bring themselves in this way that they find connections and resonances with local people, places and community narratives – and it is out of these feelings of resonance that truly creative work begins to happen. In this sense, incarnational urban ministry can be great fun and extremely energizing.

6. Characteristic of all the UE teams mentioned was a deep sense of vulnerability. This was not, however, an accidental consequence of moving into troubled and marginal places. It is not something that a team will 'recover' from once they have been around for a while; rather, vulnerability is regarded as a necessary quality for the formation of authentic relationships. If teams are to live relationally as stated by the UE values (and to live incarnationally is at heart to live relationally), then they will continue to foster 'healthy' vulnerability. Vulnerability is arguably the essence of the parable of the yeast in the dough (Matt. 13:33) – it is the quality of smallness that enables the yeast to become deeply and irretrievably embedded in its context. Yet it is precisely this quality that enables the whole dough to rise. Vulnerability, or smallness, it seems, is a prerequisite for social transformation – at least, non-violent social transformation.

Vulnerability is profoundly expressed in the Geoff Ashcroft Community. Phil, an UE team leader involved in the community, says that 'our church's vision and values understand that church is not just for people on the margins, but *of* people on the margins – people with mental health problems fit right into that'. After thirteen years in this situation, Phil and his family know what it is to be familiar with very desperate situations. They often don't have answers, and find themselves powerless in the face of overwhelming problems. Yet their conviction remains that this is exactly the kind of place that is a priority for God, and to remain there is a picture of what God is like. 'We are not just working with people, we have relationship with them,' says Phil. 'We are not an organization . . . rather, the longer we are there, the more "grass roots" we become.'

The Geoff Ashcroft Community has not become a powerful service provider; it is unable to tick many boxes in terms of the numbers of people 'helped'. It does, however, stand as a sign in its community that these people matter; they are real people, they are humans and should be treated as such.[10] It challenges a system that tends to objectify and marginalize those with long-term mental illness. Through its practice of vulnerability, it offers a hopeful way of living for those who find themselves sometimes engulfed by a sense of darkness and hopelessness.

Conclusion

The stories of convictional communities presented here are, I believe, intriguing and challenging examples of 'working faith' in marginalized urban communities. They point to certain valuable contributions being made by faith-based organizations to issues of urban social justice, and thus engage with the wider theme of this book.

Critical for the convictional community is that involvement with the practical welfare of people is neither an optional addition to faith nor a way of enticing 'non-believers' into religious belief. It would be inconceivable for a convictional community *not* to be engaged in some way in issues of social justice – and, characteristically, such engagement would be with the most marginalized in society.

The distinctive approach of convictional communities to urban social justice is centred on its radical relational and holistic values. Practical responses to social injustice arise from long-term relational engagement within an urban community and are participative in nature; they emerge precisely from the synergy of relationships that happen when people of 'difference' encounter each other in mutual respect. These practical responses are typically newly imagined; certainly they do not come from the preconceived thinking of the incoming Christian community, but are inspired through the hard work of deep engagement with others in the community.

This kind of incarnational approach to community justice and wellbeing tends by definition to empower the local community, which grows in its capacity to take responsibility for its own affairs, finds a stronger sense of its own voice, and develops a deeper sense of dignity and positive identity.

The members of convictional communities whom I interviewed all valued and promoted engagement with other groups and agencies, including welfare providers from the public and charity sectors, linking and cooperating with statutory bodies, such as the police and council services. On the whole, however, their sense of involvement was most often quite distinctive from these groups, their holistic approach standing in sharp contrast to service providers whose contact with people is so often brief and narrowly 'outcome' driven. This perhaps is the gift that convictional communities contribute – the additional quality of authentic presence that is able gently to minister to the pain of fragmentation in community, chronic loneliness, injustices based on deep-seated prejudices, and the often profound loss of hope.

Critically for convictional communities, is that this kind of patient presence that I have referred to as 'incarnational living' can only be understood in relation to the person of Jesus, who gives it both meaning and substance. He is more than a model or example; he is 'presence'. Indeed the conviction of those involved in incarnational ministry is that Jesus is the presence of God discovered and encountered as Christian communities seek to faithfully embody the values of God's kingdom of shalom. Therefore, the six points I have drawn out of these stories do not constitute a methodology for tackling urban social injustice. Rather, they are narratives of embodiment and encounter – they describe how divine presence is known and encountered in marginalized communities, and that 'presence' is specifically Jesus-shaped.

CHAPTER 6

Faith-based Youth Work in Local Communities: The Teenbridge Project

Paul Cloke

Introduction

In June 2003, a Christian faith-based organization – Teenbridge – was established in the Teignmouth-Dawlish area of south Devon, with the aim of building bridges between young people in the area and other young people, churches and the wider community. Such an event initially appears entirely unsurprising in the current UK context, for at least two significant reasons.

First, throughout the history of youth work and youth services there have been significant connections with churches and religious organizations.[1] For example, the Sunday school movement pioneered by Hannah More and Robert Raikes from the late eighteenth century onwards has grown into a wide network of church-based youth activities that stretch far beyond traditional Bible teaching on a Sunday. The Young Men's Christian Association founded in 1844 has developed into a vibrant provider of youth services, ranging from housing and employment advice to gymnasia. Uniformed organizations such as the Boys Brigade and the Girls Brigade, established in the late nineteenth century, continue to provide church-based youth services at a time when many have presumed that their brand of regimented evangelicalism has become anachronistic in the youth culture of the twenty-first century. Similarly, Baden-Powell's scouting and

Working Faith

guiding movements have in some cases continued to create links between young people and churches.

Although the post-war welfare revolution included a radical change towards state funding of and involvement in youth services, and for a period, local authorities changed the scene of youth work by setting up large-scale youth clubs and youth centres, and employing detached youth workers, faith-based organizations continued their work alongside these new vestiges of the welfare state. By the time funding for state youth work came under increasing pressure during the 1980s and 1990s, these public sector services had been overtaken by demographic and cultural events. As Mark Smith tells us:

> It was hard to make the case for dedicated buildings, a struggle to generate sufficient numbers of participants for groups and special activities, and often demoralizing for workers who had nobody to talk to but themselves for much of the time. It was also increasingly difficult to find people who were ready to volunteer to work in local groups. The traditional youth club seemed doomed to extinction. The final blow was delivered by a combination of an increasing interest in issue-based work by youth workers and a growing emphasis upon concrete outcomes by policymakers. To sustain funding for youth work there was a shift from 'open' provision toward working with groups of young people deemed to be 'at risk' in some way.[2]

With the demise of this form of public sector youth work, faith-based services once more rose to prominence. Here we encounter the second reason why the development of Teenbridge seems unsurprising. In the context of neoliberal government that emphasizes a shrinking of the activities of the state, and an encouragement of voluntary activity to fill the vacuum, there has been an increasingly warm welcome for the activities of faith-based organizations as part of the wider drift towards voluntarism and community-led citizenship.[3] Thus in the youth service sector in the UK, it is religious networks (predominantly Christian, but other religions are also involved) that have played a significant role in 'filling the gaps' in the task of serving young people. To some extent this is because these religious networks are able to provide social capital in any particular community. While Robert

Putnam[4] has sparked a widespread recognition of a general down-turn in voluntary resources, it is clear that churches and their associated networks are one of the few remaining repositories of such resources in many places. As Adam Dinham and others[5] have emphasized, church-based networks can offer the advantages of leadership, money, volunteers and buildings with which services can be established and made sustainable. This is not to suggest that these networks automatically become geared to service provision – in the youth sector, as in others, much depends on both a specific motivation to deploy resources on behalf of young people, and a further willingness to serve young people who are outside rather than already inside the church networks concerned. As with other types of organizations, churches can be prone to strategies that both 'look after their own' and seek to 'badge' wider activities as part of organizational aggrandizement. However, it has become clear that faith-based youth services are once again a prominent feature in the contemporary conditions of the UK.

It is difficult to say with any accuracy just how prominent these faith-based services are. A study in Northern Ireland[6] has suggested that around two-thirds of registered youth groups, and three-quarters of registered youth leaders are either faith-based or church-based. While the religious context of Northern Ireland may render this a special case, it seems likely that a majority of youth work in the UK is faith-based. At the local level, there is evidence that this role is becoming increasingly important. Research into youth and schools work delivered by the Christian faith community in Bath in 2010, for example, has shown that faith-based youth services involve meeting regularly with some 11.2 per cent of the city's 10 to 19-year-olds – a figure that has doubled over the previous five years.[7] These levels of activity appear highly significant, yet often seem to be under the radar of public acknowledgement. They involve particular individual churches, multi-church projects and coordinated activities from national organizations. They include church-based youth activities, school-based programmes and a range of different forms of detached youth work. They often form the backbone of in-place services for young people. It is important, therefore, to understand how such activity gets started and is sustained, and to explore the difficulties and barriers to its effectiveness.

Teenbridge: The Development of an Organization

As with many such initiatives, the inspiration for Teenbridge stemmed from the vision, energy and personal commitment of one couple – Peter and Su Twigg. Peter had previously worked for a decade as a local authority youth worker in Devon, and during that time developed a specific vision for a Christian youth project to work with young people who fell outside of the current ambit of church-based youth work. Living in the small seaside town of Teignmouth, Peter and Su had been exercised both by the numbers of young people just hanging out on the seafront, and by the apparent unwillingness or inability of local councillors and churches to act on behalf of these young people rather than viewing them as transgressors against the desired tourist image of the town. Having experienced what he describes as 'the very restrictive nature of government guidelines' for youth work in the local authority sector, Peter started to prepare the ground for the establishment of a charitable project that would enable a different kind of youth work to emerge. Peter and Su's Christian faith was an essential factor in this process; they believed that the church should have something to say to, and much to do with, these unattached young people, and they felt that a new organization could bring theological ethics into relational youth work in the area.[8]

Having liaised with local clergy, local authority youth workers and secondary school principals in the three towns of Teignmouth, Dawlish and Kingsteignton, they established Teenbridge in 2003 as a non-denominational cross-community organization designed to carry out street-based and school-based work with local young people. Undoubtedly Peter's professional experience and networks of contacts lent credibility to the project with organizational leaders, and his personal initial half-time secondment to work on the project (he later worked full-time on it) along with a new full-time youth worker was a key factor in the early energy of the project. Su's readiness to cover Teenbridge's administration as an adjunct to her existing employment was equally important. Together, the sacrificial commitment and the faith-based vision of these two people enabled the lift-off of the project. It is sometimes the case that faith-based action can be dismissed as do-gooding, or 'moral selving' – the deliberate creation of an 'on-display' ethical identity.[9] However, such analyses can seem almost flippant in the face of a willingness, as in this case, to make a total and life-changing commitment to a visionary project. There are certainly easier ways to create and display a moral self! Rather, the Teenbridge story seems to represent a determination to 'do something about something' – to put faith discourses into practice and extend the resources of the churches out into the community.[10]

From these beginnings, Teenbridge launched a series of programmes in the area, some designed specifically to meet needs, and others importing national-level resources for deployment locally. It quickly became apparent that Teenbridge needed a larger umbrella organization to help it with its work, and so it became affiliated with Youth for Christ, an international agency that was able to provide protocols for health and safety, human resources and training, and to channel gap year volunteers into the Teenbridge project, but that was also willing to allow local initiatives to respond to local needs without the imposition of centralized strategy or policy. The initial emphasis was on street-reach – an on-street presence in places such as Teignmouth seafront where young people were congregating, especially on weekend evenings, with staff and volunteers simply handing out soup and hot chocolate and providing a relational safe haven for those wishing to avoid what had become a culture of confrontation and sometimes violence. According to Peter, 'There was not a single fight on the seafront when we were out there, and we soon established a rapport with the local police who appreciated what was being done.' Similar work was done using a youth café in Dawlish.

On-street youth work was complemented by youth work in local schools, carrying out assemblies and taking Religious Education lessons. An illustration of the Teenbridge approach can be seen in their use of the nationally available GSUS Live programme in one of the local schools – Teignmouth Community College. This involved the bringing in of a purpose-built articulated trailer designed for the use of interactive multimedia techniques in Religious Education lessons. The programme uses a 3D video to draw students into particular aspects of the everyday lives of three young people. Students then follow up a particular aspect interactively in order to research and explore Christian ethical positions.

This equipment caused a considerable stir amongst students, over five hundred of whom experienced the programme during the week. The GSUS programme also enabled Teenbridge staff a further opportunity to 'know and be known' amongst the school community.

The emphasis in all of these activities was on establishing relationships with local young people rather than overt evangelism or proselytization. When challenged on this issue, Peter was clearly happy for young people to know his Christian convictions, and to discover more about Christian ethics, but he exercised his faith-voice without pressure to convert. In his words, 'On an Engel scale of 0 to 10 where 0 is getting kids to come to church and 10 is conversion, we were operating at around -10 to -5, preparing the ground, showing them the relevance and care of Christianity.' This incarnational approach chimes well with that described by Sam Thomas in chapter 4. The results of this relational approach are often difficult to measure and assess. I had the opportunity to undertake a series of psychogeographical walks[11] with Peter around the town of Teignmouth in 2011, including weekend evenings when there is some on-street activity on the part of young people in the town. During these walks we came across young people of a range of different ages and, almost without exception, they not only knew Peter but were very willing to stop for a conversation with him. 'Knowing and being known' in street and school contexts is a gradual process of relational youth work, but when carried out over several years with commitment and personal charisma the result can be that entire generations of young people in a small community can be brought into a relationship of care, and at least in some cases of trust and advice.

As Teenbridge developed, other modes of operation helped to shape the activities deployed. Sport and outdoor activity were used as further vehicles for building relationship, for knowing and being known. Staff and volunteers established both regular opportunities and school holiday visits from specialist teams of external youth workers who provided Brazilian soccer schools, basketball camps and rock-climbing programmes during school holidays. A bus was acquired and kitted out with laptops and other relevant technology, adding a further dimension to street-based work, and enabling the extension of such work in more rural places where there was no natural point of congregation. When this bus reached the end of its life in 2007, another was found with the help of the Stagecoach bus company and local councillors. Then a permanent venue was found in Dawlish; a pub (The Hole in the Wall) in the main street had closed down, and it was obtained by Teenbridge on a peppercorn lease and converted into a youth café and after-school and evening venue. In these and other ways, Teenbridge flourished for several years, with full-time workers, gap-year volunteers and local volunteers enabling a series of initiatives that added up to a significant incarnational presence in the area.

Teenbridge: Resourcing a Charitable FBO

Although the initial idea for Teenbridge was due to the vision, commitment and vitality of Peter and Su Twigg, the early impact and success of the organization depended on a much wider mobilization of resources. Here, some of the in-built advantages of faith-based networks came to the aid of the organization. Financially, regular support was received from several local churches, and from individuals within those churches. Successful applications were made to central denominational sources and to Christian charitable trusts for further funds that would not have been available outside the faith-based network. Gap-year students working with Youth for Christ but seconded to Teenbridge represented a further resource that permitted a widening of the geographical and programmatic scope of the organization.

Volunteers – as many as forty at the height of Teenbridge's operations – were drawn principally (but not exclusively) from local churches, as were a committed group of trustees who gave substantial commitment to the task of overseeing the strategy and the sustainability of the charity. Much of the fund-raising overseen by Su Twigg relied on a wide network of local supporters drawn principally from these same networks. An annual cycle of garden parties, balls, charity gigs, coffee mornings, quiz evenings, sporting challenges and recycling schemes presented regular opportunities for supporters to contribute to the cause. It is interesting to note here that such events lead to the production of interesting and important charitable spaces in small town environments.

Support for a project such as Teenbridge should not be understood simply as standardized transactions of money or time.
Instead the charitable event cycle becomes in some ways part of
the social life of the networks concerned; spaces of fun and entertainment produced as a by-product of the youth work spaces
which are the core concern of the project. Such spaces do not just
happen through the organic workings of faith-based networks.
Rather, they are themselves the product of determined and persistent fund-raising work, without which the project could not be
successful. Although faith-based services are most commonly
recognized in terms of the spaces of relationship and care
produced by staff and volunteers with particular user-groups (in
this case young people), it is equally the case that FBOs can also be
influential through the less visible but equally significant task of
producing fund-raising event-spaces in local communities.

However, the broad advantages of working within wider
church networks should not be taken to indicate that such an oper-
ational arena is unproblematic. It should also be noted that there
are also downsides to operating within and between faith-based
networks. Teenbridge was deliberately established as a non-denominational agency, so as not to be 'captured' or 'branded' by
any particular church. However, there can be a tendency for a
competitive instinct between churches, despite what is no doubt a
sincere intention to work together in a local area. This can emerge
as a desire for a local youth work FBO such as Teenbridge to focus
more of its work in a particular locality, or conversely to steer clear
of sites (such as particular schools) and client groups which are
being targeted by the in-house youth work of a particular church.
It can arise in perceptions of uneven representation on steering
groups, or of uneven levels of generosity between different
parts of the sponsoring network. It can rear its head as a clash of
particular moral or ethical stances within Christian networks, for
example, over what activities are regarded as suitable on Sundays,
or over what kinds of external grant aid is suitable for FBO operations – on this latter point, Teenbridge has refrained from applications for Lottery funds in the knowledge that such an application
would be opposed by some of its supporters. It is therefore erro-
neous to presume that the economic and social capital available
in local faith-based networks is somehow immune from these

differences in priority and competitiveness, especially given a constantly changing cast of actors both within the FBO itself and in the various churches in the network. Part of the organizational leadership role of an FBO is to negotiate these conflicts with skill and personal integrity – a task carried out very successfully in the example of Teenbridge.

In addition to resources from within faith-based networks, Teenbridge has also drawn significantly on other funding sources, including local secular networks of charitable giving, for example in civic and business arenas. It has also welcomed volunteers who are not motivated by Christian faith. For example, several volunteers at the Hole in the Wall youth café became involved specifically because of their concern over the lack of facilities for young people in Dawlish, and were happy to support the Teenbridge initiative, even though they did not share its Christian ethos. In these ways, there are some signs of openness to a broader post-secular perspective,[12] despite the unambiguous Christian foundation of the organization. Teenbridge itself has been established and developed with very clear faith-motivated perspectives and frameworks. However, its perspective is outward-looking (unlike some – but certainly not all – church-based youth work), seeking to find bridging points into the wider community and to carry out Christian service and witness without the 'strings attached' of promoting a particular church organization. Part of its success has been a willingness of local secular organizations and people to respect and work with a faith-based organization, and while much of this is down to the positive qualities of the individuals involved, there is also evidence of a wider societal trend wherein religion in this form is receiving a more positive response within the wider community than perhaps has been the case in a more stridently secular past. In this context, faith-based youth work is not simply tolerated, but there are signs that its theological basis has relevant messages, for example about ethical and moral responses to global and local issues, that are more willingly listened to than before when accompanied by relational commitment.

Perhaps the most significant source of funding outside of faith-based networks has been from 'soft' public sector funds. When interviewed, Peter reflected on 'the Labour government's policy of putting money into preventative work', and indicated that

Teenbridge had been able to draw on a range of different funding pools often disbursed by either the local council or the local police. Thus funding for different parts of the Teenbridge operation were garnered from, for example, the Crime and Disorder Reduction Partnership, the Antisocial Behaviour Unit and the Youth Offending Team. Some academic critics[13] might, therefore, regard this as simply the action of one of the 'little platoons in service of neoliberal goals'; that is as a voluntary sector pawn in the much bigger political games in which the state exercises its cost-cutting, and sometimes anti-welfare politics and policies by using agencies outside the public sector to do its work.

Such arguments need to be evaluated with care and in clear recognition of the complexity of local circumstances, as well as of grander theoretical tropes. On the one hand, FBOs such as Teenbridge can be seen as replacing public sector activity in providing youth services, providing a cut-price presence in line with wider government goals relating to the behaviour and citizenship of young people. It is clear that Teenbridge leaders perceived no incongruity between the work they wanted to carry out and the acceptance of these public sector funds (in contrast, for example, to their decision not to apply for Lottery funds). Their street-based youth work involved liaison with the local police with whom a respectful performative distance was kept to ensure that the trust of young people could be sustained. The results of their relational on-street presence were noted by local authorities in terms of a significant reduction of 'trouble'. In these circumstances, the receipt of funds designed to support preventative work against antisocial behaviour or offending posed few moral or political dilemmas. Indeed, the Teenbridge project was delighted to be awarded a Respect award by the Labour government in 2006, seeing this as a wider recognition of the stand the organization was taking with and for young people in street-based and sport-based youth work.

In this sense, then, what might be regarded as neoliberal moulding of 'respectful' youth citizenship was evidently compatible with the organization's work of engaging with young people in a positive manner, demonstrating positive adult role models, and providing positive activities by sharing the love of God in a relevant way over a hot drink or under a basketball net.

On the other hand, it is too simple to correlate an evangelical Christian approach to youth work with the wider neoliberal project. While moral conservatism may represent some over-lapping ground between the two, FBOs such as Teenbridge are by no means socially conservative in the performance of their service and care. Indeed, the relational approach adopted reflects an everyday willingness to listen to, support and care for young people, including those whose behaviour might be regarded as troublesome, and those whose way of life does not fit with that imagined in models of neoliberal citizenship. The idea here is not to clear these young people from the streets or to punish their antisocial behaviour, but rather, through the exercise of Christian values of *agape* and *caritas*, to demonstrate relations of love and care without the expectation of anything in return – an attitude that some young people often encounter for the first time through these relations. It is this performative distinctiveness that signif-icantly undermines the argument that FBOs such as Teenbridge act merely as the puppets of a post-welfare and revanchist state.[14]

Teenbridge and the 'Big Society'

Over the last two years, the stability and progress of Teenbridge have been hampered by a number of factors. Any FBO working on shoestring finances is likely to experience a regular turnover of staff, partly because the relatively low pay and uncertain nature of employment means that staff will seek out other work that offers them more stability and security, and partly because the 'full-on' nature of youth work – involving as it does long and often unso-ciable hours and intense relational demands – often necessitates that people move on after a few years to more sustainable work patterns elsewhere in order to avoid burn-out. This churning of staff often brings with it some disruption of, and maybe even challenges to, the organizational ethos and its modus operandi, as new staff members bring with them different priorities, ways of working, and allegiances within the faith-based networks of the locality. Similarly, the pool of volunteers will also be affected by this churning effect. While some volunteers are able to continue their regular commitment over many years – and Teenbridge certainly has this kind of support from key volunteers – others will drop out after shorter periods of service, and so there has to be a continual seeking out of new volunteers to take their place. By 2010, Teenbridge leaders were experiencing a shrinkage of their pool of volunteers, with the result that parts of their established programme could not be sustained. For example, the use of the Teenbridge bus has been severely restricted by the shortage of volunteer licensed drivers and support teams.

However, the most significant change for Teenbridge has been in its funding environment, and in particular the radical reduction in so-called 'soft' public sector funds. The Coalition government's policy of hard-hitting fiscal restraint and public expenditure cuts has altered the conditions within which charitable FBOs were previously sustainable. There has been a marked reduction in the support for government QUANGOs and a concomitant reduction in the funds that they were previously able to disburse into the voluntary sector. In particular, a change of approach in dealing with youth offending and antisocial behaviour has moved policy away from the funding of preventative work previously carried out by organizations such as Teenbridge. Local councils and police authorities have also been required to exercise financial cost-cutting, and inevitably, given the necessity to preserve frontline public services, it is the more peripheral funds that have previously been used to support the voluntary sector that have been the easiest to cut. While some large-scale FBOs have been able to ride out this storm (albeit with significant changes to their own operations), small-scale organizations such as Teenbridge have in relative terms been hardest hit, as the small amounts of public funding that they have come to rely on as an essential part of their budgeting are no longer available. This withdrawal of public sector support has had immediate ramifications on private charitable trusts which have become inundated with requests for support from desperate Third Sector organizations badly affected by public funding cuts. As a result, funding from these trusts has become extraordinarily competitive, and is much more difficult to access than before.

From 2010 onwards, Teenbridge was significantly disadvantaged by these changes in the funding arena, which in particular impacted on the ability to continue to pay for staffing at previous levels. A number of forward strategies were considered, ranging from keeping going in the hope that further finance could be found from somewhere, or a shrinkage of the organization back to its most basic activities, to the immediate closure of the organization. In deciding between these options, a number of interesting dilemmas came into play. For example, should Teenbridge be allowed to 'limp along' on a much more restricted basis, with the likely result that it would be unable to maintain its reputation in its host communities for high-impact relational youth work? Would it be better to stop at this point while it was still highly thought of? Had its work since 2003 actually impacted on local youth culture in the towns concerned, such that the reduction of gang-related 'trouble' meant that outreach services were no longer required? Had it effectively done itself out of a job? What would be the impact of changes on staff, both on those who had founded and run the project since 2003, and those who had been newly recruited, and had moved into the area specifically to take up this work? What would be the impact on local faith-based networks whose commitment as volunteers and charitable donors had underpinned the history of the organization? The result of these deliberations was to continue with Teenbridge, but at a reduced scale of expenditure and operation. One full-time worker was retained, but the organization's inspirational founders, Peter and Su Twigg, thought it best to leave the project that could no longer support them financially.

The financial problems experienced by Teenbridge interconnect with two wider trends in the UK. First, funding for youth services more generally seems to have been singled out for particularly severe cuts in this current period of fiscal restraint. It has been suggested that local authority youth service budgets are being cut by up to £100 million, leading both to the loss of 3,000 full-time youth worker jobs across the country, and to a starvation of funds for voluntary sector youth services.[15] The struggles discussed above in the context of one small FBO in south Devon are thus being replicated across the country due to these kinds of funding decisions. Perhaps ironically, the second trend is that faith-based organizations have been recognized as a key component of the current government's 'Big Society' discourse. In the words of government minister Greg Clark:

[Faith communities] often have the experience, volunteers and connections that can put them at the heart of their neighbourhood. Everyone has a part to play in building the Big Society. The Government's job is to make sure that religious groups and other grassroots organisations have the space in which to get on with their good work, unhindered by the barriers many of them currently negotiate.[16]

By this token, youth services provided by FBOs such as Teen-bridge can often be represented as the 'Big Society' in action, yet the discourse of 'Big Society' seems to be at odds with the practical outcomes of public sector cost-cutting which in effect are starving voluntary sector organizations of the pump-priming and sustainable funding which is often the necessary foundation on which the edifice of charitable and voluntary activity is built and kept in place.

The idea of 'Big Society' is clearly being used by government to marshal FBO activity as legitimacy for its conservative and communitarian vision, and is being received and interpreted within faith communities in one of two ways. Some faith-motivated organizations are viewing the notion of 'Big Society' as both a confirmation of and encouragement for their current social activism, and an encouragement to take this work further in the expectation that their good work will be unhindered by government action, including that of fiscal constraint. Many of these FBOs are currently discovering a fatal flaw in their expectations, as the public sector funding environment starves them of relatively minor, but essential, support funds.

In a survey of 200 faith-based youth workers throughout the UK in 2011, Nigel Pimlott asked respondents to articulate the challenges represented by the Big Society that they were regarded as being part of. He reports that the answers given were dominated by issues of funding cuts and the continual strain on resources in faith-based youth work. These youth workers, says Pimlott, 'did not, or could not, differentiate between the "vision" of the Big Society . . . and the reality of the current economic climate and the impact the Government spending cuts are having on youth work and other public services'.[17] If the 'Big Society' idea is being built on the foundations of scaled-down government and public expenditure austerity drives, then it seems unlikely to support the kind of voluntary sector activity that needs to be sponsored by some public funding. Indeed, as Pimlott suggests, 'Big Society' in this regard could be considered simply as some kind of political smokescreen behind which ideologies of the shrinking state are being implemented.

Alternatively, then, other FBOs are beginning to present dissenting voices to the idea of 'Big Society', expressing concern that it offers only a suffocating and unworkable return to a very traditional type of Christendom in which radical Christian hope and action become diluted into a rather more weary and passive acceptance of the current world order.[18] The problem here is that only a restricted number of FBOs, perhaps sited geographically or socially in the more affluent areas of the country, have the independent resources for a 'go it alone' strategy that eschews any available public sector funding, and therefore escapes this perceived translation of faith-based radicalism into pragmatic collusion. The Teenbridge experience is that such a strategy is problematic in small coastal towns such as Teignmouth and Dawlish, with high proportions of low paid or retired people. In addition, there is little sign that staff and volunteers associated with Teenbridge are devoid of radical Christian hope or sanctioning a return to non-progressive pragmatism. Indeed, the Christian foundation of the organization consistently prompts an approach in which faith-based care and service are themselves held to be a radical alternative to the stale and often uncaring nature of the current secular world order.

These models – of either the conformist FBO colluding with the 'Big Society' by taking the Queen's shilling, or the radically progressive FBO working outside of the 'Big Society' and its attendant public funding so as to retain its revolutionary Christian core – are too simplistic. As we have seen, the essential characteristics of Teenbridge are demonstrated by how its staff and volunteers perform relational care and service, rather than by the strings attached to public funding. In some ways, the Teenbridge example suggests the opening up of a Thirdspace[19] in which new forms of radical Christian performance have occurred whilst still relying on some public funding. The key question, then, is how this kind of voluntary sector effort can be sustained in the context of government financial austerity that threatens a collapsing funding environment in both the public sector and for many individual donors.

Conclusion

This book focuses on the idea of faith at work in the activities of FBOs of different scales and in different sectors. The Teenbridge project, based as it is in small towns in south Devon, represents something of the hidden face of FBO activity, operating at a relatively small local scale in a relatively marginal locality. Yet the activities and achievements of the project represent those of myriad similar projects across the country. It is founded on the vision, entrepreneurial skills and energy of one Christian couple, who saw a particular need amongst young people in the locality, and saw that by deploying a Christian relational approach that something progressive could be done about this need. They gathered around them others from their local faith-based networks: some as volunteers, others as prayerful and financial supporters. In time, these supporters were drawn not only into the charitable and caring ethics of the organization, but also into the production of local fundraising event-spaces that influenced the life of the local community, and extended beyond faith networks. Talented staff and 'year out' volunteers were recruited to join the founders in the main thrust of the relational youth work, aided and abetted by a range of volunteers. In this way, local young people got to know about these youth workers, about the Teenbridge organization they worked for, about the moral and ethical life values of Christianity, and in some cases about the love of God that underpinned the whole encounter. Relationships were formed, trust was built, and new cultures of 'knowing and being known' were constructed outside of the structures of policing and other social regulation.

These radical performances of Christian care and service were expanded out into new activities and places, to some extent changing the social landscape for young people in the towns concerned. The Hole in the Wall pub served as a living metaphor of these changes; the disused pub was transformed into a youth café, and 'hanging out with nowhere to go' was transformed into 'somewhere to go and something to do with people I can trust'. The faith-based foundations of the project did not deter the gaining of social and civic respect, or the perception that Teen-bridge was a whole-community enterprise and not just a church-based thing for church-based people. As the potential for this kind of work was increasingly realized, so a sustainable funding base was required, and this included some 'soft' public sector funds which were seen as compatible with the Teenbridge ethos and mission statement. However, the fiscal austerity of the last three years saw a downturn in available funding, and regardless of the apparent discursive support offered by the idea of the 'Big Society', the activities of the project had to be drastically scaled back, although considerable radical hope continues to be invested in what is currently being done amongst local young people, and in what will be done in the future.

The story of Teenbridge and of the thousands of small-scale FBOs like it is rarely told. Yes, it has had to negotiate the local politics and attendant propensity for micro-scale managerialism that often seem to occur in local faith networks in small towns, but it is nevertheless a testament to faith-motivated action on behalf of marginalized sectors of society. It is in many ways a radical movement of sacrificial involvement, although it rarely presents itself as such and leaves itself open to external interpretation as just another traditional voluntary agency. However, for a few short years at least, it has opened up a kind of liminal Thirdspace in these small Devon towns, where new lines of flight involving trust and respect have been nudged into being amongst young people by gifted and committed youth workers prepared to know and be known. In what form Teenbridge will survive the current age of austerity is unclear, but the potential released by its activities is much plainer. Far from being a puppet of neoliberal govern-ment, or a proselytizing self-interested device for moral selving, Teenbridge demonstrates what can be achieved progressively by a few highly motivated Christian people when they recognize and act on bridgeheads of need in their local communities.[20]

CHAPTER 7

The July Project and Big Saturdays: a Church (St Paul's, Salisbury, UK) in its Local Community

Jon Langford

Introduction

All too often, the church is known more for what it says than what it does; and all too often what it says is communicated in negative terms. You could say that Christians in the UK are, in the media at least, more often known for what they stand against, rather than what they stand for. In recent years, however, different churches and Christian charities across the UK have slowly but surely rediscovered a new awareness of the need to engage in actions rather than simply words as they have revisited God's call to serve the poor. Far from being centrally organized, the majority of movements have been initiated purely at a grass roots level, while larger organizations such as Soul Survivor, which runs annual festivals for young people, have enabled literally thousands of young people to undertake concentrated 'word and action' projects in defined weeks in Manchester (2000) and London (2004).

This movement feels somewhat different to those that have come before. Particular churches are undertaking particular works to connect with local people. From lunch clubs to food parcels, and play groups to play buses, various churches of all denominations are exploring constructive ways to serve the more vulnerable members of society. And this difference is to be celebrated, for it appears as an indigenous response to the issues of modern society, rather than a response to a national initiative. It is also a direct response to Jesus' call to 'follow him' – and is again now seen as an important part of what it is to be a follower of Christ today. Faith without actions is indeed dead (Jas. 2:17), it would appear.

Indeed, the Evangelical Alliance's report, '21ˢᵗ Century Evangelicals' (January 2011) discovered that 'evangelicals who consider their faith to be the most important thing in their life undertake an average of 2 hours of volunteering per week',[1] with 99 per cent of the 17,000 Christians surveyed stating that they undertake some form of volunteering activity each year. The church in the UK seems once again to be looking beyond its walls to the needs of the society of which it is a part – confident that it has something to contribute.

Here in Salisbury, in the south of England, we are absolutely confident that we as the local church have something to contribute, and this chapter outlines the story of our journey as we have sought to put our faith into action, and engage effectively with our local community.

Our Church: Our Community

'Last night I sat in my garden and had a coffee and a fag,' she said with a smile on her face. After a day clearing her garden, I and the crew of young people with me were delighted to hear this. We picked up our paintbrushes and got started on decorating her lounge. It was only later in the day that she took me to one side, and whispered, 'I've had this depression for six years, and haven't felt able to sit in my garden in all that time. Then yesterday the young people cleared it, and last night I felt able to sit out there and drink my coffee and have a fag for the first time in six years. I can't thank you enough.'

This brief account is but one of many we have collected as we have journeyed into community action as a youth group and as a Church of England congregation in the cathedral city of Salisbury. In many ways we fulfil the larger Anglican Church's stereotype: a clergyman, a dedicated staff team, and an equally dedicated team of volunteers that contribute to the life and mission of the church.

As you might expect, we enjoy lively worship, a committed children's and youth work, a strong focus on the Bible, and invest heavily in our relationships and community life together. What has increasingly set us apart, however, is the outworking of our faith in our local community – a faith that is increasingly shaped by the circumstances we come across in so doing.

Our story begins back in 1998 when I joined the church as its youth worker, inheriting a strong and capable youth group, but essentially an inward-looking one. As the exam season beckoned at the end of my first year in post, I saw a golden opportunity to create a new initiative which would enable those who had completed their GCSEs and A levels to look beyond themselves and invest a week of their extended summer holiday in serving the local community, very practically putting their faith into action. So, in the summer of 1999, The July Project was born as six intrepid young people and one equally intrepid youth worker let themselves loose on a community room in a local hostel for homeless people, decorating it and kitting it out with a coffee bar for the residents to both manage and enjoy. Each day the young people would work from 10 a.m. until 4 p.m., meeting and interacting with staff and residents, alongside gaining the practical skills of painting and decorating. At the week's end we had completely restored the room, and saw a delighted group of residents take charge of it. More than that, I had seen six young people learn more about themselves, more about the issues of homelessness, and more about the faith that they enjoyed. I had seen young lives changed.

Changing Lives: The July Project

'And then, this morning, after sitting in the garden like that last night, I went downstairs, and normally I open my lounge door and just, like, sigh, and feel down. But this morning I opened the door, and you'd, like, painted it, and I thought, yeah, I can do this; this is OK,' our client continued, smiling away. In twenty-four hours, we had seen her confidence rise, her self-esteem increase a little, and glimpsed a sense of humour returning as she bantered with the young people. By now the young people were painting with even more enthusiasm, and chatting away happily with the client. As we left later that day, she stretched in through the car window and said again, 'Thank you so much! You make sure you keep doing what you're doing, 'cos there'll always be people like me who need people like you to bring a little bit of hope.' Thirteen years on and The July Project is still bringing that little bit of hope to the people of Salisbury, and numerous young people have been impacted by simply giving a week of their holiday to serve others. In many ways, it is its simplicity that makes it so effective: a group of well-prepared young people, a clearly defined, accessible placement, all confined to a pre-determined timeframe, and with a sincere promise to never leave a job undone.

Perhaps our community action can best be summed up as 'targeted action'. Our regular gardening projects consist of everything from general maintenance to shed clearances, greenhouse dismantling, tree cutting, and path laying. Internally, we find ourselves decorating all sorts of rooms, generally with paint selected and supplied by the clients themselves. Increasingly, and particularly for those with enduring mental health conditions, we are often found tidying and sorting, as well as cleaning and clearing. Never underestimate, either, the great facility a vehicle offers to those without transport, as we have been enabled to remove copious amounts of waste furniture and other items from people's gardens. All jobs which primarily require people's *availability* rather than *ability* – ideal for teenagers.

In the years since 1999, we have continuously built upon and refined our model of community action, but it is the principle of defined and accessible placements which we believe to be at the heart of its success. In the months prior to July, we work with carefully selected local, and reputable, charities to gather placements, simultaneously recruiting school leavers through the church to serve with us for that particular week. Once notified of potential placements, we visit an organization or clients in their homes and assess the need and suitability of the task, determine the appropriate number of volunteers and tools required and, of course, undertake the necessary risk assessments. We then ensure an appropriate number of adult staff is also recruited, and The July Project takes shape.

Working with local charities to develop this work has taken time, and intentionally so. We naturally started small, essentially identifying local projects which had some resources but were in need of people-power in order to get a task completed. For example, in one of the first few years we worked with the Salisbury Women's Refuge to turn a redundant room into a playroom using paint donated to them by a local DIY superstore. While they had the materials, they simply did not have people available to do the work – until eighteen teenagers joined them for the week. Another year and we installed a footpath to enable easier access to the headquarters of the then little-known Trussell Trust, which was later to become significant as the provider of food banks throughout the UK. Putting a different twist on it, twice we took over empty stores in the city centre and turned them into a 'Charity Shop in a Week', stocking and setting up before trading for three and a half days. In both instances we raised over £3,000 for local charities. By now word was spreading, and with up to thirty-eight young people regularly participating, our reputation for seeing the job through was gaining us significant ground. Word was also spreading amongst the charity sector, and conversations and suggestions naturally led us from one charity to the next, gaining both placements and profile along the way.

Another essential ingredient has been discernment. We have needed to be discerning of the client's needs and our ability as a team to meet them. Often we have needed to gather further information about clients from placement providers when we have had concerns about the client's capacity to cope with the influx of a team when many of them live alone, and often in isolation. Using charities for these referrals mean a provisional assessment of a client's suitability has already been made, which we can then build on, but we have also had to be prepared to withdraw if our services are simply too much – even if this is only realized as a team arrives on site. Preparing both young people and adults for this eventuality has been essential; as has being a listening ear for frustrated and disappointed support workers when this occurs. Yet this is the reality of life for many of our clients and those who support them.

Given this, and similar difficult situations, the first morning of The July Project is an important one. Before we go anywhere near a single placement, we call the young people together for a morning of training and preparation. We explore and discuss God's call to the poor throughout the Bible. We ask what it is to talk of, and work with, the kingdom of God. We are honest about, and seek to address, our hopes, worries, and expectations for the week. We share stories of previous years, and the experiences and insights gained. We talk through the health and safety aspects, and inform ourselves of the particular needs of individual clients. And whilst most weeks begin with young people heroically stating that they are seeking to 'bring God to these people', most weeks end with them realizing that God was already there.

It is this realization that God is *already* there that has been the most profound aspect of taking 16 to 18-year-olds into community work of this nature. So their concept of God has broadened, and this learning has been rooted not simply in words but in physical and practical experience. This was perhaps best revealed when The July Project worked at the women's refuge. Although males were not allowed upstairs into the residents' rooms, they were allowed into certain areas downstairs, enabling us to transform a redundant room into a playroom. Near the end of the week, I was privileged to be in the house's conservatory with the manager and health visitor, overlooking the garden where we watched the residents' sons playing football with our young male volunteers. As we sat there, tears flowed down the faces of the manager and health visitor as they saw the progress these lads had made in just five days. Lads literally petrified of older males at the beginning of the week were now smiling, shouting, and screaming away as our young men played alongside them. We – and they – were glimpsing something of the kingdom of God at work before our very eyes.

Exploring the other side of life

Without a doubt, engagement in The July Project has been liberating for many young people as they have explored life on the 'other side' of Salisbury: that of poverty and isolation. Educationally, the impact of these weeks has been significant as young people see children sleeping on floors, elderly residents literally trapped in their own homes, and people living with the extremely limiting effects of enduring mental illness. Given these experiences, we have often needed to sit and talk through these situations with our volunteers, as they have sought to process what they have seen and heard, and indeed our initial training takes this into account. Yet this is all part of what we will experience if we genuinely wish to engage with our local community. I, for one, am proud of the fact that young people within our church understand more of our society than one might see at first glance. And I am proud of the fact that these experiences have had a profound effect on many, even influencing the shape of many July Project participants' future studies and activities. Examples range from students volunteering on nightlines to those working with the disabled and homeless. Some have even made a career of it, working in national charities and local governments. Primarily, however, these initiatives have led young people into gap years, often in the most deprived communities of the world.

Whole Church: Big Saturdays

'It's great to see these young people changing, and other people's lives changing as a result, but when do we get to join in?' A church member said this in 2003, as the pressure mounted for adult members of our congregation to also get involved. Our reputation was gaining pace in the church as well as in the wider community. Parents reported different attitudes in their teenagers, and they liked it. A few dedicated adults had volunteered to work along-side us on July Projects, and many more rejoiced with the young people as they shared stories from their placements at the front of church.

It was clear that the interest was there, and so we decided to elongate The July Project by a day to create 'One Big Saturday'. One hundred and thirteen adults and children ranging in age from 3 to 82 years old joined us on that first Big Saturday, serving in twenty-three placements across the city. This was community action in a different league, and certainly organizationally it was a different game altogether! A colleague and I coordinated this between us, drawing placements from seven agencies, and placing each volunteer in a team numbering between two and eight members. Based on my experience with The July Project, we carefully assessed all the placements, taking into consideration the skills of the volunteers, and the needs of the clients. We hired a truck to collect all the garden waste and deliver it to the tip (the license exemption was to follow when we realized we needed one). And so we entered a new era in our church's history. That first Big Saturday was a highly significant milestone as we saw families serving together, members of the church building new friendships across the generations, connections being made with our local residents, and quite literally God going ahead of us in many circumstances.

Most memorable has to be lady living just a few yards from the church which Age UK had referred to us. She was struggling to nurse her husband, who was dying of cancer, having broken her ankle. Her daughter had brought her wedding forward to the beginning of August to ensure her father could be there, and their desire was two-fold: one, that they might have photos taken in their currently overgrown garden which had been his pride and joy, and two, that he might be able to escort her down the aisle. Our team of four volunteers arrived that first Big Saturday and spent six hours clearing the garden before the truck came and disposed of the cuttings. A month later I met her in our local supermarket and, with tears in her eyes, she told me how her husband had died a few days earlier, but thanks to our work they had indeed had those photos in their garden, and he had managed a few steps up the aisle as he gave his daughter away. By now I was beginning to understand the impact we could make. A few willing volunteers, a carefully selected, well assessed, and accessible placement, and a van to take the waste away, and we could see something of the kingdom of God impact on the lives of local people in very practical ways. We could see our faith truly make a real difference. And we could see it change the faith of our church members too.

Within hours of completing this first Big Saturday, we knew we had started something we had to continue. Families talked of the joy of working together. Elderly members told stories of wonderful recollections of 'the old days' with clients as they chatted as well as painted. People enthused about the clients they had worked with, and how they would be returning to visit them regularly. Some even reported feeling closer to God in serving in this way. Others expressed disappointment that they had not been able to attend this Big Saturday, so when was the next one to be? As a result, the next couple of years saw Big Saturdays become annual events, but as demand both within and beyond the church soared, we soon settled on a termly event, which is indeed what Big Saturday remains to this day.

In essence, we have found that Big Saturdays build the church community while reaching out to the wider community. With up to one hundred and seventy people now joining us, newer members of the church feel more integrated, whilst those on the fringe of the church get drawn further in. Families get to know other families as they work together. Younger and older members mix in ways unthinkable in normal social settings. Single people experience the church 'family' at its best. And men particularly find a role within what is often the female-dominated environment of church.

We have also gained amazing insights into how the church is regarded. Whilst by far the majority of our clients have welcomed our involvement in their lives, others have been more cautious. As one client remarked, 'When my support worker said the people from the church would come and do my garden for free, I thought, "Oh no, they're weird, them religious people."' Thankfully, her perspective changed as we worked with her, but it was a timely reminder that our presumptions might not always be accurate, and approaching people carefully and sympathetically remains the order of the day.

A Journey of Discovery

Whilst the majority of our community action work brings good story, we have not had a completely smooth ride. Like any new venture, we have discovered the need for continuous refinement, and developing our community action has not been entirely straightforward. For example, an absolutely crucial aspect of enabling community action to take place is being able to make accurate assessments. The first person on the scene has to consider the suitability of the task, the optimum number of volunteers to place there, and what resources will be required – as well as starting to build a relationship with the client on behalf of the church. Thankfully, there is now a dedicated team of nine people who work with me to create Big Saturdays, and a variety of forms detail what we need to consider as we visit each placement. However, we still get this wrong on occasion, and sometimes I have simply misjudged the amount of work we are agreeing to undertake. The most extreme example was a few years ago, when a team of twelve people was clearing a garden for a man whose wife had just been sectioned under the Mental Health Act. Having cleared the garden, they called me to ask if they should keep going as in taking down the hedge at the rear of the property they had discovered *another* garden, and this one had an abandoned car in it! I decided that was beyond our remit, and the team quit while they were ahead. More seriously, allocating the correct number of volunteers to the correct project has been an essential skill – and one that we keep under constant review. Too many volunteers, and they will simply be on top of each other; too few and morale can be low, and the task incomplete.

Relationships with potential agencies have also had to be refined. Our brief foray into working with our local council found too many volunteers clearing footpaths which no one used, during the whole six hours they were on site. Now we knew why the council's own workforce had only infrequently been seen there. Inevitably, our relationship with the council was to be short-lived, as we were not convinced they understood what we were really trying to achieve. Indeed, even all these years later, we are still dependent on a key individual in each charity catching the vision of what we hope to achieve, and ensuring that both clients and placements fulfil this remit. And again, all these years later, we are still refining exactly what type of placement we can best serve, and seeking to clearly communicate this to our placement providers. Essentially, therefore, our placements fall into two categories: agency-led, such as gardening for homes for people with learning difficulties, to agency-referred, meaning we work with an individual in their own home.

These difficulties with placement providers have, however, enabled us to understand what we *are* trying to achieve: contact with *people* and an opportunity to *be* good news for them. On reflection, this rather messy process has nevertheless been a rather crucial one, and now means we will only undertake placements where contact with the client is guaranteed. While the painting and gardening might be the practical outworking of our community action, the long-term outworking is all about *people*: building relationships is key, both for clients and church members.

A New Era: Mental Health

'I just get a little bit bothered, and then I find it hard to get up and do anything. It's this blooming depression. I feel such a failure.' This client was originally referred to us by Age UK, and when we first met him he was living in a top floor flat, surrounded by stuff. And we are talking a lot of stuff. CDs, books, linen, washing – you name it, he had it. There was quite literally stuff everywhere. Six July Project volunteers initially spent a day with him, building a friendship, and gently sorting through all his belongings. It was to be the start of a long-term support relationship between the youth group and this man which saw us both sort and tidy for him, and eventually help him move into more appropriate accommodation. Four years on, and we ended The July Project with a party at this client's new supported housing complex to 'thank them for all their help and support'. A man who, when we first met him was shy and reserved, was now hosting a party for a group of teen-agers!

It was, in fact, contact with clients such as this elderly man that led directly to a highly significant conversation which was to exert a massive influence on the direction of our community action. 'Are you aware of the mental health needs in this city?' asked a worker from the homeless charity's mental health team one day. This was something different. Until then we had primarily been focused in the particular areas of the city where you might expect to see us: a large council estate and some pockets of council housing. Indeed, many people (church members and not) were beginning to question whether we should really be leaving this type of work to the churches located nearer to these specific areas. But this was different. Mental health, in the form of depression and anxiety, amongst other conditions, permeated all areas of our city, and beyond, and seemed to show no favouritism as to age, life circumstance or location. Immediately we stumbled across people within walking distance of our church door, and actually this was to have a profound effect upon many of our congregation, and the direction of our community work. No longer was our community action simply for people 'up there' or 'over there', but now the possibility arose that The July Project or Big Saturday might actually be working with your neighbour.

Young people especially have latched on to the issues of mental health. Reflecting upon this with them, they endorse many of the connections made above, but appear to be particularly sensitive to this issue. They also appreciate the impact of community action with these clients, as the changes in clients can be relatively immediate. Perhaps this is best illustrated in the story of a woman who suffered from schizophrenia, and whose partner had died in bed beside her earlier in the year. Reluctant to live in the flat alone and, somewhat haunted by this event, she had moved in with her mother, and was generally deteriorating. Her support worker first approached us to ask if we could decorate the bedroom to 'help heal the memories'. This we duly did, and subsequently she moved back into her flat. Returning to decorate her lounge at the time of the General Election, we experienced great hilarity as some of our more outspoken young people discussed politics with her for the evening. As she smiled, she confessed as we left that that night had been one of very few when she could not hear the voices in her head. An amazing impact; yet young people also recognize the long-term, slow nature of the work with people with enduring mental illness. And this brings us to another important lesson we have learnt.

This is Long Term

Community action is essentially a long-term commitment, and this has proved most effective when, as a church, we have committed to an individual or charity over a number of years. One local couple illustrate this perfectly. We first met them when they were referred to us by their support worker for mental and physical health issues. Their small ground floor flat was suffering from a lack of care, and this, coupled with a recent addiction to purchasing films on video had left them feeling isolated and low. A youth team from The July Project were first on the scene, sorting video cassettes for the charity shop and decorating their lounge. Then a Big Saturday team cleared the garden and 'redis-covered' their greenhouse. A few months on, and a team of young people returned to continue to clear the garden. By now, we were getting to know this couple quite well. They would phone when assistance was required, and they would even phone when they wanted us to pray for them as an operation or some other major life event beckoned. Then their social worker suggested that the wife should consider joining a group which consisted of a greater variety of people to those she normally met in her support groups, 'like one of the ladies' groups at the church', and within weeks she was part of a small, supportive group who have come alongside her for a number of years now. Furthermore, a couple of the ladies from this group went on to formally befriend her as government cuts meant less support from her social worker, meaning they now meet her once a month for a coffee and a chat. On a recent Big Saturday, this particular lady was our first client to go full circle and join us to serve on a team, befriending another person in need. Truly faith in action.

Young People Continuously Lead the Way

Interactions with couples such as the one cited above have also led to another initiative, this time suggested by an 18-year-old man from the youth group. Having seen the benefit of regular contact with clients, he suggested we hosted a Christmas meal and invited all our current clients along. Seven people enjoyed a four course Christmas meal – free – served by our young people one wet Friday night in December. Those attending were a healthy mix of residents from the women's refuge and mental health sufferers, and the night was a great success, again seeing confidence rise. Such meals are now a termly feature of the youth group's programme, with young people working both upfront and behind the scenes, providing food, live music, and children's entertainment. As one client put it, 'I don't know what it is about coming here, but when I'm [at the church] I feel really peaceful.' Indeed, it has seemed only logical to invite people to join us, as well as us going to join them, and this has meant significant progress in further breaking down barriers between us and them.

It has also increased the number of young people involved in our community work significantly.

This is but one example of where young people have led the way in our community action. Dissatisfied with only an annual July Project and termly Big Saturdays, a few of them suggested that we explore the opportunities to serve more regularly. As a result, we now run a fortnightly kids' club at the women's refuge, bringing fun and games into the house, as well as good company for the children. In addition, we now send small youth teams out to placements once a month on a Friday night. Whilst this has brought its limitations – there is a limit to how much gardening can be done under spotlights! – it has also liberated us to offer a more consistent service to ongoing clients, and led to deeper and more consistent relationships being formed. It has also been a great challenge to adult members of the church to see teams of young people regularly giving up their spare time to serve others.

Creating and Managing Expectations

Yet all this takes years, and any success is, whichever way we like to look at it, reliant on clients making good contacts with appropriately equipped church members. The long-term nature of these contacts has also proved a challenge to some of the keener members of the church who have expected much more immediate results, and ultimately for clients to come to faith. Continuously, we have had to pause to reflect on the theology of what we are doing (never a bad thing), and also the practice. Three things have clearly emerged:

First, church members need to be taught about God's call to serve the poor and vulnerable in any community. It has been shocking, yet enlightening, to realize the lack of awareness of this central message from the Bible amongst many of our congregation. One man who had been a Christian for over thirty years told me that he had never really noticed passages like Matthew 25[2] in all his years of following Christ. Another told me simply that she saw our church members' spiritual growth as more important than anyone else's, and so would not be joining Big Saturday on principle. Whilst having had to learn to be thick-skinned, this has

141

also led me to delve deeper into scripture for myself, and focus again on a simple verse in 1 John 3 where the apostle writes in verse 18: 'Dear children, let us not love with words or speech but with actions and in truth' (NIV). As I mentioned earlier, I am convinced that for too long the church has been best known for its words, and too often for what it stands *against*. Community action provides an opportunity for us to make clear what we stand *for*: a genuine and thought-through concern for our neighbour in need. Certainly, in our setting, we have been known as the 'happy-clappy church' in the past, but now are increasingly known as the church that serves others. I know which reputation I prefer.

Secondly, we have learnt that simply teaching scripture, and drawing people's attention to certain verses, is not enough. Rather, people respond to stories that illustrate the reality of the Bible's teaching. Increasingly we have told (anonymously of course) good stories from our experiences, and challenged church members to join in this narrative with us. We have also told of particular placements which demand our attention, and seen individuals specifically respond to be on these teams. Saving families from eviction as we clear the waste from their garden is, after all, both immediate and exciting. Undoubtedly it is a combination of both teaching and story, together with a good dose of persistence, which has resulted in increased numbers participating in our community action.

Finally, we have learnt that each of our clients is on a personal faith journey of their own, whether they realize it initially or not. We have literally been amazed at the conversations that have developed, particularly with our longer-term clients. Many tell of previous encounters with the Christian community, both positive and negative, and we have been able to build upon this. Others have discreetly asked us to pray for them. A significant few have made tentative moves towards joining our church community, and this has been much to the delight of the young people in particular. Others have simply stated that their perception of Christian people has changed as a result of our work.

We have also sought to ensure accessibility for all who wish to serve with us. Most recently, we have started using those who are less physically able to chat with clients, whilst the more able members of the team undertake the task in hand. This 'befriending' role has been highly significant for disabled members of our congregation, and also speaks loudly of an inclusive gospel. Again, with relationships as our focus, we have worked hard to ensure a more inclusive approach, and one which values all individuals – whatever their circumstances.

People are Complicated

Yet valuing individuals is costly. As we have built on our community action year on year, so we have inevitably become more involved with clients, and many of their lives are, quite simply, complicated. Whilst we have rejoiced when people feel confident to call on our services, such requests have also proved difficult to manage and – at points – limit. Of course, there is a substantial difference between clearing someone's garden on a termly basis, and fielding phone calls asking us to do their weekly shopping. Having to say no on many occasions has been difficult, and in many ways we are still learning exactly where boundaries should lie. A calling card which we leave with clients after each community action event now seeks to clarify our position and what we can realistically offer.

In response to where we have found ourselves of late, we are currently exploring the possibility of establishing a formal befriending scheme which would see our church members coming alongside our clients in a regular and well-informed way. Initial suggestions are that such a service, just like our placements, needs to be clearly defined and understood by all parties, and volunteers well-trained and accountable in what they are able to offer.

Yet whilst we can have a structured response, people are by their very nature messy – and mental health particularly only highlights this. As I said, some of my most painful telephone conversations have been telling clients that we are unable to help with weekly tasks, and that they need to seek alternative agencies for this level of support. Yet deep inside, I know only too well that charities with an ability to offer such services on a regular and ongoing basis are few and far between. And deep inside I question whether Christ is calling me to lay down my life for others.

Somehow 'structures' and termly initiatives are more attractive, and certainly much more manageable. However, as our community action story above illustrates, we have faithfully been led from one initiative to another. Whereas our community action began with simply myself and a few motley teenagers, we now have a team of nine volunteers who work with me to create the Big Saturdays, let alone the 150-plus people who join us on each occasion. In addition, a team of five young people are extremely committed to the youth group's community action, and are currently investing heavily in encouraging others to get involved, and taking full responsibility for our community meals. Furthermore, a number of our fellowship group leaders are starting to visit individual clients on a regular basis. In summary, community action is now simply part of our church's culture.

A Developing Culture

Of course, these initiatives do not operate in isolation. In recent years, and in many ways informed by our community action experiences, we have begun to explore the opportunities to develop our own purpose-built community centre to increase our service to people within our local area. To test the waters further, we began to lease rooms in our current building to a mental health charity which refers projects for Big Saturdays, enabling them to run activities and support groups for their clients on a weekly basis. It came as no surprise to us to discover many familiar faces now accessing these services within our buildings. It is this naturally 'joined up' society that has enabled us to feel that we are genuinely reaching out to people, and meeting at least some of their needs, at a variety of levels. It has also meant that their needs are continually on our radar. Informal conversations in hired rooms have resulted in more targeted community action elsewhere, and has brought with it additional referrals – often now made by clients themselves.

In addition, and to accompany the building's development, we have successfully sought funding for a community worker to join the church staff to further develop our work across the city. Once appointed, this person will take responsibility for increasing the level and range of services we are able to both offer, and signpost clients to. Our existing charity contacts should serve us well in this respect, as should our reputation.

In recent months, many other local churches have been expressing an interest in joining with us in our community action, as they too realize the many benefits this can bring. Interestingly, this is one area of the Christian walk in which a sense of unity is most clearly displayed, and a common belief in serving others in the name of Jesus has drawn a wide variety of church leaders together. Many have started to join us on Big Saturdays to experience community action in practice, and subsequently take the vision back to their churches. Plans are currently being drawn up for a large-scale city-wide weekend of community action, using members of as many churches as possible. In many ways, our story is only just beginning.

Still an Effort

Ensuring that this story continues to develop, however, requires some real effort, forward planning, and strategic thinking, and we are not naïve to the amount of work this entails. Community action is indeed a prominent part of our church culture, but keeping it in this position is an ongoing challenge. I remain very much aware that our current ventures are limited to specific dates and times, and there is much to do in resolving how we live with the organized aspect of defined projects, yet responsive to the needs of individual clients on a more regular basis. Again, the young people's enthusiasm sets a wonderful precedent here, as they regularly ask what is organized, and set plans for the next community meal, but we are yet to see this level of enthusiasm displayed in the congregation to the extent I would like to see.

We have, without a doubt, seen significant numbers of our congregation participate in our community action, but there remain many who are still to grasp this call on their lives to serve the poor. One of the members of the Big Saturday team believes that you have to coerce people to join a team once or twice before they truly understand the significance and opportunity that community action provides. I tend to agree, and indeed many of our keenest volunteers are testimony to this.

145

Our many forms of community action are but a few attempts at meeting some substantial needs in our local community, but they are attempts that we have proved can make a real difference. They are simple and accessible ways of mobilizing a congregation to serve their local community, and thus explore Christ's call to love their neighbour as themselves. Such initiatives make life a little easier for needy people, and ultimately they make us better followers of Christ.

But One Amongst Many

I am aware that this is but one church's story of faith in action. We, like any other faith organization, remain open to accusations of our community action simply being evangelism in covert clothing. Yet, as we state in the information card which we give to clients, without the love of Christ having impacted our lives, we would not be coming to them anyway. To suggest otherwise, would I believe, be fraudulent. Rather than proselytization, then, central to what we are seeking to achieve is relationship-building. Getting to know clients as genuine human beings, rather than 'old' or 'mentally ill' or whatever classification society would wish to place on them. Getting to know them as the beautiful people God created 'in [his] image' (Gen. 1:26, NIV), and treating them as such. It is these relationships that have led a significant few to pursue faith for themselves, and it is these relationships which give clients confidence to call us for further assistance. And it is the long-term, consistent nature of our work that ensures that we are respected and appreciated by the agencies who continue to refer clients to us.

We are privileged to be able to serve vulnerable and needy people in this way, and I believe we are privileged to be but one small part of a larger movement across the UK.

CHAPTER 8

Aid, Presence, Protest: Working Group, The Poor Side of the Netherlands/EVA

Justin Beaumont and Herman Noordegraaf

Introduction

'Churches should participate in the struggle against poverty, just like people experiencing poverty and their organisations fight for the improvement of their position. So churches should want to be involved in combating the causes of poverty.'[1]

These words were taken from the declaration of the conference of Churches Against Impoverishment that took place on 29 September 1987 in Amsterdam, The Netherlands. The conference was the starting point of an ecumenical and religiously influenced movement against poverty in The Netherlands that took the form of the working group, The Poor Side of the Netherlands.[2]

The conference had been organized by the Council of Churches in The Netherlands, and affiliated organizations in the realms of church and society. The conference and the foundation of the Working Group must be seen against the backdrop of neoliberal restructuring of the welfare state that took place after the economic crisis in the early 1970s, plus the ideological shifts that put emphasis on less state spending, more free market, more individual responsibility and the resulting increased income inequalities.[3] These changes meant that people were increasingly turning to the churches for material support. After the accomplishment of the welfare state in the mid 1960s, church involvement in aid relief for the poor had declined. So, the establishment of a working group heralded a renewed interest among churches and related organizations in the reality of problems of poverty in The Netherlands.

The Poor Side of The Netherlands movement was unique in that it combined three things: (1) relief aid to poor people, (2) it followed a model of communication and presence with people experiencing poverty, and (3) it mobilized politically to contest injustice and to lobby government for social justice in The Netherlands. The movement fruitfully operated a signalling function as well as an advocacy role, alerting society and politics to the realities of poverty and bringing together organizations across ideological, denominational and theological divides to help shape an agenda for social justice. Taken together, these features reflect the way that a variety of organizations display postsecular partnership that constitute a new form of resistance to state policy within a specific context of shadow state corporatism in The Netherlands.

First, we deal with the background of the involvement of churches in the Netherlands with the problem of so-called 'new poverty' in the frame of wider debates on neoliberal welfare reform. Secondly, we pay more attention to the campaign against poverty which reached its zenith in the 1980s and continues today under the auspices of a social justice agenda. A number of working principles are discussed. Thirdly, we provide an overview of the activities within the working group, followed by recent developments in the network from 2000 onwards. Finally, we offer some conclusions.

Background of Church Involvement in Welfare

The background to this new expression of church involvement had to do with the confrontation with problems of 'new poverty'.[4] From the mid 1970s, there was structural change in the economy that resulted in a massive increase in unemployment. It was also the time that witnessed the beginnings of neoliberal welfare reform as a result of financial problems levelled at the rising amount of benefit receivers and a fundamental criticism of mounting state dependency. Neoliberal welfare restructuring is nowadays the name of the game. The result of this ongoing process of restructuring will be a different type of society to the one experienced in the libertarian 1960s: more sober, selective and severe, and where living on benefits is more difficult because eligibility and levels have been restricted. The Dutch welfare state these days is no longer a compensating welfare state (income for unemployed people) but an activating one, meaning that people are increasingly required to follow training courses to improve their emloyability, otherwise to face sanctions.[5] The restructuring of welfare has rebalanced the relations between state and civil society, with a revival of attention in particular to that of the churches as deliverers of welfare services.

The resurgence of churches in questions of poverty relief should be viewed in the context of the history of the welfare state in The Netherlands.[6] The General Assistance Law (1965), the apex of the welfare state in The Netherlands, secured the responsibility for social welfare in the hands of the state. The law ended a long period in which churches were the primary organizations responsible for aid to the poor as a result of the Poor Law of 1854. Now that aid for the poor became the sole responsibility of the state, it was assumed that the involvement of churches would be reduced to a minimum. Over the years, the Poor Law had been adjusted several times, but not with respect to the fundamental principle of assistance as a favour and not a right. The General Assistance Law broke with that principle, rendering welfare a right for all.

In the post-war period just prior to the General Assistance Law, churches of various denominations began to focus their ministries in factories through the work of industrial pastors who built on connections with people working in the factories. The aim of Industrial Mission was to assist workers in all aspects of life inside and outside the factory, and to reflect together on their work. Industrial Mission workers, who were involved in those factories and who had contacts within companies employing workers in key sectors, remained in contact with those factory workers after they were dismissed and forced to go on the dole, or those who were officially designated as disabled or in another way dependent on welfare benefits. Industrial pastors and ministers visited these people in their homes, and organized group meetings. During these encounters, these pastors and ministers witnessed first-hand how people suffered as a consequence of their social and material hardship. These problems included a deep sense of loss, particularly of financial income and the ability to enjoy the standard of living their hard work had brought them; a loss of personal and social contacts and relationships and a general sense of social isolation; an existential questioning of the meaning of life as hitherto layers of certainty withered away. The people now out of work were also forced to restructure their daily routines and sense of time; overall their predicament imposed a major threat to their personal sense of dignity.

At the same time, various local churches were confronted with similar problems, particularly among single women as widows or divorcees, as a result of their unpaid care activities. Industrial Mission and local churches noticed that the social and economic situation for vulnerable and marginalized people progressively worsened as the direct result of government policies for lowering benefit levels and savings on provisions in the field of (health) care, education, housing and other essential public services.

By the first half of the 1980s, churches in The Netherlands were seeking their way in a new social, economic and spiritual situation of modernization and secularization of society and the rise of mass structural unemployment.[7] It was increasingly recognized that a new way of working should be to organize meetings with unemployed people, disabled persons, single parents (mostly women), elderly people with only a state pension (again, mostly women) and other people on low income. People from the churches began to listen more closely to the life stories and experiences of these people as a starting point for more critical reflection on the tasks of the church in these affairs and within society and politics more generally. Initiatives were also taken to provide material aid, for instance help at Christmas-time by giving gifts to people and their families. But quite understandably, these activities aroused a lot of criticism, particularly from the more secular organizations that lobbied on behalf of benefit recipients themselves (e.g. in the 1980s, Sjakuus Foundation; today, Stichting CLiP)[8] who felt that these acts of kindness were subjugating and demeaning of the people suffering poverty. Instead these groups urged the churches to show real human and social solidarity by supporting their struggle for alternative politics, one centred on the betterment of the position of people who are dependent on welfare. The risk was, they argued, that churches would fall into the trap of charity while it was the task of government to guarantee social participation for all citizens. The argument was that it was undesirable to return to the former days of 'soup kitchens' and paternalistic handouts administered through churches that had characterized social provision prior to the introduction of the General Assistance Law.

When it became clear that new forms of poverty were here to stay and not merely temporary 'blips' in an otherwise relatively cohesive and egalitarian society, the Council of Churches[9] and the National Organisation for Industrial Mission (DISK)[10] took the initiative in 1987 to hold a national conference on The Poor Side of The Netherlands. The aim was to send a clear signal to the churches' congregations, church boards, institutions and church members, as well as politicians and society at large, that the problem of impoverishment was one that should not be sidelined any longer and had to be taken seriously. The term 'Poor Side' was deliberately chosen in order to point to the situation of those who live at or under the social minimum over extended periods of time, and to formulate an indictment against society in its process of growing wealth, on the one hand, and a society that appeared to tolerate the exclusion of some of its members from full social participation on the other. A clear position was taken regarding the question of material aid: if people were in need, churches should help, but at the same time they should make clear that this aid was offered *under protest*; in other words, while immediate support was required, the purpose was to raise political awareness that these requirments should not have been necessary in the first place. In a declaration which was widespread within and outside the churches, these principles were formulated and became trend-setting for the involvement of churches in the struggle against poverty from that moment on.

Campaign Against Poverty

An anti-poverty campaign was initiated as a response to the conference. For that reason the working group The Poor Side of

The Netherlands was established that was from inception also rooted in regional and local church groups. A network of relations at national, regional and local levels emerged, sometimes official church institutions, sometimes so-called 'Poor Side' groups, where local and regional churches interacted with others such as organizations of benefit-entitled people, trade unions, organizations of handicapped people, of migrant workers and so on. In this way, the working group shows some parallels with the neo-Alinsky-style broad-based organizing efforts within London Citizens and Birmingham Citizens in the UK.[11] Recent analyses of postsecular partnership within these forms of political and ethical mobilization are relevant to the working group too.[12] The working group became an ecumenical network that continues to operate to support religious organizations at a local and regional level, those working to improve the living conditions of people in poverty. Decisions are made for the course of action for a period of three years. Annual reports are produced. The working group operates within a broad mandate.

It is striking that the working principles show a great continuity over time. From the start there was always the recognition that *churches should cooperate with poor people*: 'working with' and not primarily 'working for'. This principle has practical consequences in that working group meetings at all levels should actively involve people experiencing poverty. In this way the activities were reminiscent of how scholars such as Auge have differentiated between 'with' or 'for' the other, as well as Sandel's work on empowerment within justice.[13]

A connected element of this working principle was that churches should become acquainted with the life-worlds of the poor. It was deemed crucial that the churches were familiar with the circumstances in which deprived people were living, and importantly, the ways that the people themselves give meaning to their predicament. The churches should be aware of their grievances, sorrows, but also their joys. These elements of the working group amounted to an intense process of communication between churches and people experiencing poverty as a continual process of mutual learning and adaption. In this way the churches entered into alliances with people experiencing poverty, listening to their stories and making these stories more widely known. This way of working – connecting to the life-worlds of the poor – formed the basis of all activities of the working group. The theologian Andries Baart's 'presence model' comes the closest in theorizing this approach to empowerment, justice and engagement.[14]

A second working principle was that churches should not limit themselves to the provision of aid to poor people, but should *strive for justice*; that is to say, to a society that offers possibilities for everyone for a decent life and for social participation more generally. This justice ideal requires a decent social security system, access to public services and the creation of jobs, that are realistic for people facing multiple forms of exclusion.[15] So, aid to poor people should be connected with protest and signalling the needs of the poor to the wider society and political system.

A third working principle is the attention paid to *gender aspects of poverty*.[16] Women are overrepresented in the figures on poverty. Of course that has to do with the inequality between men and women in education and employment; it is also a fact that in The Netherlands it was not until the1970s that the 'norm' that men worked outside the house and women inside began to change. Paid work for married women was considered extraordinary.[17] The effect is that many divorced women or lone older women were and still are dependent on minimum level benefits, sometimes with a small amount from a pension. For that reason, within the anti-poverty movement a separate project was set up that focused on the position of women: church women and benefit-entitled women (*kerkvrouwen-bijstandsvrouwen*). National church bodies in the field of church and society organized meetings between women who were active in the church, and also with benefit-entitled women. From these meetings, groups of women formed a network at local, regional and national levels. Later on, this network was called *Economie, Vrouwen en Armoede* (EVA) ('Economy, Women and Poverty'). In 1997, the working group The Poor Side of The Netherlands and EVA joined forces as the working group The Poor Side of The Netherlands/ EVA.

The implication for the anti-poverty movement and alliance is that links were made with ways of thinking about family and marriage that puts women in a position of economic and legal dependency, and with the specific problems of women experiencing poverty. Special attention is asked for the value of unpaid work in the field of care within and outside the household. This type of work should also be valued as a basis for economic and legal rights. In the course of the project, women from a variety of ethnic and cultural backgrounds entered into discussions. At a national level, encounters were organized where participants entered into the life-worlds of women and their families experiencing poverty. A particularly heart-rending activity combining sorrow and joy has been the choirs that made emotional songs from well-known melodies. These songs are also emotive expressions of protest. Since 1995, there has been an annual festival for these activities. To quote one:

> Big is the injustice and big are the differences.
> Big is the heart of those persons who share.
> Now share your sorrow and share your joy,
> By which the wounds are cured here.[18]

A fourth working principle is *networking*. The Poor Side network operates within a network arrangement. The national working group is connected with local and regional groups, but not in a hierarchical way. The working group takes care of exchange of information and experiences at the local and regional levels, supports these groups with information and knowledge and advocates over the plight of the poor and the causes of poverty within public debates at the national level. An important part of the networking activities is to link with churches; to raise awareness among church members about poverty and to encourage them to support antipoverty efforts. This way of working makes it possible that the anti-poverty movement profiles itself in society, and that local and regional groups do not feel isolated or powerless – that they are part of a larger movement. The journal *De Arme Krant* ('The Poor Journal') appears every three months and fulfils a useful networking and connecting function. In this journal we find news about the working group and from the regional and local groups, information about developments, discussions, and publications in politics and society as regards poverty and, of course, current affairs.

The working group also connects with other closely related groups fighting against poverty at all levels, including the national level. At the national level it is vital to mention the *Alliantie voor Sociale Rechtvaardigheid* ('Alliance for Social Justice'; in short, the 'Social Alliance').[19] The Social Alliance broadened the previously existing *Platform Armoedebestrijding KHV* ('Platform for Combating Poverty Churches, Humanists and Trade Unions'). At the start, more than thirty organizations joined the Alliance, and in 2011 there were more than sixty members, again, reminiscent of the broad-based organizing and postsecular partnership principles noted in the UK. Besides the churches, variou organizations are involved, including trade unions and humanists, regional Poor Side groups, organizations of benefit-entitled people, of handicapped people, and organizations for migrants. The Working Group The Poor Side of the Netherlands is one of the active groups in the Social Alliance at the national level. The Social Alliance has a flexible structure based on central themes that are formulated together. The function of chair circulates annually among the Council of Churches, the trade unions and the humanists. The Alliance's council meets twice a year to decide about the working plan and other courses of action. The Alliance organizes annual conferences at a regional level to discuss current themes regarding poverty. More and more the relations with the local authorities received attention because their role in poverty policies has become more important. So, in the European Year for Combating Poverty and Social Exclusion (2010), the Social Alliance cooperated with twenty-three cities that were prepared to stimulate anti-poverty policies. The result was a 'local agenda' with concrete points of action. Ultimately, in eighty cities, local groups and authorities decided to work together in their city on the basis of this agenda.

Debates were also organized at the national level to challenge dominant visions on work and poverty, and manifestos were published challenging the government's narrow definition of workers as about paid work only, income (against the growing inequality, for raising the levels of minimum benefits), and against blaming the victim and pointing instead to structural causes of poverty. An annual and biannual delegation of the Social Alliance has a meeting with the responsible person of the cabinet about issues regarding poverty. The Social Alliance is fully recognized as a partner in the discussion. In the last manifesto, 'The Netherlands Free from Poverty', the Social Alliance expressed the vision:

155

... a society in which all citizens experience respect, in which security of existence for all and the care for each other are guaranteed. Poverty can be conquered and be prevented if good public provisions enable people to own capabilities to contribute to a good society for all and the own security of existence [sic] for everybody. With solidarity and own strength it succeeds to banish poverty and keep it away from our society.[20]

It is in these ways that one might characterize the working group and the Social Alliance as an example of *shadow state corporatism* in The Netherlands.[21]

Activities of the Working Group

Various types of activities took shape over the course of time. Echoing the remarks in the previous section, it remains fundamentally important that there is an encounter between churchgoers and activists, on the one hand, and the people facing poverty and worsening situations on the other. A commonly used model in this regard is where poor people are given the opportunity to tell their stories as the starting point of an intensive process of communication. These efforts to give voice to the poor and to raise awareness about their life-worlds remains fundamentally important, because the stories of poor people are far less heard and known about than they should be within wider institutions of the church, politics and society. The non-poor must be made aware of the life-worlds of the poor, to become motivated towards the improvement of the position of the poor. The poor are a minority and without a great deal of political and economic influence. So, solidarity provided by other groups is essential to work politically towards their social and economic betterment. *This raising of awareness* takes place within churches and society at large. A much-used method is the budget game. People have to make clear how to deal with benefits at a minimum level. How does one adjust expenses to make ends meet? Time and time again, this gaming demonstrates vividly how difficult it is to live on the minimum for many years.[22]

Encounters and communication are the basis for the forging of alliances between churches and poor people directed towards a

common social and political agenda. This alliance involves advocacy, financial assistance to organizations of poor people, accommodation, knowledge, social relations and so on.

Group work to advance *empowerment* is another important
ingredient of this alliance.[23] Poor people are often seen as a collection of failings, as people who is unable to participate in society
on the basis of their own capabilities and strengths. The working
group and the wider network emphasize the need to look beyond
this narrow view and look at the possibilities that each and every
person has. With an attitude of respect, churches should listen to
people, connecting to their life-worlds and looking together for
possibilities to develop their capabilities and strengths. Assistance
is offered on a mutual basis and provides a radical and people-centred alternative to currently in-vogue approaches within the policies of the 'activating welfare state'. Current activation policies
are concerned with objective targets to get numbers of people
into paid work as soon as possible. This kind of empowerment
is instrumental and gives little attention to structural problems of
poverty, and betrays scant regard of the obstacles that come to fore
in the life stories of people experiencing poverty. The churches
therefore are actively pursuing an alternative based on presence,
communication and the building and sustaining of meaningful
relationships.

Specific activities are developed to strengthen empowerment. For instance, training programmes are offered on lobbying
work, on planning activities, but also at the individual level: for
example, how to remain strong and how to promote your interests
at benefit offices or in the company of politicians, as well as how to
present yourself when applying for jobs and attending interviews.
The initiative 'dress for success' provides people who apply for
jobs with suitable clothes, free of charge, for the interview. The
initiative originated within the churches, but has now become an
organization in its own right.[24]

Attention also gets paid to *individual aid and social assistance*.
Activities of this kind can be spiritual, social and emotional (or
immaterial), service-orientated (for instance, taking care of children, accompanying and supporting people in their contacts
with social welfare institutions, offering possibilities for cheap
holidays, etc.), as well as material support. To take the example

of holidays: each year a guide for affordable trips away (cheap and possible for families on low incomes) is published.[25] To take instance, a number of local churches makes available a house or a caravan. There are different types of services in this field: holidays with children or without children, holidays for children and young people, holidays for people with a handicap, exchange of houses and funds that subsidize these vacations.

Time and time again it is stated by the national working group that these activities should be part of signalling protest and political action and not relief aid on its own. There is awareness among local groups that this political role should be the case, but in practice few find it easy or straightforward to engage politically and often remain more service-orientated than politically active.[26] For that reason, the national working group continues to emphasize the need to provide 'aid under protest'. This 'aid under protest' takes a number of different forms.[27] Strengthening and supporting people experiencing poverty to express themselves in the public domain is a main thing. They should have the possibility to have their voices heard. Churches should be aware of this priority, advocate with the poor themselves, and refrain from taking over.

Local authority policies are of relevance, too, because local authorities have acquired greater responsibility in recent years for local poverty policies. To what extent can local authorities genuinely improve the livelihoods of their poorest inhabitants within their regulatory limitations? Does the relevant information reach the people who need it most, and is this information easily understood? Do local authorities work together with the people who are involved in anti-poverty efforts? These are enduring questions that need to be asked in the current phase of activation policies in the welfare state and decentralization of responsibilities to local authorities in the field of welfare services. However, protest and signalling new developments on the ground do not only refer to local authorities but to all kinds of organizations. Schools (for instance: school fees; travel on school trips), housing corporations (for example: policies towards the expulsion of tenants with rent arrears) and public utilities (such as policies towards cutting off the supply of gas, electricity or water because of payment arrears) are all areas where discussion and intense communication with people experiencing poverty needs to continue and deepen.

Protesting and signalling also occurs within *national politics* in the form of letter writing to government, MPs and political parties, inviting them for discussions with people in poverty. A special project was the 'adopting' of members of parliament by local Poor Side groups. Those politicians were invited to visit projects of people experiencing poverty, and to talk with them. In this way, the MPs could learn from the people themselves about the problems of poverty on the ground, and became aware of their living conditions.

Connected with this letter writing and invitation activity is the role of *stimulating public debate* about relevant issues, as well as more fundamental questions. The working group has organized debates about the growing wealth among particular sections of society and the widening gap between rich and poor. These debates were organized at a local, regional and especially national level. Politicians, representatives from social organizations, academics and other interested parties were challenged to react on questions of poverty, the meaning and purpose of (paid and unpaid) work, social inequality and related concerns.[28] Issues like just distribution of income and properties are hardly ever found on the political agendas of the day. Exceptions include inordinately high salaries and bonus shares enjoyed by those at the top of enterprises, and in the organization of social care and housing that were previously non-profit, but are now referred to as 'social enterprises'. The campaign against deepening inequalities meant that a number of shareholders called for more taxation on the revenues of their shares. Though this action received a great deal of media attention, the campaign as a whole was not that successful in setting the issue of inequalities on the agenda.

The strength of churches in advocacy work and the public debate is that they can work with the knowledge of the life-worlds of the poor, while many other organizations operate at a greater distance because of their instrumental way of working, or their more abstract, dehumanizing approaches with statistics.

Recent Developments

There are four recent developments that have focused attention within the working group. First is the relatively new phenomenon of *food banks* in the Netherlands.[29] Food banks arose as a result of deepening need, and while there is no direct link to the working group, it felt nonetheless compelled to confront the phenomenon. The first food bank was founded in 2002 in Rotterdam. By 2011, there were about 130 food banks in nearly every region of The Netherlands, and there are still more locations for distribution. The aim of the food banks is aid for people in need (the criteria are described precisely) and to counter the waste of goods. There are agreements with enterprises that food that otherwise would be disposed of is delivered to food banks. This second aim (against waste) is less known among the public than the first. On a weekly basis, 8,000 volunteers are delivering 25,000 food parcels (and sometimes other goods such as soap, toothpaste, serviettes) for 50,000 people. Most food banks are not religious organizations but independent foundations. However, many church members are involved on the board of such foundations, and churches are involved by way of volunteers, the availability of church buildings for distribution, financial and material aid and by signposting people with specific needs to the centre and other agencies.

The development of food banks raises a fundamental question over how the working group and the wider network relate to the phenomenon. To address this question, the working group organized a conference, *More Than Only Food*, on 21 April 2006, where people from churches and food banks were present. A draft declaration was drawn up and distributed after the conference. The declaration contained the main principles, as in the original declaration in 1987; that the working group should give aid to people in need, but should make clear that food banks are a signal that structural measures are needed to combat poverty.[30] The fact that food banks are needed was seen as a contradiction to the fundamental principles of the social rights underlying democratic society. At the conference there was a clash between some people working as volunteers in the food banks who at first saw the draft as a rejection of their work. At any rate, the recommendations that were formulated for the national government, local authorities, churches, social organizations and food banks themselves were ultimately agreed by all and brought into effect.

The same points of view can be found in a report of the Social Alliance based on research among food banks and their clients.

This research was made possible by the Ministry of Social Affairs and Employment in The Hague.[31] Recommendations included:

- a higher level of minimum benefits;
- more respectful ways of giving aid;
- improvement of the cooperation between organizations that people living on the minimum level are dependent on;
- improvement of the relations between local authorities and food banks;
- strengthening the position of people with debts;
- more attention to prevention.

Secondly, research has been undertaken by the working group, alongside several other church organizations, on the activities of *local churches towards vulnerable, marginalized and deprived people.* The aim of this research was to make clear to society and politics the problems the churches encounter in their work on behalf of the poor and to promote solutions to these problems. Further research was done and published in 2005, 2006, 2008 and 2010.[32] The amount of churches that were taking part was growing: the Roman Catholic Church, the Protestant Church in The Netherlands, smaller Protestant churches, among them Orthodox Protestant churches, and also the Evangelical Alliance (where Pentecostals and evangelicals are working together).[33]

The most recent report on poverty in The Netherlands provides an insight into the activities of local churches.[34] Three-quarters of social provision organizations are involved in support for people with financial problems. Of these, 95 per cent supply, in one way or another, financial and material aid; they received in the region of 34,000 requests for financial assistance, of which nearly 30,000 were honoured, mostly as gifts, sometimes as a loan. These actions cost in the region of 12,327.739 euros. Besides the financial aid, 86 per cent of the social provision organizations are involved in emotional, spiritual and psychological assistance by visiting people at home and listening to their stories and needs. Accompanying people to offices and assisting in dealing with forms and so on also fall under this category. More than four-fifths (82 per cent) of the local churches are also participating in collective forms of assistance such as food banks, participation in a fund for people in need, financial support for organizations, stores for clothes and exchange of goods and so on. The amount of money that is spent on these provisions is 12,206.330 euros. Over half (52 per cent) of the social provision organizations supply parcels at Christmas-time (131,120 parcels, amounting to 3,369.915 euros). More than a quarter of the social provision organizations have given money for walk-in houses (1,715.562 euros). In total, churches have spent nearly 30 million euros on combating poverty.

Thirdly, exploratory research has been carried out among *migrant churches*.[35] These churches are an important group with an estimated 800,000 members. The investigation was done by means of in-depth interviews with representatives of nine migrant churches. The results show that migrant churches are doing important work in the field of support and assistance by financial and material aid, advice and information for finding their way in Dutch society (regulation, forms, rules of the game and so on). These churches support people seeking a legal status in The Netherlands; they also provide spiritual guidance and empowerment, assistance and practical help (such as baby-sitting, homework assistance, furnishing and renovating houses, transportation, etc.). All these activities involve individual and collective ways of assisting and supporting. Most assistance is provided via informal channels, not officially via the church, but among the church members. Migrant churches themselves also have too few financial resources to be able to provide sufficient help. They also have other expenses, such as the church rent, or payment of loans for the construction of the church building. It also became clear that poverty is not just a material matter, but intertwined with all aspects of life and reflecting the variety of issues that migrants in Dutch society are confronted with, including psychological and spiritual aspects and, for those without papers, the legal obstacles. The hope is that the report can be a stimulus for migrant churches to reflect on strategies to combat poverty and to work together with other churches to find solutions.

And finally, a new area of concern since 2007 is *debts and indebtedness*. This problem was already well known prior to the current financial crisis, but has increased in relevance since then. Debts can have social and/or individual causes: too low incomes, overspending, adjusting to a new situation when the income from paid work falls, or because of addiction to drugs, alcohol and/or gambling. In 2010, nearly one million people could not fulfil their monthly financial obligations. A publication for churches was made with information and suggestions for dealing with problems of debt. The report, *Eerse Hulp bij Schulden*[36] ('First Aid for Debts') was presented at a conference that was visited by 300 people from churches. The financial crisis also affects middle class people, and problems of debts are also found in the more affluent sections of society. Together with the Social Alliance, an expert meeting (with people who provide assistance and experts, on the basis of their experience with indebtedness) was organized that focused on women who have debts because of the spending habits of their partners. In cooperation with national and local authorities, a project has been set up where volunteers from churches become companions or friends to people suffering from debt problems, to assist them so that they are able to control their finances, and to offer emotional, spiritual and psychological support. The volunteers receive special training for their work. The working group The Poor Side is involved in this project, together with other religious groups. The Evangelical Alliance cooperates too.

Conclusion

Churches in the Netherlands have tried to put their faith into action in small-scale activities, as well as in advocacy and participation in the public debate at local, national, and sometimes also at European and global levels. The latter have been the result of interaction with international ecumenical organizations. The anti-poverty campaign continues to try to combat poverty and create a fairer and more just society in The Netherlands; however, it is difficult to continue motivating people within and outside churches, and also the poor themselves, after so many years of effort. The campaign has contributed significantly to the raising of awareness and recognizing the problems of poverty within the churches. It is striking to note that evangelical churches are now participating in the Poor Side movement as a result of their growing interest in social issues and the increasing visibility of activities. In this way, traditional ecumenical churches and these churches are now ever more working together.

The working group has provided an impulse to political agenda-setting, and demonstrates important ways of how aid and justice can be brought together in action. Sometimes it has directly influenced concrete policy measures at national and local levels, as well as providing emotional, spiritual and psychological support, alongside material aid, to people in need. There is a significant continuity in the way of working, but there are shifts in approaches and activities. The local level has received more attention because of decentralization from national to local authorities. Levels of individual aid have increased due to the persistence of poverty and the acceptance of aid efforts. Empowerment at the individual level has received greater attention in supporting people to cope with their situation. It must be admitted, however, that the activities of the network and the various political campaigns have not significantly altered the overall neoliberal direction of politics and society in a way that would help realize effective anti-poverty and social justice policies. The tendencies in politics are now in the direction of a further worsening of the income and rights of poor people and still more focus on instrumental activation policies. The tough struggle against poverty and injustice continues in The Netherlands.

CHAPTER 9

Adventures at a Border Crossing: The Society for Diaconal Social Work in Rotterdam, The Netherlands

Maarten Davelaar, Andrew Williams and Justin Beaumont

Introduction

Faith-based organizations occupy an ambiguous position within neoliberal urban politics, and are often regarded as buying into the political values of welfare dependency, individual responsibility and self-help.[1] However, as the introduction and other chapters in this volume indicate, faith-based social action can prophetically challenge the 'powers that be' – unbinding individuals from years of marginalization and oppression, and redeeming the social, economic and political structures that, directly or indirectly, do the binding.[2] In this chapter we present the story of the Society for Diaconal Social Work by the churches in Rotterdam (in Dutch: *Stichting voor Kerkelijk Sociale Arbeid*, hereafter KSA), as one of the oldest and at times highly influential examples of urban faith-based social action in The Netherlands. Its story has much to say about the potential for faith-based involvement in radical social action, and the possibility of the church tempering conservative moral stances in order to reach out effectively (rather than half-heartedly or even in a pseudo-condemnatory way) to people living highly precarious lives.

The evolving history of the organization highlights the swings of radicalism and conformity that can occur within a single FBO, and we draw attention to the different actors (church, state, both) and political contexts that regulate these swings towards, or away from, more non-conformist and sometimes politically controversial forms of faith-based social action. Parts of its story also exemplify what Cloke and Beaumont call 'spaces of postsecular rapprochement'[3] where secular, humanitarian and religious motivations come together over shared ethical impulses.

The KSA has long been a border crossing for the church and society, with the dual aim to bring society and its problems and debates into the church, on the one hand, and on the other, to help the church to reach out to, affiliate with and strengthen vulnerable groups in the different parts of the city. In this sense, its purpose as a diaconal organization has been to bridge the gap between the marginalized and the better-off inhabitants of the port city of Rotterdam, between the urban outcasts – the sex worker, the street heroin user, and the rough sleeper – and the executive boards of welfare services and the municipality. Working with the local churches, the KSA seeks to facilitate spaces of engagement for church members to connect to the issues facing the 'least among them'.[4] This involves discerning and naming the conventions and beliefs held by church members and religious bodies that contribute to the status quo in society and leave structural injustices unchallenged. These spaces of dialogue go hand in hand, and often arise from mobilizing (new) forms of engagement for church members; for example, volunteering in or financially supporting local projects for socially excluded and vulnerable groups in the city. These practical 'contact spaces'[5] can be understood as instrumental in soliciting an ethical citizenship which is emotional, committed and grounded in a 'sense for the other', rather than a distanced 'sense of the other' based on secondary sources.[6]

Over the course of its history, the KSA has set up or participated in numerous services and networks, with a particular focus on the homeless, people experiencing poverty, abused women/victims of domestic violence, and vulnerable groups in migrant and ethnic minority populations. Perhaps the most famous and contested of these was the Pauluskerk (St Paul's Church) and its work with the homeless, with drug addicts and with 'illegal' asylum seekers and labour immigrants. The story of the KSA tells how an FBO with relatively conservative beginnings has become, more than any comparable organization, at the forefront of combining direct service delivery with political advocacy and political protest.

In this chapter, we describe and analyze the development of the KSA through the years, with a stress on the last two decades. We highlight changes and continuities in vision, policies and practices, as well as its position vis-à-vis (local) governments. We pay particular attention to the swings towards more radical and conformist stances with respect to the dominant policies at a given moment in time. Due emphasis is given to the more outspoken part of the KSA, carried out under the banner of the Pauluskerk, but we seek to contextualize these activities within the development of the KSA in general, and draw attention to other less well known aspects of the activities of the KSA which contribute to the welfare of the city. The changes and continuities are organized in six short episodes: (1) 1947–1969: Rebuilding Society Together; (2) 1969–1979: Losing Direction; (3) 1979–1986: The Sixties in the Eighties; (4) 1986–2000: Challenging the Powers That Be; (5) 2000–2007: Under Fire; and (6) 2007–2011: New Horizons.

This chapter builds extensively on annual reports of the KSA and on previous work by one of the authors (Maarten Davelaar) published in 1997.[7] These are supplemented with other documents and interviews conducted over the period 1997–2007 and on research material gathered during the European FACIT-research project (2008–2010), including interviews with the previous and current director.

1947–1969: Rebuilding Society Together

The KSA was founded in 1947 as an association of the diaconal bodies[8] of the highly independent Dutch Reformed churches in the Greater Rotterdam area. Some leading vicars and laymen took the daring attempt to put an end to the isolated diaconal work of the Dutch Reformed churches in the different parts of Rotterdam. In the short-lived post-war optimism, attempts were made to put an end to the segregated social, cultural and political life under the Protestant, Catholic and social-democratic 'pillars' in society.[9] The KSA's founders sought to enlarge the level of solidarity between the churches and the various districts of the city. The limited social cohesion between different parts of the city was then, and still is, an issue for religious and urban politics ever since the rapid expansion of the port city in the nineteenth century.

The creation of the KSA was an explicit attempt to join forces with other groups in the city, initially with the dominant social-democratic movement. There was also a strongly perceived need to establish an effective organization that could help public authorities reconstruct the largely devastated city and regenerate its impoverished communities – regardless of their belief – in the aftermath of the Second World War. The KSA thus brought together nine district orientated branches of the Reformist Church of the Netherlands in Rotterdam, churches ranging from strongly orthodox (in the traditional Calvinist sense),[10] to liberal, with the majority of the churches belonging to the mainstream of the former Dutch state church.

Initially the KSA worked to modernize and coordinate work in the fields of social work and family care, plugging a gap where public services were still non-existent at that time, and to prevent a simple return to pre-war charity. The KSA welcomed the state's move to provide public services directly rather than dispensing state funds and support through each of the channels set up by different pillars. Financially, the KSA was working hand in hand with the local government, which was dominated by the Social-Democratic Party, and even at this early stage helped to deliver government policies on the ground – for instance, by providing social work aimed at families that had to leave their homes because they were to be demolished for the sake of urban renewal plans:

> The people concerned have to be informed of the necessity of carrying out certain projects, so that they will more easily conform and reconcile themselves with their compulsory removal.[11]

Working closely with the state on such a project immediately raises questions about whether the KSA was entirely in agreement with the wider politics of urban planning, or had they been caught up in contractual requirements with the state. From the KSA report, we can gather that the organization deliberated over a possible equilibrium between general interests and the interests of individuals, but tended to position itself as a loyal servant of the collective 'good'.

1969–1979: Losing Direction

The second half of the 1960s and the 1970s saw the government and subsidized secular services gradually take over most of the tasks in the field of traditional social or welfare work (including family care and youth work).[12] The annual report in 1973 still proudly mentions a growth in family care (including services for the elderly) with a growth in staff from 749 to 972, mainly subsidized by the municipality. But by 1980 this work had also been detached from the KSA and thus from the diaconates of the Dutch Reformed churches. The KSA became less involved in direct welfare work and repositioned itself as primarily a 'second-line' organization; it was responsible for the recruitment and support of volunteers, and for reflection on social issues. The city of Rotterdam continued to subsidize this part of the work, classified as social activation work or faith-based community work (*maatschappelijk activeringswerk*).

This transition led to a reduction in staff and an organizational identity crisis, which brought about renewal. Yet in this period, the role of the KSA was not self-evident any more. The annual reports from this period reflect this: in lengthy articles, the staff tried to identify and establish the role of the KSA within the shifting terrain of public services, neighbourhood community development work and at the level of the deaconates themselves. During this period of introspection, new trends and issues were detected and analyzed, like joint decision-making, democratization and the presence of guest workers. Within the annual reports, there is a clear tone of 'playing it safe' and fear of creating unrest in the churches as they experience declining church attendance and membership. As such, the new social movements, and social and political turmoil of the 1970s, seemed to bypass the KSA. Its vision was not driven by the wish for social change, but resembled that of 'enlightened conservatism' content at working at the level of the individual and civil society. Interestingly within this new socio-political context, the KSA veered away from previous allies – the Social Democrats – who ruled the town hall at the time with an exceptional near-absolute majority (which is remarkable for Dutch politics) during much of the 1970s and 1980s. During a time of perceived secularization of social and moral life, the Social

Democratic and socialist activists working in the neighbourhoods were met with suspicion by many in the KSA.

1979–1986: The Sixties in the Eighties

However, this conservative stance soon was challenged with the appointment of Reverend Hans Visser as the new director of the KSA. From 1965 to 1979, Revd. Visser served as a missionary in Indonesia (Central Sulawesi), working in a church combating rural poverty, and managing projects for community development. He had been expelled from the country by the authorities because he was openly criticizing government, and refused to see his role as purely religious. It is unclear whether the KSA knew what they were getting when they appointed Revd. Visser, but he was given the freedom to pursue a much more radical stance on social, economic and political issues and adopt a more demanding and confrontational approach to government.

Just when the economic crisis hit The Netherlands hard, and in politics the conservative restoration set in, the KSA pronounced social change as its new overarching goal. It seemed that the sixties culture of political activism had finally arrived in the KSA. The deacons ran a series of meetings on 'processes of change in society' in 1980. Themes were, among others, 'tradition and change' and 'practice of change'. The director-general of Rotterdam's Social Service – a latter Social-Democratic minister of Internal Affairs – was one of the speakers. She advised the KSA to become less internal orientated and to focus more on the outside world. Experienced in cross-cultural mission, Visser also believed that the church must be a creative institution that adapts to the society it is in without jeopardizing the core Christian story. However, the maverick manner in which Visser took up new activities and allied with new target groups soon led to unrest and turmoil inside the Reformed churches in Rotterdam. The 'tread carefully' way of operating of his predecessors had been abandoned overnight. For Visser, every single injustice in society had to be addressed immediately. Addiction, homosexuality, nuclear weapons, prostitution, the energy crisis and migrants were put within a one term course on the agenda of the churches:

We try to start movements, that will meet each other, eventually. One movement from the world in the direction of the church. We are concerned about groups and individuals in society, that call upon their fellow men, for solidarity. One [other] movement from the church in the direction of the world. It is about motivating members of churches to . . . create space for people in problematic situations, so that they will get new perspectives.[13]

The church, far from being a bastion of 'enlightened conservatism', was taking this call for solidarity literally, as the list of activities shows – a working group on gays, transvestites and Christian faith, an inter-church committee on addiction, a group on church and industrial relations, a working group on women in church and society and, even as early as 1980, the need to get more information on Islam was reported.[14] With the Moroccan workers committee, a sit-in protest of thirty illegal immigrants was supported. The church supported Turkish and Cape Verdean worker organizations. Visser was active in the labour movement and delivered speeches at large and highly disputed strikes in the harbour. The reaction from more conservative churches was mixed, and Visser barely survived his first year as director – that he remained was largely due to the support of a few members of the board of the KSA and an influential diaconal chairman. His radical engagement gives him the benefit of the doubt under the traditionally cautious and moderate diaconal leadership:

People in a scrape are a precious gift to us. In them we meet Jesus. The unemployed, the unfit for work . . . illegal immigrants, migrants, squatters, small shop owners that face bankruptcy . . . are no threat or burden to us. They are a blessing to us. Jesus is among them[15]

In 1980, Visser 'took over' an inner-city church, the Pauluskerk, at that time still home to a church community. Located in a deprived part of Rotterdam well known for drug-related problems, Visser sought to create a church that would serve the outcasts of society, not in a manner that keeps its distance from the people and issues involved, but in a way that was truly incarnational – entering the worlds of 'others' in a way that seeks understanding.[16] From this position of relational care and trust, the Pauluskerk was able to

171

have direct and regular contact with the excluded, and able to work on solutions for these people.[17] The centre provided support services – such as a walk-in centre, emergency shelter, social work, pastoral care and medical care – as well as direct action and protest for improving policies targeting marginalized people including drug addicts, alcoholics, homeless people, asylum seekers, sexual deviants and prostitutes. The church was home to a series of sit-in and hunger strikes by guest workers without a permit to stay. By 1981, the Pauluskerk was integral to establishing a broad coalition for the renewal of drug policy.[18] Despite heavy internal conflicts and criticism from businesses, the police force and sections within the municipality, Visser succeeded in expanding the work of the centre to better meet the needs of drug users.[19]

The work of the KSA-Pauluskerk was proving that government policy and mainstream services had been underestimating developments like the marginalization of large groups of daily users of hard drugs, which was connected with criminal activity and negative effects on several neighbourhoods in the city. Another development that manifested itself in this period was the impoverishment among (illegal) migrant workers who had en masse become jobless or declared unfit to work in the period of rapid de-industrialization and unemployment from the late 1970s on.[20] As public attitudes began to harden towards those deemed as the 'undeserving' poor, it seemed Visser operated on an alternative ethical register – not based on utility value or a behavioural credit rating – but based on a theo-ethics of agape and caritas informed by the example of Jesus Christ's own ministry.[21] By standing in solidarity with 'the least of these',[22] accepting people where they are (although it must be underlined that the Pauluskerk did not give their approval to drug addiction), Visser would enter into direct confrontation with authorities.

1986–2000: Challenging the Powers That Be

The church adopted St Paul's slogan 'Overcoming Evil with Good' as its guiding philosophy. Rather than representing typical bourgeois charity (although gladly drawing on its resources), Visser's perspective for radical opposition began with the view that marginalized people have little or no political voice. While conceding that local voluntarism cannot alter the structures of the global capitalism, he sided with Castells,[23] claiming that local networks of solidarity can counter state-dominated structures. Visser advocated grassroots solidarity for gradual reform based on Castells' philosophy,[24] while engaging in direct action against social exclusion, often in open conflict with the local state. The Pauluskerk openly encouraged the full participation of individuals, where collective resistance through civil disobedience is the preferred route to social justice. Visser is nonetheless candid about the problems in mobilizing individuals at the grass roots. He claims desperately poor and marginalized people are tired and lack energy, possess a hopelessly pessimistic sense of the future where, in their view, it often makes little sense to participate, and whose lives are debilitated by short-term strategies in the search for cash and other immediacies for survival. Under these circumstances, it is difficult to motivate the populace towards political action.[25]

From this basis, and engaging in networks and coalitions in an ad hoc and issue-sensitive manner, the Pauluskerk provided several functions.[26] First, a campaigning function on behalf of urban marginalized people, including street demonstrations, sit-ins in front of the town hall, support to bus tours of undocumented people, and creative actions such as caravanning with street sex workers under a bridge to put pressure on better facilities, or the never accomplished announcement of Revd. Visser to urinate against the national diaconal headquarters of the Reformed Church, to show his disagreement with a decision of the national board. Secondly, a controversial liberal drugs policy aiming to regulate drug dealing and use (including hard drugs such as heroin), by permitting these activities on the church premises. The church pioneered the development of harm reduction services and established official 'user rooms' in the cellars of the church where several hundred drug users passed through every day to use their cocaine, crack and heroin in a supervised, safe and sanitary environment. This scheme was the first of many in the country. Another experiment was the establishment of Platform Zero (*Perron Nul*) near the Rotterdam Central (station) in 1987, offering day centre care for the most marginalized and criminal parts of the drug scene. This was a source of ongoing tensions

173

between Visser and the mayor, responsible for public safety, as the project developed into one of the biggest open drug scenes in Europe. There was no alternative but to close the spot in 1994. It led to months of unrest in the city and demonstrations of inhabitants of neighbourhoods concerned by the likely 'water bed' effect of the closure. In the aftermath, the Pauluskerk attracted new staff (guards, medical personnel) with financial support from the city. After 1995, the Pauluskerk was experimenting with so-called house dealers (*huisdealers*) – trusted, less criminal, dealers 'appointed' by the church. It proved to be a bridge too far for the public prosecutor, and after some years of negotiation, the construction was forbidden. Thirdly, through different charities and projects, the KSA and Pauluskerk provided emergency shelter for individuals and their families, in addition to organizing protests to draw attention to the plight of asylum seekers and 'economic' refugees, especially those within groups still awaiting legal decisions on their request to stay in The Netherlands, or those who had never been eligible to enter an asylum procedure and were left destitute. Fourth, empowerment and activation of individuals from the streets – homeless people, undocumented migrants, etc., who could work in security and cleaning jobs, furniture production, sell the 'street magazine' or participate in cultural projects.

Regardless of his radical criticisms of local and national politics, and his love for civil disobedience, Revd. Visser was keen to look for opportunities to do business behind the scene for the long-term undocumented families and individuals cared for by the church. He was also consistent in his wish to meet his opponents and debate with them, although he seldom change his policies after these dialogues. As a consequence of his fame, notoriety as wel as what the church was standing for, (prime-) ministers, members of parliament, public officials, writers and other artists were always willing to attend discussions and meetings in the church.

It was sometimes hard to see the organization and people behind the charismatic Revd. Visser. Soon, the Pauluskerk and Visser made it to nationwide fame, with documentaries on television, frequent contributions to newspapers and equally frequent discussions and questions in the local council and the parliament in The Hague. In the meantime, the rest of the work of the KSA was less visible. Yet, the KSA and the Pauluskerk were firmly intertwined. KSA staff were taking care of specialized projects, concentrating on groups that the Pauluskerk was not catering for but that were clearly at risk and certainly part of the solidarity networks that the churches sought to establish in the city. Examples include a service for victims of domestic violence; solidarity networks with people experiencing poverty and with refugees; building up a social movement with a range of other organizations in Rotterdam. Staff of the KSA also established links with national organizations and platforms working with refugees, undocumented migrants and homeless people, especially the 'Platform for migrants without permit to stay', where religious organizations and radical urban solidarity networks met, and the Frayed Fringes committee.[27]

Moreover, the involvement of the local diaconates has always been essential for maintaining the necessary basis for the policies. Visser always had support from influential people in the churches in Rotterdam. From time to time, he drove his 'allies' and supporters/colleagues mad with his solo actions, sudden changes in policies and his provocations, but his charisma, his steadfast devotion to marginalized people, and his national fame meant he retained support for what the Pauluskerk was doing. However, it is likely that some activities and policies of the KSA and Pauluskerk would have been stronger and more effective if he had been willing to cooperate more.

In financial terms, between 1990 and 2002 just over one-third of the money of the KSA-Pauluskerk came from the churches in Rotterdam (in particular the diaconal committees). Several interviewees mentioned a gradual but constant shift in the number of volunteers in projects travelling in from towns around Rotterdam.[28] For this reason, organizations like the KSA have been intensifying their relations with churches in the broader region. In the same period, approximately one-third of funds came from the municipality and the remainder from charitable funds and hundreds of individual supporters. The Pauluskerk was supported by the relatively wealthy churches in the surrounding areas and by individuals all across the country.[29] This 'division' in funds was remarkably constant over the years, regardless of the tensions between town hall and Visser – until the radical change in local politics in 2002. As we will see later on, the more cooperative way

175

of his successors did not increase or decrease the amount of public funding the Pauluskerk received from the municipality. However, after 2002 the government began to roll out more intense coordination of its public services and non-governmental welfare agencies through technologies of control (audit, best practice, and performance targets).[30]

Interestingly, the work of the KSA and the Pauluskerk were – at least until the great change in the political climate from 2002 onwards – in general appreciated by both sides of the political spectrum, and the organizations received influential supporters in all sectors of society. The Remonstrant chair of the board of the KSA, for example, was a supporter of the right-wing Liberal Party (VVD), and the treasurer of the board of the diaconal centre Pauluskerk was owner of one of the biggest estate agencies in the city.

The staff and volunteers running the Pauluskerk came from vast sections of society. Initially, the Pauluskerk had been run by members of local churches, ranging from Dutch Reformed to those with a more evangelical background. As the organization grew in size and reputation, not only did professional medical staff paid for by social services get appointed to work in the centre, but a broad set of motivations were at play. The largest group of volunteers identified themselves as 'post-Christian', people brought up in the faith, but now considered to be on the edge of the church (*randkerkelijken* in Dutch). They still consider themselves to be Christians, do not regularly go to church any more, but are driven to 'practise what you preach' in serving other people in need. Similarly, many volunteers worked at the centre as an outworking of a humanist ethic driven by the concern to 'do something about' particular injustices in the city, and 'do something for' people who live precarious lives there. Evangelical and more conservative volunteers continued to volunteer and support the Pauluskerk.

Interestingly, as the Pauluskerk expanded its activities in the direct care for homeless people and drug addicts, the proportion of 'post-Christian' volunteers increased. Whereas activities such as holiday weeks for elderly disabled people, abused women and victims of trafficking, the solidarity networks (e.g. with people experiencing poverty and with refugees) and new activities – such as awareness-raising working groups on sustainable urban development and environmental issues – continued to attract mostly Christian volunteers. The KSA also established partnerships aimed at integrating different strands of social and political grass roots protest, such as the rather short-lived Third Chamber movement. This saw KSA staff cooperating with activists with an overt atheist, radical-left background in order to achieve change in government policy.

In this sense, the work of the KSA-Pauluskerk represents a melting pot of ethical motivations that converged over a shared desire to care for, and stand with, marginalized groups in Rotterdam. Although this was not an intentional aim of Visser, who himself would have preferred more Christians to be involved in the Pauluskerk,[31] the crossover space between humanitarian, secular and religious ethics created by the Pauluskerk is notable.

Under the leadership of Revd. Visser, the KSA evolved from something of a quietist, even socially conservative, social welfare organization, into a radical and highly provocative voice in Dutch politics. However, the success of Visser's push towards a more radical faith involvement in social action and civil disobedience very much benefited from the progressive tide in main Protestant churches in the 1980s (although many ordinary members were and stayed more conservative). It was also a period of polarization in the church, and in Dutch society, on issues such as disarmament, welfare, the economy and, importantly, drug use. The political climate in the 1980s permitted Visser to pursue a more ideological and confrontational urban politics. The political context is integral in delineating the possibilities for radical faith-based social action, both through changing institutional environment (in terms of funding, policy) on which FBOs act, but also in shaping the ways churches come to understand, and subsequently get involved in, social problems.

2000–2007: Under Fire

Rotterdam was a frontrunner in more progressive new social services and programmes during the 1980s and 1990s. The Social Democratic Party had dominated every municipal executive since the Second World War, except for 2002 to 2006, when the

177

right-wing, populist party Leefbaar Rotterdam (LR), took over control of the municipality. The LR members of the municipal executive expressed very clearly that the Pauluskerk had to stop its activities for drug users and the homeless, whereas previous executives had tried to cooperate with the church, advocating its policies or – since the mid 1990s – tried to incorporate the church services into the broader municipal policies.[32] Public perception gradually brought into arguments that the Pauluskerk facilitated people's adherence to antisocial or unhealthy habits and lifestyles and functioned as a pull-actor in attracting urban marginals to the city, and this view gained rapidly in influence.[33] As early as 2000, Revd. Visser started a discussion on the future of the church. Demolishing and rebuilding the church was his own option. But the new right-wing coalition took the initiative and tried to get rid of the church totally – a strategy that was blocked by the right-wing liberal mayor.

A few years before his retirement, in the midst of grim negotiations between municipality and church on the future of the Pauluskerk, Visser was aware of losing the battle to provide – as the church – user-orientated services for drug users. That function was transferred to a government-controlled organization. Yet, Visser was still convinced of the necessity of a liberal drug policy and a mix of approaches – individual treatment and places where people could be themselves:

I see the promised land, but I will not enter it.[34]

In 2007, shortly after Visser's retirement, the old Pauluskerk was demolished.

2007–2011: New Horizons

With the retirement of Visser and the closure of the worn-out Pauluskerk, the double function of diaconal minister of the Pauluskerk and director of KSA was split. With a much smaller staff, and operating simply as a drop-in centre from a temporary location adjacent to the old building, Revd. Dick Couvée is working on the rebuilding and opening of a new style Pauluskerk.

It will open its doors in 2013 or 2014, although on a smaller scale. The expensive land value of the church-owned plot of land where the 1950s building of the Pauluskerk was demolished in 2007 has made it possible to redevelop the site into – at least on paper – an architectural masterpiece, luxurious apartments, social housing, a café and new church facilities for the urban outcasts and the surrounding residents. However, the church is no longer permitted to set up services for addicts who, after intervention by the mayor of Rotterdam in 2006, have been expelled from the church and directed to several more regular, secular projects in the city.[35] This was part of the contain and discipline tactics deployed under the LR executive; however, since the re-election of the Social Democrats in 2006, this national and local drive to clean up the streets has been matched with large-scale state investment in homeless service infrastructure.[36] Local government has increasingly placed restrictions on the expected behaviour of service providers and service users. Couvée has argued that this system, although bettering the standards of care in the sector, still fails some groups of homeless people and homeless undocumented migrants who cannot access these services, either because of restrictive eligibility or idealistic behavioural requirements (for instance, no alcohol or drug use on site) tied to residency agreement in the hostels.

In 2010 the Pauluskerk has twelve paid employees and about 100 volunteers (in previous years, there were fifty and more than 150 respectively). Among the employees the proportion of men / women and young/old is quite equal, but among the volunteers, women are overrepresented. In addition, there are more older than younger volunteers, although the church always succeeded in attracting students and other young people to its work throughout the years. The Pauluskerk serves as an important day centre, where undocumented migrants and homeless people can still come for help and assistance. However the old night shelter function will not return.

One might have expected that KSA – after loosening its strong relationship with the Pauluskerk – was doomed to fall into oblivion. However, under the leadership of director Hanny de Kruijf, the organization has succeeded in opening up new perspectives. KSA started to work closely with its Catholic counterpart – the organization Mara – in Rotterdam. In organizational terms, it was further strengthened by other bodies joining the KSA, including TRAIN, a training agency working for mainly migrant groups, and a Protestant partner organization. The municipality, still subsidizing KSA for its contribution to the local policy goals on volunteering, is driving an agenda to avoid duplication in the welfare sector which makes further integration with other organizations promoting volunteering likely. The government is heading for more cooperation, directing new initiatives towards the KSA and Mara, including an umbrella organization of migrant churches and an inter-religious platform of churches, mosques and temples, which the local government hopes to develop as a main point of entrance to the religious field in Rotterdam.

In 2010, KSA counted twelve professionals. While these professionals largely come from the city, the volunteers increasingly come from the suburbs. Therefore, KSA is thinking about expanding their field towards the suburbs. The beneficiaries are mainly from deprived neighbourhoods in the city. There is a great deal of continuity in these groups: these are people in poverty, with debts, occasionally depending on food aid, migrants, refugees, victims of domestic violence and people with little or no social support network. The KSA continues its political advocacy on issues of poverty, domestic violence, refugees and family care. Besides this advocacy work, the KSA supports voluntary organizations dealing with these problems. Ms Kruijf also notes that the mainstream institutions let the 'difficult cases' pass to the KSA.

> We try to fill gaps that are left by the government, and if the government fills that gap, we start to do something else.[37]

In many ways, the KSA has returned to its original foci from sixty years ago, providing essential social services which the government at the time failed to provide. With the implementation of the Social Support Act 2007, social and care services are being brought under one system, managed by municipalities and largely privatized/market driven, in terms of service delivery.[38] Civil society organizations, including churches and mosques, are asked to act as intermediary organizations between clients and social service agencies.[39] Underpinning this policy shift is a drive towards personal responsibility, independence and participation of all citizens, which

Mrs De Kruijf feels might guide the KSA back into a more direct service provider role, and possibly closer partnership with local government.

For instance, the KSA currently runs a guest house – 'The Neighbours' – for people whose doctor has told them that they can leave hospital, but have no one to look after them. In the guest house, people can stay up to six weeks. It is funded as an innovative project within the Social Support Act framework by the local authorities, and has been adopted by the Order of St John (*Johanniter Orde*).

Other new activities include shelters for men who are victims of violence, and providing training for public officials on religion and philosophies of life in Rotterdam. KSA continues this emphasis on building bridges between groups in society – faithful to its original old mission. Supported by the municipality, the KSA is trying to open a new community centre where every Somali – whatever clan background, gender or age – is welcome. Somali organizations can get support and are involved in setting up educational and cultural activities, aiming at empowerment and participation of Somalis in Rotterdam.

The municipality sees the KSA as a connector to religious communities and as a source of citizenship and social cohesion. Between 2008 and 2010, cooperation between the KSA and the local government has been growing. However, to avoid over-reliance on the state, or possible co-option into 'doing what the government wants', the KSA recognizes the importance of a varied source of funding, and is working closely with the churches. This enables the KSA to provide services that appear out of sync with the prevailing assumptions of government policy.

Hence, KSA's service delivery role is often coupled with milder forms of political advocacy. For instance, one of the activities which Mrs De Kruijf does not regard as a task for the KSA but one for the government, is the care of refugees who are awaiting their procedure. The KSA does not receive a subsidy for this, but does it because of the destitution of the group. According to KSA, the government should provide 'bed, bath and bread' for this group, highlighting the injustice that refugees, while waiting for the outcome of their asylum claim, are legally not entitled to receive social benefits, subsidized housing, or to financially support themselves through paid work.

Meeting unmet need is an ethical imperative; however, filling the gap is a deeply ambiguous political position. At times it can be seen as a powerful form of political protest to achieve change, and at other times it can be regarded as a placatory device that justifies state retrenchment in direct provision. Faith involvement that identifies itself purely as a social service provider runs the risk of losing sight of the church's prophetic role to redeem the 'powers that be' and address the uncomfortable questions about why people live highly precarious lives.

Conclusion

This chapter has provided an historical account of the evolving character of the KSA, Rotterdam. By outlining the shifting politics and service portfolios of the KSA[40] we have highlighted the swings of radicalism and conformity that can occur within a single FBO, and the reasons underpinning these manoeuvres. From its early days of collectivism and the 'public good' in the post-war optimism, the KSA found itself estranged in the fast-moving social and cultural context of the 1970s as the state took over many of the service functions of the organization. Becoming less involved in direct service provision, the KSA became a hub for recruiting volunteers and community/social activation work. Its philosophy was generally conformist, in part as a response to declining church membership and perceived tide of secularization in public politics.

As a result, the KSA became suspicious of the radical left's demands for change at the structural level; indeed, some members distanced themselves completely from what was considered 'worldly' affairs and, subsequently, the KSA became more acquiescent with the parameters of government policy. The arrival of Visser saw a radical positioning of the KSA on social, economic and political issues. Through the development of the Pauluskerk, civil disobedience and political confrontation with the authorities over the neglect of marginalized groups became core faith-inspired involvements of the churches, echoing Proverbs 31 verse 8: 'Speak up for those who cannot speak for themselves; ensure justice for those being crushed.'[41]

The radicalism of some of Visser's activities, however, soon led to frictions in the local municipality, whose initial pragmatic accommodative stance towards the Pauluskerk turned increasingly hostile. The 2000s backlash against antisocial behaviour, drug users and street homeless, under the right-wing popularist party, culminated in the Pauluskerk closing its doors and legally prohibited from establishing services for drug users. The new Pauluskerk, under the direction of Couvée, retains many of the theological and political views held by Visser, but has adopted a more cooperative stance towards government, although it continues to operate outside integrated and coherent partnership arrangements in the city. Today the KSA is an organization at the crossroads, following various approaches to social challenges, some old, some new. It is currently being repositioned by local government as a fit partner in the delivery of a number of welfare services, and the organization has to some extent returned to focus on social work, activation and community empowerment, with less emphasis placed on social change.

In its history, the KSA has occupied several extreme positions on urban justice issues, ranging from the collectivist, the conservative, the radical and the pragmatist. It would be easy to conclude that the more radical expressions of the KSA were exclusively driven by the charismatic leadership of Revd. Visser, whose theological and political values undeniably shaped what came to be known as the Pauluskerk. However, it is important not to underestimate the wider political and cultural contexts in the church, and beyond, that regulate, even mitigate, against such radical social action. This is where the example of Hans Visser and the KSA is both inspiring and challenging, because it pinpoints the core tension in the potential for radical faith-based social action: discernment and discipleship. Radicalism requires a prophetic imagination to see past the prevailing parameters of the current order. It requires the nurturing, nourishing and evoking of a consciousness and perception which is the alternative to the consciousness and perception of the dominant culture.[42] For Visser and others, this involved contesting the mistreatment of drug users in the city, and the discursive representations that strip people of their humanity and normalize practices of neglect. These alternative discernments, informed directly by a passionate faith commitment and through engagement in the lives of drug users, helped illuminate the current landscapes and practices of power within the city, 'joining the dots' between the spiritual interiorities and exteriorities of oppression.[43] It was this that fuelled the radical politics that called into question how the 'least of these' are treated in contemporary society.

CHAPTER 10

Faith Community Works
in Sweden

Charlotte Fridolfsson and Ingemar Elander

Introduction

Together with other Nordic countries, Sweden differs from most
European welfare states with regard to the role of FBOs. From the
1930s and onwards, the Third Sector charities and popular movements in the social welfare domain willingly handed over much of
their social responsibilities to the state, especially its local institutions. Public child care and care for elderly, for example, are results
of demands advocated by the women's movement.[1] However, as
articulated by Olsson et al.,[2] the popular movements and related
charities kept something of their 'avant-garde' role for advocacy
and innovation, and a need for the competence and avant-garde
role potentially provided by FBOs still remains important, especially in times of Welfare State retrenchment.[3] As demonstrated
in this chapter, FBOs in Sweden still take action where public
authorities, for a variety of reasons, fail.

   With a very broad categorization, three forms of FBO activities
can be identified, i.e. *service delivery*, including relational as well
as infrastructure service provision; *capacity building*, including
resourcing and networking; and *political activism*, including
advocacy and representation of marginalized groups, consultation, lobbying and protest.[4] Although all three kinds of activities
are in practice parallel and/or overlapping, this chapter will in
particular focus on capacity building and political activism by

Swedish FBOs. We use examples taken from Church of Sweden parishes, but work carried out by other faith communities such as Christian free churches and Muslim congregations are included too, as well as examples of faith-driven actions taken by Christian and Muslim individuals. Ecumenical and inter-religious activities are also presented.

Swedish FBOs and the Welfare State

It is important to mention the widespread FBO support for the universalistic Swedish welfare systems, and the conviction that public authorities ought to have a general responsibility for social welfare. Many of our informants describe cut backs in public welfare as a problem, which also put heavier burdens upon the FBOs.

> Today social secretaries working for the city are sometimes forced to tell people in need to turn to the church instead, because there is not enough money in the municipal budget to guarantee the basic rights anymore.[5]

Similarly, another interviewee states:

> Beneficiaries have confidence in the mosque and therefore turn to the mosque for support. This confidence is good, but we would . . . like the public welfare institutions to adapt to needs among new groups of citizens in order to safeguard also their constitutional rights.[6]

'The state should provide welfare services such as schools, care for elderly, social workers and health care' another informant typically states.[7] Thus, Swedish FBOs rather push the government to take responsibility for citizens' rights than wanting to be the providers of welfare services. In other words, FBOs should not spend their money on things that ought to be financed by taxes. Nevertheless, most FBOs with public contracts also argue a qualitative difference and an added value of their own targeted activities, in relation to other publicly financed service providers:

We believe that we can provide better welfare services than the state in certain areas, for example when it comes to addiction. We think that the spiritual is yet another factor to help people to a new life. The faith in Jesus Christ is a power that can help, together with health care of course.[8]

There is an added value, they [tax payers/beneficiaries/municipality] get something a little extra; we can hire more staff at the elderly care facilities for the same money. And this then means better nursing care here, as we are not commercial and do not need to give the Chief Executive Officers all their millions.[9]

The Church of Sweden Defending the Swedish Welfare State

In 2000, formal ties between the Church of Sweden and the state were cut. The former state church changed from a powerful institution with wide-ranging statutory ties to the government, and became a relatively independent faith community with its own agenda. Although remaining neutral in terms of party politics, Swedish FBOs in general increasingly voice concerns about poverty and social exclusion to the media and the public – usually opposing central and local government welfare cut backs. The Church of Sweden, for example, expresses its social mission with the following words: 'The church should be a voice for the vulnerable and the weak – in Sweden and abroad.'[10] As stated by an official responsible for diaconal concerns at the Central Church Office, the Church is 'a complement to the public sector, an alternative and a critical voice'.[11] In other words diaconal work is all about standing on the side of the unfortunate, giving them a voice to target responsible actors, e.g. local government officials. In line with this mission, and without siding with any particular political party, the church should defend public health and wellbeing.

In 2005, the Church of Sweden declared September as 'The Month of Deacony', stating that even in Sweden there are poor people. The main theme of the September campaign in 2010 was 'Vulnerability – Lack of Opportunities', stating that poverty contributes to social exclusion: 'For example there are 850,000

187

people who can't afford going to a dentist.' The cooperating partners in this ecumenical campaign were the Swedish Church, Interact (*Evangeliska frikyrkan*), the Salvation Army, the Swedish Alliance Mission, the Swedish Baptist Congregation, the Swedish Mission Church and the Christian Council of Sweden (an umbrella organization including the Church of Sweden and other Christian congregations in the country). In line with this initiative, the council in November 2010 organized a conference targeted at poverty and social exclusion: 'Together we can challenge, influence, create opinion, change and let ourselves be transformed.'[12]

In March 2011, yet another political initiative was taken by the Christian Council of Sweden. An open letter was sent to the government demanding revisions of socially devastating rules in the health insurance system:

> . . . because we have seen . . . how people are hit, how the social and economic platforms of many people are eroded. Our mission is to be an ethical voice in society following Jesus Christ, his words and deeds. But our churches are not political parties, we have no party programs, investigation committees or civil servants mandated to bring forward solutions. Solutions must be presented by politicians in government and parliament as well as by civil servants in the public administration.[13]

The Mosque as an Urban Social Hub and a Platform for Capacity Building

Muslim congregations regularly use non-religious activities such as playing sports, study circles, adult education and other social activities as means to indirectly prevent social exclusion and promote integration.[14] In other words, the mosque is a crucial arena where people can find friendship, connection with others, and a sense of belonging. As shown by many researchers, first generation immigrants often stay close when they first arrive, developing a sense of community within their new country, and then gradually begin 'a transition from internal bonding to external bridging capital'.[15] Often, activities such as learning computer skills may help someone to stay in touch with former fellow countrymen, but also help the same person to get a new job in Sweden. Other actions include helping and representing people that for one reason or another have experienced problems in their relations with the public authorities. The Stockholm Mosque provides support on an individual basis and refers people onto local government institutions or other statutory FBO and NGO organizations when necessary.

Thus, aside from being important spaces for worship and celebration, mosques also function as community centres, including the development of contacts with non-Muslims. For example, although the Stockholm Mosque is basically a house of prayer, other cultural and welfare activities are now dominating. These activities include marital support sessions, youth activities, female gym classes and swimming lessons. 'We are part of society. Saving souls is not enough,' president of the Islamic Association in Stockholm, Abdallah Salah, told us in an interview, and continues:

> [there] is in essence no limit for what kind of activities . . . can be carried out at the mosque. The problem is that a mosque is immediately associated with religion. But a mosque is more like a Community Centre [*Folkets Hus*]. Out of the fifty to sixty activities organized at the mosque each week, a maximum 10 per cent has religious content. People want to spend time in the mosque also doing other things; it is a good environment where people feel comfortable.[16]

Any week day, up to eight groups with around thirty people in each, predominately teachers with their school classes, visit the mosque. Politicians and public servants are also frequenting the place on a regular basis. The contact is quite friendly with homeless people and/or people with drug problems hanging around the adjacent Medborgarplatsen (which literally means 'Citizen Square') and its subway station. During Ramadan, people can also stay overnight in the mosque. The location close to the subway also means that Muslim people from other parts of the city, as well as visitors from other areas of Sweden and abroad, can easily reach the Stockholm Mosque: 'The mere location of the mosque at the centre of Stockholm is the greatest integration project.'[17] In line with this, the goals of the United Islamic Congregations in Sweden are 'integration of Muslim people in society', 'helping Muslims to keep their cultural, social and religious identity' and 'working as a bridge builder between the Swedish authorities / majority population and Muslims'.[18] A spokesperson for the Islamic Association in Göteborg says:

> the role of our organisation is for our members to feel safe and secure socially, in society and within Islam. That is a prerequisite for peace for the ethnic or religious minority, but also for the society at large.[19]

A Muslim Adult Education Association, Ibn Rushd[20] was founded in 2007. This association institutionally links the Swedish Muslim community to the Swedish corporatist tradition with strong ties between civil society / popular movements and the state. A current project by Ibn Rushd, 'The promotion of Islamic Peace Culture', is targeting Muslim youth across the country trained to become Peace Agents:

> The long term aim is to combat Islamophobia (fear and animosity towards Islam, mainly by people in the West) and Westphobia (fear and animosity towards the West, mainly by Muslims). Within the framework of the project a foundation has been laid for a Muslim peace movement.

Mosques and other Islamic centres can also offer advice and support on matters of great diplomatic concern. In connection with the controversial Mohammed caricatures republished by a Swedish daily newspaper, the Stockholm Mosque met with the prime minister and other government officials and 'we contributed to limiting the problem, so that it would not become the same as in Denmark', Abdallah Salah says, referring to racist, Islamophobian, anti-immigrant flavoured social unrest in the wake of a similar publication there.[21]

> Fredrik Reinfeldt [the prime minister] asked us, 'What can we do to avoid things to become the same as in Denmark?' we told him, 'You don't need to do anything; we have already sent press releases to all the international news media.' International media contacted the mosque to get statements on the development but the mosque did

not want to inflate the issue. 'This is Sweden, this is a local problem, we can handle it here and we are capable of solving this,' was our message to the journalists.[22]

Thus, the mosques are places where social services to Muslims are offered, and where important community service information is communicated, which is also important in terms of increasing the capacity of Muslim immigrants to learn about and participate in Swedish society. Similar to the Ibn Rushd projects, these activities also contribute to the establishment of a Swedish Muslim identity in a broader sense.

FBOs Outside State and Market

Given the vast responsibilities by local government in Sweden, FBOs typically carry out their social work in fields where the public sector has 'given up', 'failed' or has not yet imagined or acknowledged new needs and demands. As mediators, they can represent people that for one reason or another have problems in their relations to the authorities, thus guiding them through the labyrinths of bureaucracy, i.e. as the ones needing public services the most, they may have greater difficulties to navigate in the system due to language or other barriers. Their non-party political position also grants them possibilities to raise important questions in the media without compromising themselves.

In the case of people with a foreign background, the official jargon among the public servants can be difficult. The activities may be illegal, but more often they are just incompatible with government responsibilities. These FBO actions include helping and representing people that for one reason or another have experienced problems in their relations to the public authorities. It sometimes also involves appealing against public authority decisions, which of course cannot be part of the authorities' practice. Modes of actions targeting poverty and social exclusion in these areas can be direct and carried out with a pronounced purpose to assist individual persons or groups of individuals that need support; they include the homeless, mentally ill, and people

191

with addictions. The measures taken include advice and support centres, legal aid receptions, debt remedy solutions, soup kitchen types of charity offering food, job training programmes, or help for ex-convicts to adjust to life outside prison. The Church of Sweden's diaconal operations also hand out small amounts of cash support. Indirect measures of targeting poverty and social exclusion range from family counselling sessions and choir singing to Swedish language training workshops. These are sometimes pronounced preventive measures, aimed at youth at risk, or people with poor language skills.

Hiding refugees by organizing countrywide networks, organizing study circles for various immigrant groups, language and civic courses colleges for adult education (*folkhögskola*), and homework support for immigrant children are only a few of the activities undertaken by local branches of FBOs and ecumenical networks. One interesting process of building up interreligious and secular support for undocumented and hidden asylum seekers in Sweden is the Easter Call (*Påskupppropet*).[23] Around Easter-time in 2005, the Christian Council of Sweden came together in a joint protest against tougher policies making it more difficult for refugees to get residence permits. The Easter Call used the watchwords:

> WE MOURN that the rights of the child is not given priority in decisions made about resident permits in our country.
> WE WELCOME a court procedure that grants asylum seekers legal security.
> WE URGE the Swedish government to grant amnesty to all previously denied asylum.
> WE DEMAND that the right to asylum is restored and broadens in a way worthy a humane society founded on the rule of law.

In total, 157,000 people responded to the call and signed the petition that was later turned over to the minister for Migration and Asylum Policy. The result from this was that 20,000 asylum seekers were granted a residence permit in a second trial.[24] Although the Easter Call was organizationally initiated by the ecumenical Christian Council of Sweden, it did not only gain support from most of the Christian congregations, but also from

192

the Islamic Council of Sweden (Sveriges Muslimska Råd), and more than sixty non-religious NGOs and party organizations, e.g. the Green Party, the Young Left, the Centre Party Women, the Male Network, Reporters without Borders, the Borås Students, the Iran Music and Cultural Association, the National Association of Somalian People etc. Notably, several organizations that do not normally join collaborative demonstrations like this one actively supported the Easter Call. For example, the coordinator of the thirteen Orthodox churches in the Christian Council of Sweden says that 'the support was never questioned. The Orthodox churches live close to the asylum seekers and the statement was self-evident'. The Islamic Council of Sweden supported the Call, although renaming it 'the Refugee Call'.[25]

However, what may in retrospect look like an initiative from above by the Swedish Church and its archbishop, Karl Gunnar Hammar, had a pre-history of local engagement and strong criticism of the Swedish Church for not acting on behalf of the asylum seekers. Professionals and volunteers, who in many parishes had begun hiding refugees on their own initiative, explained the illicit actions taken with arguments such as 'I simply had to' or 'It had to be done'. One priest in a parish in west Sweden says:

> To me it is about preserving my freedom, my conscience and my belief. One must be able to act and make such choices that one gets adversaries and ends up in minority. I don't see any difference between hiding Kosovo Albanians today or hiding Jews during World War II . . . People have always done . . . this. Just as they have always loved, given birth to children, and died, they have hidden others if necessary. Josef and Maria were offered a place in the stable. And you can ask people in Jämtland and Värmland what they did during World War II.[26]

Notably, most of the refugee hiders said they did not see themselves as making politics, just doing what they should do as believers. Nevertheless, their engagement and the Easter Call as such became a hot political issue or, as formulated by one representative of the Swedish Christian Council: 'We were on time on a question where moral and politics converge, were on top of the agenda and deeply touched the soul of the people.'[27]

Inter-religious Networks

Although the Easter Call was an exceptional event gathering an impressive, nationwide variety of FBOs, there are many other examples of everyday cooperation between FBOs in Swedish towns and cities.

Abraham's Children's Christmas Crib

Several Swedish municipalities and Church of Sweden parishes each year set up a special inter-religious Christmas crib called 'Abraham's Children's Christmas Crib'. This modified version of the ordinary crib from the Christian tradition builds on features taken from the Bible, but also from the Koran and the Torah. The scriptures all have passages recounting the events that are the foundation for the celebration of Christmas and the birth of Christ in the Christian tradition. Additional attributes for decorating Abraham's Children's Christmas Crib are a date palm and a waterfall, elements that are mentioned in the Koran and Torah. The Church of Sweden parish of Skärholmen outside Stockholm cooperates with the public library, where it has become a tradition to set one up.[28] In the autumn of 2010, the one-man play *Abraham/Ibrahim* was performed in senior level schools (*högstadieskolor*) in the Örebro region. As formulated by the actor Peter Bergared: 'The play was written because of the mad polarisation that has emerged between Christians and Muslims.'[29]

Christian-Muslim Social Service Centre

The Stockholm City Mission cooperates with a mosque and a Church of Sweden parish at a joint social service venue in Nacka. It is called The Well (*Källan*) and they offer counselling and advice on practical matters in relation to public authorities and other organizations. A social worker and a deacon work at the support centre, and they offer consultations with a priest from the Church of Sweden or the Catholic Church or with an imam. There is also a room for prayer that is open to anyone. The Well is not an authority, so the visitors may remain anonymous. The centre is a joint project between Stockholm City Mission, the Church of Sweden Parish, the Muslim Association and St Konrad Catholic Church in Nacka.[30]

Celebration of midsummer, inter-religious prayers and public dialogues in Malmö

There have been some common activities jointly undertaken by the Christian and Muslim faith communities in Rosengård (Malmö), for example, a celebration of the Swedish National Day (6 June 2010). The Islamic Centre of the Malmö Mosque sent an invitation to the Västra Skrävlinge parish about jointly celebrating the day. Notably, the invitation (see Figure 1), illustrated by a painted picture of the Malmö Mosque, was published in the parish newsletter.[31]

ISLAMIC CENTER
INBJUDAN

Välkomna att fira
Sverige nationaldag
hos oss på Islamic Center
söndagen den 6 juni , kl 11.00

Figure 1. Invitation from the Islamic Centre to the Church of Sweden Parish in Västra Skrävlinge, Skåne.

Inter-religious public prayers have been held at centrally located squares in Malmö. Religious leaders from the Church of Sweden, the Catholic Church, Muslim and Jewish communities joined together in common prayers. The purpose has been to make a collaborative intervention for the spreading of knowledge at the same time as getting rid of prejudice and improving security.[32] There have also been organized joint FBO demonstrations against the violence that has lately plagued the city.

Figure 2. Inter-religious prayer in Malmö city centre.
Photo: Kicki Strand-Larsson

From the left: The Malmö Fire Brigade Band; Dharmavaja Detlef Schultze, Malmö Buddhist Centre; Frank Kelber, The Jewish Community of Malmö; Father Gabriel Felipe Baldostamon, Roman Catholic Church; Priest Blazo Kazarski, Macedonian Orthodox Church; Imam Junus Latifov, Islamic Centre; Bishop Antje Jackelén, Church of Sweden; Reverend Lennart Henriksson, The Mission Covenant Church of Sweden.

Inter-religious, municipal advisory board

In one city, Örebro, with about 135,000 inhabitants, the local government in 2007 launched an inter-religious advisory board comprising of representatives of the local branches of the Church of Sweden, the free churches, different Islamic groups, the Syrian Orthodox Church, and people representing the municipality. Among the latter was the chairman of the city council, a Christian Democrat, who also became the chairman of the board. The stated aims of the board are to increase citizens' knowledge about different cultures and religions, stimulate inter-religious and intercultural dialogue, support civil society in developing complementary social services, and creating an 'integrated Örebro'.[33] However, except for one member, the inter-religious board is totally male dominated, something that was critically noticed by some women who decided to initiate a parallel women's intercultural network. The network, that was established within the United Nations' UNIFEM framework, and has some financial support from the central government, promptly started ten working groups around specific topics such as women's health, violence against women in the family, and safety in the street. Notably, the women's network is explicitly intercultural and not inter-religious.[34]

Faith-driven Initiatives by Individuals

FBO activities relate in different ways to the legal framing of social services and care for the poor and socially excluded. Some of the parishes on occasion accommodate families that have nowhere else to turn, for example refugees threatened with expulsion. They take an active stand in deportation cases, either by supporting networks that are hiding refugees/illegal immigrants, or by offering temporary sheltering, as has been done on several occasions, for example at the Church of Sweden in Bergsjön parish in Göteborg.[35] Others regularly provide healthcare and legal aid for undocumented immigrants, who cannot easily acquire services elsewhere.

A number of FBOs provide healthcare to undocumented people. Emergency care is offered to all residing in Sweden, but non-life-threatening conditions are not covered by public money for those without legal papers. In Sweden, the vast majority of medical staff work for the county or regional governments. After working hours some are involved in these volunteer programmes, providing aid for non-official residents at Church of Sweden premises. These activities are often clearly contrary to the legal framework regulating heathcare in Sweden. Public authorities stand by in compliance.

In everyday life there are often actions undertaken by faith-committed individuals, not necessarily in the name of a particular congregation. A few such examples will be given, all from Örebro, a city with a fairly strong free church tradition. In May 2010, a 24-year-old Muslim man received the Swedish King's Grant for youth, due to his engagement in a large multiethnic housing estate. Being a resident in the area for six years, he has initiated a number of social activities: teaching women to cycle, opening the youth centre (*fritidsgård*) on weekends, organizing football games for youth, educating young people about Islam and Christian faith traditions, and much more. In his blog on 21 May 2010, he wrote:

> I humbly receive the grant, and it is a great honor for me . . . The grant should rather be from me to the Swedish people for their warm hospitality and the opportunities I got in this country. For me it is a repayment to the Swedish society for all good they have done to me and my family.[36]

In the same housing estate (Vivalla), one Muslim woman, born in Casablanca, taught 120 girls how to play basketball. For this she was awarded the local sports journalists' grant, the 'Sports Leader of the Year'.[37] Looking upon her as a role model for young women in the area, the employed (male) manager of the neighbourhood centre said: 'Malika mirrors the women here and is one of them. As a Muslim and woman they have a special trust in her. She is a star in the neighbourhood.'

Another individual faith-based initiative was taken in the autumn of 2011 by a woman who was connected to the evangelical free church. She discovered the temporary hut where a Roma family was staying close to the Varberga housing estate. The family had been unable to sustain themselves by begging in Örebro city centre, and their plight had been ignored by social services, the police, and the municipal housing company who owned the land on which the hut stood. However, they were invited to a nearby church where parents and daughter were given temporary assistance in the form of warm clothes, food and shower facilities. The woman from the evangelical free church then used her Facebook network to gather money to cover bus tickets for the family back to their home in Romania. This promptly resulted in enough money for return travel, including a surplus that became a foundational source of support to the family when back in Romania.[38] The woman gave a strongly faith-motivated reason for her action: "I feel good inside. This is important, for real. And then it is a question of my belief in Jesus. She says: 'What you do to one of the most vulnerable, that you also have done to me.'[39]

Conclusion

Aside from their evangelistic mission, FBOs in Sweden engage in service delivery, capacity building and political advocacy/ activism to support people in need. This goes for the Church of Sweden as well as for free church and Muslim congregations. Thanks to their long-standing social tradition, many FBOs are motivated, competent and experienced enough to manage soup kitchens, homeless shelters, old people's homes, walk-in centres in neighborhoods, and other social services. In the case of asylum seekers and, in particular, undocumented people, there is very little, if any, support these people can get from governments. In this case, there are numerous examples in which FBOs, or individuals affiliated to FBOs, circumvent the legal system, sheltering and supporting people in distress as exemplified in the case of the Easter Call in 2005.

Other FBOs concentrate on groups whose needs are recognized by official policies, but fall outside the view and reach of the authorities. They assist people who are entitled to, but make no use of, debt-related advice, visit people who lead isolated lives and might be helped out with informal care, etc. They are working for people who have – for very different reasons – lost faith in regular services, or who have made themselves 'untraceable' for the public authorities.

Although public welfare provision is increasingly handed over to big profit-making companies, FBOs still have an important role in combating poverty and social exclusion. Muslim FBOs are developing at the local level, often facing an environment with anti-Islamic sentiments. Independent Islamic organizations, cellar mosques, and a few big Mosques are important centres, serving Muslim immigrants with social support. Occasionally, Christian, Muslim, Jewish and other FBOs even cooperate in activities to combat social exclusion and help people in need. As formulated by Paul Cloke, FBOs

> represent some of the last islands of social capital as well as spiritual capital in some urban communities . . . and present potential resources (buildings, volunteers, social leadership and so on) as well as a sense of longstanding local presence and commitment to local areas.[40]

Notably, there is a striking gender dimension to this, as women are generally more active than men in voluntary work at the face-to-face level of society, whereas the reverse goes for men in leading FBO positions.[41]

However, despite a growing need for private, non-profit engagement in welfare provision and non-public activities to counter social exclusion, FBOs in Sweden seem to have a general trust in public welfare provision. They rather expect and demand central and local governments to take responsibility for poor families, vulnerable children, disabled elderly, drug addicts, homeless, and other people in need. They deliberately concentrate on offering complementary care at the margins only when public provision of welfare wavers. Thus, the FBOs themselves are hesitant when considering the opportunities to increase their responsibilities in welfare provision, partly because they lack the financial and professional muscles of the profit-seeking actors, and partly because they expect public authorities to be main responsible for provision of social welfare.[42] As formulated by one of our informants:

> The danger is, since Sweden joined the EU, how large multinational corporations now are entering the Swedish market. First dumping the market, [getting rid of] all the competition in the area, and then after a while . . . dominating the market completely. They can have a price-tag of zero SEK for the entire elderly care in a municipality; no NGOs and FBOs can compete with that.[43]

In other words, there is a fear among many FBOs that the increasing habit of tendering in the social sector will primarily favour profit-making rather than non-profit provision of welfare, thus pressing FBOs to professionalize and become more profit-orientated themselves, i.e. to the potential detriment of the socially deprived, and excluded groups they want to support. This may create a risk for diluting the deeper ethical motivations traditionally driving voluntary work.

CHAPTER 11

Central Welfare Office of the Jews in Germany

Jennifer Klöckner

Introduction

ZWST (*Zentralwohlfahrtsstelle der Juden in Deutschland*; Central Welfare Office of the Jews in Germany) is the umbrella organization of Jewish welfare associations, and a non-political representative of Jewish communities in Germany. During the First World War, ZWST was founded to take care of the Jewish survivors and to alleviate their suffering. Before the Second World War, about two hundred facilities were under ZWST's leadership and approximately six hundred thousand Jews lived in Germany. Only 15,000 Jews survived the Nazi regime, and relatively few refugees came back to Germany. While the membership figure in East Germany decreased to an extremely low level during the times of the Iron Curtain, tens of thousands of Soviet Jews immigrated to the reunited Germany after 1989. By 2008, ZWST served about 104,000 clients, 90 per cent of which were migrants, the majority from Russia and the former Soviet Union. This has changed the tasks of ZWST dramatically.

This chapter addresses the conflicts between the old-established, more orthodox and the 'new', more liberal Jews in Germany, and examines the crucial role that a single FBO – the ZWST – plays in reconciling these wider shifts in religious culture, ethnicity and population mobility within Jewish communities.

Foundation and History of the Organization

ZWST is a non-political umbrella organization of Jewish welfare communities in Germany.[1] It is the smallest of the six independent welfare umbrella organizations in Germany, and its tasks comprise social, cultural and youth work. In 1917, ZWST – then under the name '*Zentralwohlfahrtsstelle der deutschen Juden*' (Central Welfare Office of the German Jews) – was founded to coordinate various local initiatives which were taking care of the Jewish survivors after the First World War.[2] Since the Emancipation Edict in 1812, Jewish women had banded together to fight against the poverty and discrimination the Jewish people had to face.[3] Their main domains were running hospitals and homes for the elderly, serving the poor, disabled and invalid persons.[4] By this time, Jewish welfare services were mostly organized as a means of self-help because the Jews were largely excluded from governmental help and had only marginal civic rights.[5] But besides social welfare, religious education, especially for poor Russian Jewish immigrants, was a major task of Jewish organizations; for example, the Benevolent Society of the German Jews for Eastern Jew's Relief, which was founded in 1901.[6] In the Weimar Republic, Jewish welfare communities were established and gained influence and, by 1923, they had more than 200,000 members in Germany.[7] In 1926, ZWST succeeded in becoming a member of the (Christian) League of the Umbrella Organizations of the Independent Welfare Work (*Liga der Spitzenverbände der freien Wohlfahrtspflege*).[8]

With the takeover of National Socialism, ZWST's almost equal position in welfare society disintegrated. ZWST's primary task was to care for emigrants – to provide famine relief in winter as well as other emergency relief in all social domains, a task that became necessary because of increasing discrimination and prosecution.[9] The association had to resign from its membership in the League in 1933. After successive expropriation proceedings, the Nazis prohibited the association in 1939.[10] The board members and employees either fled abroad, were deported into concentration camps or executed immediately.

After the Second World War, reconstruction of the Jewish community slowly began. Only 22,000 Jews – some survivors, some returnees – organized new religious communities, and a welfare association which since operates under the new name *Zentralwohlfahrtsstelle der Juden in Deutschland* (Central Welfare Office of the Jews in Germany).[11] This name expresses that while the Jews are living in Germany, they are not German Jews, as they had named themselves before.[12] During the times of the Iron Curtain, the number of members in East Germany decreased to less than four hundred, and the number in the West German communities increased only marginally as well.[13] But immediately after the opening of the border in 1990, tens of thousands of Soviet Jews immigrated to the reunited Germany.[14]

ZWST today

Table 1 reports the population figures of Jews in Germany since 1987. In 1987, 27,533 Jews lived in Germany. The figure has remained more or less constant over the years. In comparison to 1987, after the opening of the Eastern borders, the figure of 1991 increased by 5 per cent to 29,089, and almost doubled until 1996 to 53,797. From 1997 on, the increase attenuated year by year until 2007, when the migration balance was negative for the first time after decades. After 2006, when the Jewish population reached its peak of 108,289, the figures again decreased. The last official figures from 2010 report that Jews constitute a percentage of 0.13 of the German population, and that about 90 per cent of them are immigrants of the former Soviet Union, mostly from Ukraine or the Russian Federation.[15]

In 2010, ZWST had twenty-three federal associations serving 104,241 clients (Table 1) with more than seven hundred and forty-nine[16] employees in 440[17] facilities and clubs for the elderly, youth, families and the disabled, and 108 Jewish communities.[18]

The Jewish welfare system operates on the principles of *Zedaka* (justice), which obligates every Jew to protect vulnerable community members.[19] Its main tasks are to strengthen Jewish identity, offering social and youth work and orientation seminars for immigrants, caring for the elderly and for people with intellectual, mental and physical disabilities, and the promotion of volunteer activities.[20]

In regard to their history, ZWST has an exceptional position among the welfare organizations. They are forced to participate in various committees and public events. Politicians regularly try to adorn themselves with 'the very good relationship' to the Jewish community.[21] Because of the small and limited clientele, ZWST is no competition for the other organizations.

Jews in Germany since 1987[22]

Year	Total number of migrants*	Total number of ZWST members	% increase since 1987	% change in comparison to previous year	New Jewish immigrants	New Ethnic German repatriates**
1987	4,286,472	27,533	100.0			
1988	4,623,528	27,612	100.3	0.3		
1989	5,007,161	27,552	100.1	-0.2		
1990	5,582,357	27,711	100.6	0.5		
1991	6,066,730	29,089	105.7	5.1		221,995
1992	6,669,568	33,692	122.4	16.7		230,565
1993	6,977,476	36,804	133.7	9.2	16,597	218,888
1994	7,117,740	40,917	148.6	11.2	8,811	222,591
1995	7,342,779	45,559	165.5	11.3	15,184	217,898
1996	7,491,650	53,797	195.4	18.1	15,959	177,751
1997	7,419,001	61,203	222.3	13.8	19,437	134,419
1998	7,308,477	67,471	245.1	10.2	17,788	103,080
1999	7,336,111	74,289	269.8	10.1	18,205	104,916
2000	7,267,568	81,739	296.9	10.0	16,538	95,615
2001	7,318,263	87.756	318.7	7.4	16,711	98,484
2002	7,347,951	93,326	339.0	6.3	19,262	91,416
2003	7,341,820	98,335	357.2	5.4	15,442	72,885
2004	7,287,980	102,472	372,2	4.2	11,208	59,093
2005	7,289,149	105,733	384.0	3.2	5,968	35,522
2006	7,255,949	108,289	393.3	2.4	1,079	7,747
2007	7,255,395	107,794	391.5	-0.5	2,502	5,792
2008	7,185,921	107,330	389.8	-0.4	1,436	4,362
2009	7,130,919	106,435	386.6	-0.8	1,088	3,360
2010*		104,241	378.6	-2.1		

ZWST's share of financial governmental support is about 3 to 4 per cent, much less than other organizations receive. Hence, to some extent, ZWST is belittled as insignificant by other government and non-governmental organizations.

As part of the FACIT research project we conducted five interviews with different Jewish communities in Cologne, Hamburg and Leipzig. Participants consisted of local board members or chairmen and women of the federal state or city associations. The queries included general questions on the organization, the religious dimension, organizational goals and activities, on service delivery, and referred to the Welfare State, the organizational network, policy dimensions and the urban context.

The representatives of the local ZWST facilities reported that the relationship to local affairs is fairly good. Because of the historical events during the Second World War, ZWST is well accepted and the municipalities are well disposed towards Jewish communities. They participate in 'inter-religious round tables' where representatives from different religious communities meet and they sit on advisory boards for the construction of places of worship for other religious communities (e.g. a mosque in Cologne). The relationship to other religious or non-religious NGOs in general is good, based on the connection of BAGFW, although they compete for funding.[23]

ZWST Leipzig sees its main challenge as the integration of Jews, both into the Jewish community and German society. In addition to social provisions, they offer several cultural services with the aim to pass on Jewish culture, identity and history. ZWST Cologne seeks to be a community hub for contact for Jews,[24] for immigrants who came to Cologne since 1990 as well as for those who lived there before. Most of the workers are not professional social workers, but take care of the community needs as well as they can. They work true to the motto 'trial and error', and have accumulated a large amount of know-how in these fields over the years.[25]

ZWST Hamburg is also primarily specializing in social services for ethnic German repatriates from the former Soviet Union. In addition to accompanied visits to authorities, search for housing and employment exchange, they provide a kindergarten for forty children and a school with more than forty pupils, as well as legal advice, language courses, care for the elderly and Jewish religious education. ZWST also offers a wide variety of leisure time activities such as dance and yoga groups, swimming club, music and literature events, cultural journeys to Jewish places of interest, and holiday camps for the youth. ZWST Hamburg is very important in a cultural way, too. Before the Second World War, the Jewish Talmud Torah school, built in 1805, was the largest school in north Germany, with 800 Jewish pupils.[26]

The following discussion present the results from the interviews, along with statements from an interview with Dr Michael Bader, alternate director of ZWST Germany, leader of the ZWST project on the integration of the disabled into the community, and initiator of the Network for Down's Syndrome, which was conducted in Frankfurt on 7 October 2008.

The focus of the presented material is on the changes which appeared when the borders of the former Soviet Union opened and the Jewish immigrants came to Germany. In particular we highlight how the ZWST has adapted to the flood of new members after 1990, and consider some of the new challenges the organization faces.

New Challenges

Until 1989, the Jewish community was comprised of a disproportionately high number of elderly persons and Holocaust survivors. Those persons are marked by the brokenness of the wish and the ability to live in the German society, a problem which illustrates their continued feelings of persecution and alienation. They have experienced trauma through long confinements in concentration camps and existential threat. Many survivors and their families could not find a home in Germany again and always kept in mind the possibility of going to Israel. Germany was mostly seen as transitional solution and not as a place for re-establishing Jewish life.

> I believe that these Holocaust survivors are always living in this ambivalent stance towards Germany . . . Most of those who were here before 1989 were survivors of concentration camps or ghettos and their descendents, who always lived here in this situation where they

actually did not want to live in this country and with some [thought of maybe moving] on or [going] to Israel. But [they] never [had] the status to build a long-term Jewish life here.[27]

After the fall of the Iron Curtain, and based on the wish of preserving the Jewish community, Jewish quota refugees were allowed to immigrate under certain limited conditions. Hundreds of thousands of Jews took the chance to leave their home countries which were stricken by the economic and political crisis, in addition to the oppression many people had to suffer from. The law on measures for refugees taken in during humanitarian relief actions (*HumHAG, Gesetz über Maßnahmen für im Rahmen humanitärer Hilfsaktionen aufgenommene Flüchtlinge*) offered an opportunity for 'persons of Jewish ancestry from the former Soviet Union, their marital partners and their unmarried underage children' to come to Germany and to be granted permanent residence.[28]

> We now have asylum seekers and refugees. Quota refugees have a secure status, so that means they are not in this process of recognition, but are already accepted when they arrive. That means, theoretically there's the liberation option, so they're migrants rather than refugees. They are coming – they came with the formal status, that has changed now, there's no status of quota refugee [any more]. The immigration law has changed. That means, [though] this immigration has significantly decreased, it is assumed that in the future, at most 2,000 to 4,000 persons of this group will immigrate annually.[29]

This caused a large influx of Soviet Jewish immigrants from 1990 until 2005, when the immigration regulations were retightened again. While the German government initially let everybody immigrate who had at least one Jewish parent, Jewish religious laws usually imply a different procedure. Further, the Soviet Union treated Judaism not as a religion but as the nationality. National identities were deemed transmitted from father to child, thus contradicting the traditional Jewish religious inheritance rules which focus on links through the female gender.

> It's a bit because being Jewish in the former Soviet Union wasn't a religion but a nationality. And that referred to the father. And this

contrasted with exactly this, that Judaism otherwise refers to the mother . . . frankly, for the German society and the Jewish community, it's a very difficult situation. Because for religious reasons, you cannot accept these people into the Jewish community; on the other hand, we naturally have to help.[30]

ZWST's task was to care for the newly arrived Jewish immigrants. But after legislation amendments in 2005, there were requirements the immigrants had to comply with, barring those with persecution experiences: They had to prove their financial independence, that they had no dual citizenship, their German language proficiency, and that a Jewish religious community would support and integrate them. ZWST's tasks were extended to checking the Jewish identity, which proved extremely difficult. They faced the duty of deciding who was Jewish and could immigrate and who was not.

This agreement means that we consequently are asked in terms of recognition procedure, and the ZWST basically has to give a statement whether these people can be accepted by them yet . . . The only thing that the ZWST does at this point is that it checks by means of the submitted documents whether the person is Jewish from a religious point of view.[31]

On the one hand, religious persons who had tried to maintain their religious traditional rites and practices on the quiet during the communist regime, which was hostile to the free practice of religion and even temporarily forbade it, were suddenly no Jews any more. On the other hand, 'legal Jewish persons' without any religious socialization could immigrate unmolested, this group representing the larger one of the two. Hence, only half of those who immigrated under the conditions of *HumHAG* were integrated in one of the Jewish communities.

The new clientele, the so-called 'Ostjuden' (Eastern Jews), had experienced deaths in their families as well, mostly through mass shootings in the German-occupied territories. But they had fought as soldiers in the Red Army during the Great Patriotic War rather than falling victim to the Nazi's Europe-wide euthanasia. After the end of the German Reich, the veterans had been venerated as heroes and had been highly decorated. Those who were killed were remembered as patriots rather than as Jews. Hence, the immigrants do not share the entire Holocaust trauma and consequently, coping with the past has a different meaning emotionally as well as historically.

The main task of ZWST today is split into two issues: providing religious and cultural services for the old-established members, and fighting problems of poor people from the 'Eastern bloc', which includes various social services. The most important problem for the immigrants is integrating in a new society where their degrees and diplomas are not recognized, where they depend on transfer income, where they are unemployed and do not speak the native language.

> But we have the problem that we naturally also have many immigrants . . . between 40 and 60, and with these people the professional integration is a . . . huge problem . . . in contrast to the repatriates, we deal with a group of people 70 per cent of which have a university degree . . . So there are very, very many poor persons . . . because very many of the target group receive basic social welfare [*Grundsicherung*] or long-term unemployment benefits [*Arbeitslosengeld II*] . . . This means that the status loss is very, very high and someone who has had such a high status has little motivation [to try especially hard] for [a job as] an assistant . . . that he could maybe get.[32]

The group of persons who came to Germany is highly selective. Those whose chances on the labour market were low because of their age, and who had difficulties in making ends meet, emigrated to make a better living.

Indeed, many of the immigrants turned to the ZWST and asked for help with services which the organization had rarely provided before.

> . . . these people with migration experience shape our welfare situation at the moment . . . There are people who expect new answers of this welfare association; that means, the answers that this welfare association has given for decades in the post-war period have to be partly modified.[33]

The organization as a whole is still on the way to becoming a welfare organization. It had to establish services such as interpreting, accompanying visits to authorities, medical care, care for the elderly with home visits and funeral services, assistance with house and job hunting, but also several cultural services, preserving music, language and literature of their home countries.

> That means . . . the Jewish communities have a special interest in these immigrants . . . we support [them] in every regard, especially, let's say, in counselling – we work towards their social and professional integration and basically combine the integration into the Jewish community with [integration] into the German society.[34]

Additionally, the new members were instructed in the Jewish religion, with the goal of reviving the identification with the Jewish belief which was repressed and forgotten during decades of communist regimes.

> . . . These people have to want it, to be guided towards Judaism; [they] have themselves very little knowledge about being Jewish. It can be compared a bit with the situation of repatriates who . . . were also nationally considered Germans in the former Soviet Union, [but] come from Kazakhstan and suddenly are considered Russians here. And . . . if you ask them, 'So what is the cultural commonality with the Germans?', [they] don't know exactly.[35]

Liberal and Orthodox Communities

Although the orthodox communities believe that a Jew is someone who has a Jewish mother, the federal office of the ZWST reported that liberal facilities integrated those whose Jewish identity was not given from the religious point of view.[36]

> . . . And then there are the other people [where] the mother was [not] Jewish, but the father was Jewish . . . there . . . can be the verification that he basically can immigrate; he can then also become [a] member for example of a liberal Jewish community.[37]

211

Despite the fact that the liberal communities work under the auspices of the old-established Jewish communities, they are less orthodox, for financial reasons, among other things. They established different and less tight rules, e.g., not separating males and females at the synagogues and accepting female rabbis, and homosexuality. They see the Jewish religion as 'cultural tradition and the historical experiences of the Jewish people as part of their own identity', but they believe 'that every generation should interpret the Jewish doctrine itself' considering ethical and humanitarian aspects which are more important than rites.[38]

While ZWST's services before 1990 had mainly focused on preserving the memory of the victims of death-camp atrocities and euthanasia, lobbying for the Jewish society, cultural activities and religious education for the shrinking proportion of Jewish youth, the situation and work totally changed with the new Jewish immigrants. Since that time, ZWST's work has been characterized by the migrants of the former Soviet Union and their needs and problems.[39]

The less strict rules and openness of the liberal communities provide a huge attraction for the immigrated Jews. The fact that the communities not only support those immigrants with a Jewish background in the sense of maternal ancestry but create an inclusive environment, premised on less mandatory religious effort and space for interpretation and dialogue within and between different expressions of Judaism, gave 'new Jews' a wider sense of belonging, especially for the majority of the immigrants for whom the practice of religion might have decreased in significance during its oppression in the Soviet Union.

So by now there are about a hundred Jewish communities in Germany again, entirely new communities . . . there are Jewish communities that, especially in East Germany . . . are . . . more than 90 per cent immigrants. And then it's just the task of the ZWST to not just build a welfare system, but basically provide infrastructural help and build a community in the first place. It's basically that the Jewish communities and especially the ZWST are seen by the German state authorities, especially by the Federal Office for Migration and Refugees, as integration accelerators.[40]

New associations without a connection to the old-established communities were founded based on different traditions. Some community members see this as a regular evolutionary process which society as a whole goes through and which opens new possibilities. Some feel threatened and consider the Jewish religion weakened.

> Since there are different stances . . . there are political tensions . . . But it's also about the question, 'What is a Jewish community, what is there at all?' So it's really about very basic questions. You just have to acknowledge that, and that's also the challenge, for the welfare association as well. That means, many things have to be clarified. We come from a field where all of this was very straightforward . . . and today we are in a different time. And not everything can be managed centrally, but there will be diversity . . . For some, that's threatening . . . and others can see an opportunity in that . . . At the moment we are also in a phase like that, where you also still have to learn a lot, together.[41]

Outlook

The interviews with the Jewish representatives left a lasting impression on the German FACIT team. We met deeply committed personalities and were told inspiring stories about voluntary work which had been taken on by the Jewish communities for the last twenty years. Many of the facilities serve as a device through which old-established Jewish members and new members can belong, organize events, meetings, counselling and leisure facilities, and therefore contribute to the integration of their own group. The ZWST represents a key hub for immigrants in generating relationships of trust, developing language skills and accessing vital services. Most of all, in a context of increasing population mobility, these community facilities, although much smaller than prominent welfare providers, are crucial services for meeting the needs of migrants in a manner which is culturally relevant. The increasing membership of the ZWST is seen by Dr Michael Bader and others as a chance to consolidate and to reinvigorate the Jewish community, by creating an encounter view that enriches different denominational cultures, whilst avoiding the recognizable danger of failing to cross group boundaries among non-Jewish affiliations. Hence, the new situation is not simply seen as a difficult task of integration, but as a fruitful path for German Jews in the twenty-first century.

Endnotes

Chapter 1

1 Our interest in FBOs has been formed in part during an EU Seventh Framework research programme: 'Faith-based Organisations and Social Exclusion in European Cities' (FACIT). The academic findings of that programme are published in J. Beaumont and P. Cloke, eds., *Faith-based Organisations and Exclusion in European Cities* (Bristol: Policy Press, 2012).

2 See P. Cloke, J. May and S. Johnsen, *Swept-Up Lives?: Re-envisioning the Homeless City* (Chichester: Wiley-Blackwell, 2010).

3 J. Caputo, *On Religion* (London: Routledge, 2001), p. 92.

4 See for example, S. Murray, *Post-Christendom: Church and Mission in a Strange World* (Carlisle: Paternoster Press, 2004).

5 For a detailed discussion of theo-ethics, see P. Cloke, 'Theo-ethics and Radical Faith-based Praxis in the Postsecular City', in *Exploring the Postsecular: The Religious, the Political and the Urban* (eds. A. Molendijk, J. Beaumont and C. Jedan; Amsterdam: Brill, 2010), pp. 223–41.

6 Prominent contributions of this group include: R. Dawkins, *The God Delusion* (London: Bantam Press, 2006); D. Dennett, *Breaking the Spell: Religion as a Natural Phenomenon* (Harmondsworth: Penguin, 2006); D. Hitchens, *God is Not Great* (London: Atlantic Books, 2007).

7 A key author of the Third Way philosophy is A. Giddens, *Where Now For New Labour?* (Cambridge: Polity Press, 2002); see also A. Dinham, 'From Faith in the City to Faithful Cities: The "Third Way", the Church of England and Urban Regeneration'. *Urban Studies* 45 (2008): pp. 2163–74.

8 P. Scott, C. Baker and E. Graham, eds., *Remoralizing Britain?: Social, Ethical and Theological Perspectives on New Labour* (London: Continuum, 2009).

9   A. Dinham and V. Lowndes, 'Religion, Resources and Representation: Three Narratives of Faith Engagement in Urban Governance', *Urban Affairs Review* 43 (6) (2008); pp. 817–45.

10 In this context, see A. Aldridge, *Religion in the Contemporary World* (Cambridge: Polity Press, 2000); G. Davie, *The Sociology of Religion* (London: Sage, 2007).

11 See C. Baker, *Hybrid Church in the City* (Aldershot: Ashgate, 2007); C. Baker and H. Skinner, *Faith in Action: The Dynamic Connection Between Spiritual Capital and Religious Capital* (Manchester: William Temple Foundation, 2006).

12 This is discussed in detail in V. Lowndes and R. Chapman, *Faith, Hope and Clarity: Developing A Model of Faith Group Involvement in Civil Renewal* (Leicester: De Montfort University, 2005).

13 P. Cloke, J. May and S. Johnsen, 'Ethical citizenship? Volunteers and the Ethics of Providing Services for Homeless People', *Geoforum* 38 (2007): pp. 1089–1101.

14 V. Lowndes and G. Smith, *Faith-based Voluntary Action* (Swindon: ESRC Seminar Series, 2006), p. 7.

15 See P. Cloke, 'Geography and Invisible Powers: Philosophy, Social Action and Prophetic Potential', in C. Brace, A. Bailey, S. Carter, D. Harvey, and N. Thomas, eds., *Emerging Geographies of Belief* (Newcastle: Cambridge Scholars, 2011), pp. 9–29.

16 See W. Brueggemann, *The Prophetic Imagination* (Minneapolis, MA: Fortress Press, second edn, 2006); W. Wink, *Naming the Powers* (Fortress Press, Minneapolis, MA: Fortress Press, 1984).

17 Key sources include: B. Cairns, M. Harris and R. Huchinson, *Faithful Regeneration* (Birmingham: Centre of Voluntary Action Research, Aston Business School, 2005); A. Dinham, *Faith, Public Policy and Civil Society: Policies, Problems and Concepts in Faith-based Public Action* (Basingstoke: Palgrave-Macmillan, 2009); A. Dinham, R. Furbey and V. Lowndes, eds., *Faith in the Public Realm: Controversies, Policies and Practices* (Bristol: Policy Press, 2009); R. Furbey and M. Macey, 'Religion and urban regeneration: a place for faith?', *Policy and Politics* 33, (2005): pp. 95–116; V. Jochum, B. Pratten and K. Wilding, *Faith and Voluntary Action: An Overview of Current Evidence and Debates* (London: NCVO, 2007; Lowndes and Chapman, *Faith, Hope and Clarity*, op cit.).

18 P. Cloke, A. Williams and S. Thomas, 'Faith-based Organisations and Social Exclusion in the United Kingdom', in (eds. D. Dierckx, J. Vranken and W. Kerstens), *Faith-based Organisations and Social*

Exclusion in European Cities: National Context Reports (Leuven: Acco, 2009), pp. 283–342.

19 W. Larner, 'Neoliberalism: Policy, Ideology, Governmentality', *Studies in Political Economy* 63 (2000): pp. 5–25.

20 See J. Peck and A. Tickell, 'Neoliberalising Space', *Antipode* 34 (2002): pp. 380–404; J. Hackworth, 'Compassionate Neoliberalism?: Evangelical Christianity, the Welfare State and the Politics of the Right', *Studies of Political Economy* 86 (2010): pp. 83–108; J. Hackworth, 'Faith, Welfare and the City: The Mobilisation of Religious Organisations for Neoliberal Ends', *Urban Geography* 31 (2010): pp. 750–73; J. Hackworth, *Faith-based: Religious Neoliberalism and the Politics of Welfare* (Athens, GA: University of Georgia, 2012); D. Trudeau and L. Veronis, 'Enacting State Restructuring: NGOs as "translation mechanisms"', *Environment and Planning D: Society and Space* 27 (2009): pp. 1117–34.

21 W. Connolly, 'The Evangelical-Capitalist Resonance Machine', *Political Theory* 33 (2005): pp. 869–86; V. Lyon-Callo, 'Cool Cities or Class Analysis: Exploring Popular Consent to Neoliberal Domination and Exploitation', *Rethinking Marxism* 20 (2008): pp. 28–41.

22 J. Wolch, *The Shadow State: Government and Voluntary Sector in Transition* (New York: The Foundation Center, 1990).

23 Peck and Tickell, 'Neoliberalising Space', op cit., p. 20.

24 See for example, M. Harris, *Organising God's Work: Challenges for Churches and Synagogues* (Basingstoke: Macmillan, 1998); M. Harris, P. Halfpenny and C. Rochester, 'A Social Policy Role for Faith-based Organisations? Lessons from the UK Jewish Voluntary Sector', *Journal of Social Policy* 32 (2003): pp. 93–112.

25 See R. Edwards, *Believing In Local Action* (London: Church Urban Fund, 2008); Home Office Faith Communities Unit, *Working Together: Co-operation between Government and Faith Communities* (London: Home Office, 2004); Department of Communities and Local Government, *Face to Face and Side by Side* (London, DCLG, 2008).

26 See Common Wealth, 'Common Wealth: Christians for Economic and Social Justice' (2010)
http://commonwealthnetwork2010.blogspot.com (accessed 9 October 2012).

27 See especially, A. Williams, P. Cloke and S. Thomas, 'Co-constituting Neoliberalism: Faith-based Organisations, Co-option and Resistance in the UK', *Environment and Planning A* 44 (2012): pp. 1479–1501.

217

28 D. Conradson, 'Expressions of Charity and Action towards Social Justice: Faith-based Welfare in Urban New Zealand', *Urban Studies* 45 (2008): pp. 2117–41.

29 Conradson, 'Expressions of Charity and Action towards Social Justice', p. 2129.

30 See M. Barnes and D. Prior, eds., *Subversive Citizens: Power, Agency and Resistance in Public Services* (Bristol: Policy Press, 2009).

31 C. Barnett, N. Clarke, P. Cloke and A. Malpass, 'The Elusive Subjects of Neo-liberalism: Beyond the Analytics of Governmentality', *Cultural Studies* 22 (2008): pp. 624–53; C. Barnett, 'Publics and Markets: What's Wrong with Neoliberalism', in *The Handbook of Social Geography* (eds. S. Smith, S. Marston, R. Pain and J.P. Jones; London: Sage, 2009).

32 Cloke et al, 'Faith-based Organisations', op cit.

33 Williams et al, 'Co-constituting Neoliberalism', op cit.

34 Dinham, 'Faith, Public Policy', op cit.

35 Williams et al, 'Co-constituting Neoliberalism', op cit., p. 29.

36 P. Cloke, S. Thomas and A. Williams (2012) 'Radical Faith Praxis', in *Faith-Based Organisations* (eds. P. Beaumont and P. Cloke), op cit.

37 R. Coles, *Rethinking Generosity: Critical Theory and the Politics of Caritas* (Ithaca, NY: Cornell University Press, 1997).

38 See for example, J. Beaumont and C. Baker, eds., *Postsecular Cities: Space, Theory and Practice* (London: Continnum, 2011).

39 P. Cloke and J. Beaumont, 'Geographies of Postsecular Rapprochement in the City', *Progress in Human Geography*, 37 (2012), p. 28.

40 P. Cloke, 'Emerging Postsecular Rapprochement in the Contemporary City', in *Postsecular Cities* (Beaumont and Baker, 2011), op cit.

41 P. Berger, ed., *The Desecularization of the World: Resurgent Religion and World Politics* (Grand Rapids, MI: Eerdmans, 1999); D. Martin, *On Secularisation: Towards a Revised General Theory* (Aldershot: Ashgate, 2005); J. Wilford, 'Sacred archipelagos: geographies of secularization', *Progress in Human Geography* 34 (2010): pp. 328–48.

42 P. Cloke, J. May and S. Johnsen, 'Exploring Ethos? Discourses of "Charity" in the Provision of Emergency Services for Homeless People', *Environment and Planning* A 37 (2006): pp. 385–402.

43 L. Jamoul and J. Wills, 'Faith in Politics', *Urban Studies* 45 (2008): pp. 2035–66; A. Ivereigh, *Faithful Citizens* (London: Darton, Longman and Todd, 2010).

44 Cloke, 'Emergent Postsecular Rapprochement', op cit.

[45] P. Blond, 'Introduction: Theology Before Philosophy', in *Post-secular Philosophy: Between Philosophy and Theology* (ed. P. Blond; London: Routledge, 1998), pp. 1–66.

[46] J. Milbank, 'Materialism and Transcendence', in *Theology and the Political: New Debates* (eds. C. Davis, J. Milbank and S. Žižek; Durham, NC: Duke University Press, 2005), pp. 393–426.

[47] J. Birdwell and M. Littler, *Why Those Who Do God, Do Good: Faithful Citizens* (London: Demos, 2012), p. 20.

[48] R. Hutter, *Suffering Divine Things: Theology as Church Practice* (Grand Rapids, MI: Eerdmans, 1997); M. Oakley, 'Reclaiming Faith', in *Spirituality in the City* (ed. A Walker; London, SPCK 2005), pp. 1–14.

[49] T. Wright, *Surprised by Hope* (London: SPCK, 2010); Cloke, 'Theo-ethics', op cit.

[50] J. Habermas, 'An awareness of what is missing', in *An Awareness of What is Missing; Faith and Reason in a Postsecular Age* (eds. J. Habermas, J. Brieskorn, M. Reder, F. Ricken and J. Schmidt; Cambridge: Polity Press, 2010), pp. 15–23.

[51] Cloke and Beaumont, 'Geographies of Postsecular Rapprochement', op cit., p. 37.

[52] Baker and Beaumont, 'Postsecular Cities', op cit.

[53] Cloke and Beaumont, 'Geographies of Postsecular Rapprochement', op cit., p. 34.

Chapter 2

[1] This idea is commonly illustrated by the biblical statement that 'He who oppresses the poor shows contempt for their Maker, but whoever is kind to the needy honours God' (Prov. 14: 31, NIV).

[2] Christian Aid, *Doing Justice to Poverty* (London: Christian Aid, 2008).

[3] J. Kirkby, 'The Silent Misery of Britain's Indebted Poor', *Parliamentary Brief Online*, 1 September 2010 (accessed at: http://parliamentarybrief.com/2010/09), p. 2.

[4] J. Kirkby, *Nevertheless* (Bradford: CAP Books, 2010).

[5] Kirkby, *Nevertheless*, p. 22.

[6] Kirkby, *Nevertheless*, p. 23.

[7] Kirkby, *Nevertheless*, p. 103.

[8] Kirkby, *Nevertheless*.

[9] J. Kirkby, 'The Silent Misery', p. 1.

10 A. Hawthorne, CEO and founder of The Message Trust, cover review of CAP, *Journeys of Hope* (Bradford: CAP Books, 2009).
11 CAP, *Journeys of Hope*, p. 23.
12 CAP, *Journeys of Hope*, p. 25.
13 P. Cloke and J. Beaumont, 'Geographies of Postsecular Rapprochement in the City', *Progress in Human Geography* 37 (2012), pp. 27–51.
14 I. Gallagher, 'Christian group ditched by charity . . . for offering to pray for debt victims', *Mail Online* (2011) http://www.dailymail.co.uk/news/article-2033456) (accessed 2 September 2011).
15 R. Murphy, *The Case for an Interest Rate Cap in the UK*, report prepared for Church Action on Poverty, The New Economics Foundation and Debt on our Doorstep (2003) www.church-poverty.org.uk (accessed 2 September 2011).
16 C. Howson, *A Just Church: 21st Century Liberation Theory in Action* (London: Continuum, 2011), p. 117.
17 See the discussion in A. Williams, P. Cloke and S. Thomas, 'Co-constituting Neoliberalism: Co-option, Resistance and Faith-based Organisations in the UK'. *Environment and Planning A* 44 (2012): pp. 1479–1501.
18 Interview with Niall Cooper, 2011.
19 N. Oakley, *Engaging Politics: The Tensions of Christian Political Involvement* (Milton Keynes: Paternoster, 2007).
20 This phrase is commonly attributed to the biblical verse, 'I have come that they may have life, and have it to the full' (John 10:10, NIV).
21 Interview with Niall Cooper, 2011.
22 Maria Miller, minister with responsibility for Child Poverty, speaking at an All Party Parliamentary Group on Poverty, 4 July 2011, in N. Cooper, *The Pain of Poverty: Does Income Matter?* (2011) http://niallcooper.wordpress.com/2011/07/08/the- pain-of-poverty-does-income-matter (accessed 9 October 2012).
23 T. Campolo, *Red Letter Christians: A Citizens Guide to Faith and Politics* (Ventura: Regal, 2008); R. Sider (2008) *The Scandal of Evangelical Politics: Why are Christians missing the chance to really change the world* (Grand Rapids, MI: Baker Books, 2008); J. Wallis, *God's Politics: Why the American Right Gets it Wrong and the Left Doesn't Get It* (Oxford: Lion Hudson, 2005).
24 G. Gutierrez, *A Theology of Liberation: History, Politics and Salvation* (New York: Orbis Books, 1971); P. Freire, *Pedagogy of the Oppressed* (New York: Continuum, 1970).

[25] R. Furbey and M. Macey, 'Religion and Urban Regeneration: A Place for Faith?', *Policy & Politics*, 33(1) (2005): pp. 95–116; V. Lowndes and G. Smith, *Faith-based Voluntary Action* (Swindon: ESRC Seminar Series, 2006).

[26] Interview with Niall Cooper, 2011.

[27] Interview with Niall Cooper, 2011.

[28] C. Howson, *A Just Church*, p. 118.

[29] Howson, *A Just Church*, p. 119.

[30] Common Wealth, 'Common Wealth: Christians for Economic and Social Justice' (2010), available online from http://commonwealthnetwork2010.blogspot.com/ (accessed 2 September 2011).

[31] B. Walsh and S. Keesmaat, *Colossians Remixed: Subverting the Empire* (Westmont, IL: IVP, 2004).

[32] D. McIntyre, A. Stewart, L. Brill and J. Jarman, *Invisible Workers: The Informal Economy* (Manchester: Community Pride Initiative/Oxfam UK Poverty, 2009).

[33] Interview with Niall Cooper, 2011.

[34] Methodist Conference, 'Tax avoidance impoverishes the vulnerable and is morally unacceptable, says Church' (2011) http://www.methodistconference.org.uk/news/latest-news/tax-avoidance-impoverishes-the-vulnerable-and-is-morally-unacceptable-says-church (accessed 9 October 2012).

[35] In addition to those already mentioned, CAoP has contributed heavily in several broad-based campaigns (namely, Living Wage, Still Human Still Here, Robin Hood Tax) and national demonstrations such as the March for the Alternative in London, 26 March 2011, against the coalition government's cuts in public spending, and their disproportionate effect on poor and vulnerable people.

[36] J. Ranciere, *Dissensus: On Politics and Aesthetics* (London: Continuum, 2010). However, the concept of the 'post-political' can be overly generalized in its application, and can be critiqued for conflating politics with democracy, both narrowly defined. See N. Gill, P. Johnstone and A. Williams, 'Towards a Geography of Tolerance: Post-Politics and Political Forms of Tolerance', *Political Geography*, 31 (8) (2012); pp. 509–18..

[37] Williams et al., 'Co-Constituting Neoliberalism,' op cit.

[38] W. Connolly, *Why I Am Not a Secularist* (Minneapolis, MN: University of Minnesota Press, 2000).

39 See P. Cloke, 'Theo-ethics and Faith Praxis in the Postsecular City', in *Exploring the Postsecular: The Religious, the Political and the Urban* (eds. A Molendijk, J Beaumont and C Jedan; Amsterdam: Brill, 2010), pp. 223–43; P. Cloke, S. Thomas and A. Williams, 'Radical Faith Praxis', in *Faith-based Organisations and Exclusion in European Cities* (eds. J. Beaumont and P. Cloke; Bristol: Policy Press, 2012).

40 See Isaiah 10:1,2, 'Woe to those who make unjust laws, to those who issue oppressive decrees, to deprive the poor of their rights and withhold justice from the oppressed of my people' NIV.

41 K. Brewin, *Other: Loving Self, God and Neighbour in a World of Fractures* (London: Hodder & Stoughton, 2010), p. 123; A. Kaplan, *Development Practitioners and Social Process – Artists of the Invisible* (London: Pluto, 2002).

42 See J. Edwards, *An Agenda For Change* (Zondervan, MN: Grand Rapids, 2007).

Chapter 3

1 Practical theology broadly denotes the application of theological reflection to areas of Christian ministry. Here I focus primarily on the self-other relations visible in the ethos and practice of Christian organizations serving drug users.

2 My focus on Christian organizations here is simply a matter of discussing what I know best. By using two Christian organizations which have distinctive styles of ministry, I wish to centre analytical attention on the practical theologies and contexts that inspire such action. My decision to illustrate issues of care ethics and how people deal with 'otherness' through case studies of Christian organizations does not imply a neglect of other faith positions. Broadening out analysis to cross-faith comparisons would foreground dimensions that are not the prime concern of this chapter.

3 The book documents the founding of Teen Challenge, a ministry started in the 1950s with New York gang and drug culture drug users. See D. Wilkerson, *The Cross and the Switchblade* (London: Marshall Pickering, 1963).

4 This book tells of Pullinger's work with St Stephen's Society, which provides rehabilitation homes for recovering drug addicts, prostitutes, and gang members in Hong Kong. See J. Pullinger, *Chasing the Dragon* (London: Hodder & Stoughton, 1980).

5 This book is a collection of testimonies of the early days of Betel, an international network of Christian communities for the addicted. See S. Dinnen and M. Dinnen, *Rescue Shop within a Yard of Hell* (Fearn, Tain: Christian Focus, 1995, 2000a).

6 This is most explicit in US watchdog groups which call for the investigation of coercive 'behavioural manipulation' in faith-based organizations such as Teen Challenge. See https://teenchallengecult.blogspot.com/andhttp://www.dailykos.com/story/2008/4/28/17428/8172/453/503981 (accessed 22 October 2012).

7 O. Elisha, 'You can't talk to an empty stomach: Faith-based Activism, Holistic Evangelism, and the Publicity of Evangelical Engagement' in *Proselytisation Revisited: Rights Talk, Free Markets and Culture Wars* (ed. R. Hackett; London: Equinox Publishing, 2008).

8 E. Thiessen, *The Ethics of Evangelism: A Philosophical Defence of Ethical Proselytising and Persuasion* (Milton Keynes: Paternoster Press, 2011).

9 P. Cloke, J. May and S. Johnsen, 'Exploring ethos? Discourses of "Charity" in the Provision of Emergency Services for Homeless People', *Environment and Planning A* 37 (2005): pp. 385–402.

10 G. Chereau, *We Dance Because We Cannot Fly* (Lancaster: Sovereign World, 2003), p. 195.

11 WEC International is a large inter-church evangelical mission body with a membership of 1,600 organizations working in fifty-five countries around the world. Its outreach activities are often with the world's poorest, most marginalized and forgotten peoples, and have given birth to several ministries in addition to Betel. For example, Rainbows of Hope works with children across the world suffering pain and trauma – victims of war, HIV/AIDS, sexual exploitation, child labour, life on the streets and poverty.

12 'Not in my back yard' attitudes; for instance, the acknowledgement that drug services are needed in society but should be located elsewhere.

13 Chereau, op cit.; Dinnen and Dinnen, op cit.; and S. Dinnen and M. Dinnen, *Sacking the Frontiers of Hell* (Fearn, Tain: Christian Focus, 2000b).

14 The majority of drug treatment services in the UK are geared towards 'in the community' care. Residential treatment tends to be increasingly focused on outputs rather than outcomes. It is clear that faith-based residential rehabilitation services are filling a gap left

after the paradigm change from therapeutic communities towards user-involvement services. On the rise and fall of secular therapeutic communities: R. Yates, 'A brief moment of glory: the impact of the therapeutic community movement on the drug treatment systems in the UK', *International Journal of Social Welfare* 12 (2003): pp. 239–43; On the changing role of the voluntary sector in drug services, see A. Mold and V. Berridge, *Voluntary Action and Illegal Drugs: Health and Society in Britain Since the 1960s* (Basingstoke and New York: Palgrave Macmillan, 2010). For further information on the historical and contemporary role of faith-based drug services in the UK, see A. Williams, 'Geographies of Faith, Welfare and Substance Abuse: From Neoliberalism to Postsecular Ethics', unpublished doctoral thesis, University of Exeter, 2012.

[15] Interview with several of the Betel residents, 2010, during a four-week residential placement in one of the UK centres.

[16] Interview with one of the Betel leaders.

[17] Focus group with residents.

[18] E. Tepper, 'Why Community' in *Sacking the Frontiers of Hell* (eds. S. and M. Dinnen; Fearn, Tain: Christian Focus Publications, 2000b), pp. 202–6.

[19] Tepper, 'Why Community' in *Sacking the Frontiers of Hell*, p. 204.

[20] E. Thiessen, op cit.

[21] Interview with Betel pastor, 2010.

[22] E. Tepper, op cit., p. 203.

[23] Louise Newman, a professor of psychiatry at the University of Newcastle and a former director of the NSW Institute of Psychiatry, quoted in 'They sought help, but got exorcism and the Bible' (R. Pollard; *The Sydney Morning Herald*, 17 March 2008; R. Pollard, 'Lives at risk when vulnerable patients taken in by cult-like groups' (R. Pollard; *The Sydney Morning Herald*, 17 March 2008).

[24] A striking geographic feature of Rotterdam is the fact that its low income and deprived neighbourhoods and districts are located just outside the city centre, more than in the periphery areas (the opposite of Amsterdam or Paris). Rotterdam has the most segregated areas of the Dutch cities.

[25] For further information on postsecular caritas, see: R. Coles, *Rethinking Generosity: Critical Theory and the Politics of* Caritas (Ithaca, NY: Cornell University Press, 1997); P. Cloke, 'Theo-ethics and Faith Praxis in the Postsecular City', in *Exploring the Postsecular: The Religious, the*

Political and the Urban (eds. A. Molendijk, J. Beaumont and C. Jedan; Amsterdam: Brill, 2010), pp. 223–43.

26 This echoes Proverbs 14:31: 'Whoever oppresses a poor man insults his Maker, but he who is generous to the needy honours him' (ESV).

27 M. Volf, *Exclusion and Embrace: A Theological Exploration of Identity, Otherness, and Reconciliation* (Nashville: Abingdon Press, 1996).

28 For more on the notion of postsecular reapprochement: P. Cloke and J. Beaumont, 'Geographies of Postsecular Rapprochement in the City', *Progress in Human Geography*, 37 (2012), pp. 27–51.

29 H. Bey, T.A.Z. Autonomedia (2003), access online http://www.hermetic.com/bey/taz3.html#labelTAZ, p. 95 (accessed 9 October 2012); also see K. Brewin, *Other: Loving Self, God and Neighbour in a World of Fractures* (London: Hodder & Stoughton, 2010), p. 191.

30 See the chapter by M. Davelaar, A. Williams and J. Beaumont (this volume) for further development of this idea.

31 Interview with Reverend Dick Couvée, 2009; Website: http://www.pauluskerkrotterdam.nl/ (accessed 9 October 2012).

32 For more details on contemporary changes in evangelical theology and postmodern belief in the context of social activism; see P. Cloke, S. Thomas and A. Williams, 'Radical Faith Praxis', in *Faith, Welfare and Exclusion in European Cities: The FBO Phenomenon* (eds. J. Beaumont, P. Cloke and J. Vranken; Bristol: The Policy Press, 2012).

33 P Cloke, op cit.

34 K. Brewin, op cit.

Chapter 4

1 For further analysis see P. Cloke, A. Williams and S. Thomas, 'Radical Faith Praxis', in *Faith, Welfare and Exclusion in European Cities: The FBO Phenomenon* (eds. J. Beaumont, P. Cloke and J. Vranken; Bristol: The Policy Press, 2012).

2 Cloke et al., 'Radical Faith Praxis'.

3 A. Grinnel, 'The Forgotten Five%' (2010). Research paper, available at: http://www2.salvationarmy.org.uk/uki/www_614uk.nsf/0/CA2B6C898B35E39E802576AA003DDB70/$file/Forgotten5-January2010.pdf (accessed: 5 February, 2012).

4 614UK (2010) Salvation Army 614UK. Available at: http://www2.salvationarmy.org.uk/uki/www_614uk.nsf (accessed: 5 February 2012).

5   614UK, as above.
6   The research forms part of the author's current ethnographic PhD research in Human Geography at Exeter University.
7   See http://www.edn-network.org.
8   Statistics from http://www.neighbourhood.statistics.gov.uk
9   See D. Ritchie, 'One Oldham One Future' (2001), available at: http://resources.cohesioninstitute.org.uk/Publications/Documents/Document/Default.aspx?recordId=97 (accessed 29 October 2012) and T. Cantle, 'Review of Community Cohesion in Oldham' (2006), available at http://www.oldham.gov.uk/ (accessed 4 February 2012).
10 Statistics from http://www.neighbourhood.statistics.gov.uk (accessed 9 October 2012).
11 Statistics from http://www.neighbourhood.statistics.gov.uk (accessed 9 October 2012).
12 For more details, see both M. Wilson, *Eden: Called to the Streets* (London: Kingsway Publications, 2005), and D. Green, *Redeeming our Communities: 21st Century Miracles of Social Transformation* (Chichester: New Wine Press, 2008).
13 Eden Oldham, 'Vision and Values' (2010). Available at: http://www.edenoldham.com/vision-and-values/ (accessed 17 February 2012).
14 Eden Oldham, 'Vision and Values'.
15 See parallels with case study in the Netherlands, 'Faith-based Organizations and Urban Social Justice in the Netherlands', in *Tijdschrift voor economische en sociale geografie,* vol. 99, no. 4 (J. Beaumont and C. Dias; 2008), pp. 382–92.
16 See Beaumont et al., as above, pp. 387.
17 Personal interview, March 2010.
18 See P. Cloke, J. May and S. Johnsen, *Swept-Up Lives?: Re-envisioning the Homeless City* (Chichester: Wiley-Blackwell, 2010).
19 Personal interview, March 2010.
20 See www.hchealthcare.org (accessed 9 October 2012).
21 See criticisms of contemporary humanists, for example Richard Dawkins, *The God Delusion* (London: Transworld Publishers, 2006).
22 See Rebecca Allahyari, *Visions of Charity* (Berkeley and LA, CA: University of California Press, 2000).
23 See for example S. Claiborne, *Irresistible Revolution: Living as an Ordinary Radical* (London: Zondervan, 2006).

[24] See for example E. Graham and S. Lowe, *What Makes a Good City?* (London: DLT, 2009).

[25] See M. Frost, *Exiles: Living Missionally in a Post-Christian Culture* (MA: Hendrickson Publishers, 2006).

[26] www.justlife.org.uk (accessed 9 October 2012).

[27] G. Bishop, *Darkest England and the Way Back In* (Milton Keynes: Authentic Media, 2007).

[28] Bishop, *Darkest England and the Way Back In*, p. 60.

[29] Bishop, *Darkest England and the Way Back In*, p. 65, emphasis added.

[30] See S. Claiborne, op cit., and www.thesimpleway.org (accessed 9 October 2012).

[31] See for example, Mission Year UK www.missionyear.org.uk and the Eden-Network www.eden-network.org (accessed 9 October 2012).

[32] See Urban Expression chapter by Mike Pears this volume and www.urbanexpression.org.uk.

[33] For a great discussion of the church after Christendom, see S. Murray, *Post-Christendom: Church and Mission in a Strange World* (Milton Keynes: Paternoster Press, 2004).

[34] D. Guder, *The Continuing Conversion of the Church* (Grand Rapids, MI: Eerdmans, 2000).

[35] See Matthew 9:13 (ESV).

[36] See www.eden-network.org.uk (accessed 9 October 2012).

[37] See Wilson, *Eden: Called to the Streets.*

[38] See for example T. Wright, *Virtue Reborn* (London: SPCK, 2010), and L. Bretherton and R. Rook, *Living Out Loud: Conversations About Virtue, Ethics, and Evangelicalism* (Milton Keynes: Paternoster, 2010).

[39] Personal interview, October 2009.

[40] P Cloke, 'Theo-ethics and Radical Faith-based Praxis in the Postsecular City', in *Exploring the Postsecular: The Religious, the Political and the Urban, International Studies in Religion*, 13 (ed. Arie Molendijk, Justin Beaumont and Christoph Jedan; Amsterdam: Brill, 2010).

[41] G. Ward, 'Suffering and Incarnation', in T*he Blackwell Companion to Postmodern Theology* (ed. G. Ward; Oxford: Blackwell Publishing, 2001), pp. 192–208.

[42] See S. Žižek, *The Fragile Absolute: Or, Why is the Christian Legacy Worth Fighting For?* (London: Verso, 2000).

[43] See for example Luke 7:36; Mark 1:41; Luke 5:13.

[44] For interesting critical analysis of liberal tolerance see www.lacan.com/zizek- inquiry.html (accessed 9 October 2012).

45   See M. Volf, *Exclusion and Embrace: A Theological Exploration of Identity, Otherness, and Reconciliation* (Nashville, TN: Abingdon Press, 1996).
46   L. Bretherton, *Hospitality as Holiness: Christian Witness Amid Moral Diversity* (Aldershot: Ashgate, 2006).
47   See K. Brewin, *Other: Loving Self, God and Neighbour in a World of Fractures* (London: Hodder & Stoughton, 2010).
48   See Brewin, *Other: Loving Self, God and Neigbour in a World of Fractures*.
49   See L. Bretherton, *Christianity and Contemporary Politics* (Oxford: Blackwell Publishing, 2010).
50   See H. Halter and M. Smay, *The Tangible Kingdom: Creating Incarnational Community* (San Francisco, CA: Jossey-Bass, 2008).
51   See Bretherton, *Christianity and Contemporary Politics*.
52   See Cloke, 'Theo-ethics and Radical Faith-based Praxis in the Postsecular City'.
53   1 Peter 3:15, NIV.
54   See Owen Jones's insightful book entitled *Chavs: The Demonization of the Working Class* (London: Verso, 2012).
55   See J. Caputo, *On Religion* (London: Routledge, 2001).
56   See J. Caputo, 'The Poetics of the Impossible and the Kingdom of God', in *The Blackwell Companion to Postmodern Theology* (ed. G. Ward; Oxford: Blackwell Publishing, 2001), pp 469–482.
57   See Anna Thompson (2010) 'Eden Fitton Hill: Demonstrating and Becoming in Oldham', in *Crossover City* (ed. A. Davey; London: Mowbray).
58   Micah 6:8, NIV.

Chapter 5

1   The mood of the urban church, and the challenges they sought to engage with through this time are well documented by the Urban Theology Unit in Sheffield. See for example John Vincent, *Into the City* (London: Epworth Press, 1982) http://www.utusheffield.org.uk/ (accessed 9 October 2012).
2   For a vivid account of the transformation of London, see Doreen Massey, *World City* (Cambridge: Polity Press, 2007).
3   For an account of growing social engagement amongst Pentecostals, see Donald E. Miller and Tetsunao Yamomori, *Global Pentecostalism: The New Face of Christian Social Engagement* (Berkeley and LA, CA: University of California Press, 2007).

4 Oasis and Faithworks are two related organizations that grew out of this period and represent well the kind of work that churches were engaging in. See http://www.oasisuk.org/ and http://www.faithworks.info/ (accessed 9 October 2012).

5 Virtue and virtue-ethics have a rich theological heritage. See for example Stanley Hauerwas, *The Peaceable Kingdom: A Primer in Christian Ethics* (London: SCM Press, 1984); John Howard Yoder, *The Politics of Jesus* (Grand Rapids, MI/Carlisle UK: Eerdmans and Paternoster, 1972, 1994); James Wm. McClendon Jr, *Ethics: Systematic Theology* vol.1 (Nashville, TN: Abingdon Press, 2002); Glen H. Stassen and David P. Gushee, *Kingdom Ethics: Following Jesus in Contemporary Context* (Downers Grove, IL: IVP, 2003); Tom Wright, *Virtue Reborn* (London: SPCK, 2010).

6 UE is an urban mission agency that 'recruits, equips, deploys and networks self-financing teams pioneering creative and relevant expressions of the Christian church in under-churched areas of the inner city. Urban Expression is committed to incarnational ministry on the margins and amongst the poor, and encourages teams to move into urban neighbourhoods to work with others to pioneer exciting, grassroots, transformative ways of being church which seek God's kingdom of justice and peace' from: http://www.urbanexpression.org.uk/ (accessed 9 October 2012).

7 For introductions to this methodology see: Laurie Green, *Let's Do Theology: Resources for Contextual Theology* (London/New York: Mowbray, 2009); Gerald O. West, ed., *Reading Other-wise: Socially Engaged Biblical Scholars Reading with Their Local Communities* (Atlanta, GA: Society of Biblical Literature, 2007); Richard R. Osmer, *Practical Theology: An Introduction* (Grand Rapids, MI/Cambridge: Eerdmans, 2008).

8 For more information on the development of the Claypits see http://sites.google.com/site/possilgreenspace/ (accessed 9 October 2012).

9 The community was named after a young man who lived locally and was well known in the area. He eventually committed suicide in a secure psychiatric unit.

10 For an insightful and challenging discussion about the theology and spirituality of communities where those with physical and mental disability live as equals with able-bodied people, see Jean Vanier and Stanley Hauerwas, *Living Gently in a Violent World* (Downers Grove, IL: IVP, 2008).

Chapter 6

[1] M. Smith, 'Youth Work: An Introduction', in *The Encyclopaedia of Informal Education* (2002), p. 6 www.infed.org/youthwork/b-yw.htm (accessed 10 October 2012).

[2] Smith, 'Youth Work: An Introduction', p.6.

[3] J. Beaumont and P. Cloke, eds., *Faith-based Organisations and Exclusion in European Cities* (Bristol: Policy Press, 2012).

[4] R. Putnam, *Bowling Alone: The Collapse and Revival of American Community* (New York: Simon & Schuster, 2000).

[5] A. Dinham, *Faith, Public Policy and Civil Society: Policies, Problems and Concepts in Faith-Based Public Action* (Basingstoke: Palgrave-Macmillan, 2009); A. Dinham, R. Furbey and V. Lowndes, eds., *Faith In The Public Realm: Controversies, Policies and Practices* (Bristol: Policy Press, 2009).

[6] T. Macauley, 'Faith Based Youth Work in Northern Ireland', Youthnet, 2006.

[7] J. Vaughton, 'Report on Youth and Schools Work Delivered By the Christian Faith Community in Bath', Bath Youth For Christ (2010), www.bathyfc.co.uk (accessed 2 September 2012).

[8] P. Cloke, 'Theo-ethics and Faith Praxis in the Postsecular City', in *Exploring the Postsecular: The Religious, the Political and the Urban* (eds. A. Molendijk, J. Beaumont and C. Jedan; Amsterdam: Brill, 2010), pp. 223–43.

[9] See for example, R. Allahyari, *Visions of Charity: Volunteer Workers and Moral Community* (Berkeley and LA, CA: University of California Press, 2000).

[10] See P. Cloke, S. Thomas and A. Williams, 'Radical Faith Praxis', in *Faith-based Organisations and Exclusion in European Cities* (eds. J. Beaumont and P. Cloke; Bristol: Policy Press, 2012).

[11] On psychogeography, see M. Coverley, *Psychogeography* (Harpenden: Pocket Essentials, 2006). On psychogeographical walking, see: I. Sinclair, *Lights Out for the Territory* (London: Granta, 1996); J. Davies, *Walking the M62*, (2007) http://www.johndavies.org (accessed 10 October 2009).

[12] P. Cloke and J. Beaumont, 'Geographies of Postsecular Rapprochement in the City', in Progress in *Human Geography*, 37 (2012), pp. 27–51.

[13] See for example, J. Peck and A. Tickell, 'Neoliberalising Space', *Antipode* 34 (2002), pp. 380–404; J. Hackworth, 'Faith, Welfare and the

City: The Mobilization of Religious Organizations for Religious Ends, *Urban Geography* 31 (2010), pp. 750–73.

14 These issues are discussed in the context of homelessness and employment training respectively, in P. Cloke, J. May and S. Johnsen, *Swept-Up Lives?: Re-envisioning the Homeless City* (Chichester: Wiley-Blackwell, 2010); and A. Williams, P. Cloke and S. Thomas, 'Co-constituting Neoliberalism: Co-option, Resistance and Faith-based Organisations in the UK', *Environment and Planning A* (2012) 44: pp. 1479– 1501.

15 False Economy (ND), 'Youth services are being savaged by government cuts', from http://falseeconomy.org.uk/blog/youth-services-in-crisis (accessed 10 October 2012).

16 Greg Clark, minister for Decentralisation, quoted in: N. Pimlott, *Faith-based Youth Work and the Big Society* (Newark: Staffordshire University/Oasis College/Christian Youth Mission, 2011), p. 10.

17 Clark, in *Faith-based Youth Work and the Big Society*, p. 24.

18 See for example, Common Wealth, 'Common Wealth: Christians for Economic and Social Justice' (2010) http://www.commonwealthnetwork2010.blogspot.com (accessed 9 October 2012).

19 See for example, C. Baker, *The Hybrid Church in the City: Third Space Thinking* (Aldershot: Ashgate, 2007).

20 In 2012 (after the completion of this chapter) it was announced that Teenbridge would cease operations. The financial perils described in the chapter led to the decision by the trustees that Teenbridge could not continue to be funded at a sustainable level.

Chapter 7

1 '21st Century Evangelicals', an Evangelical Alliance report. See http://www.eauk.org/church/resources/snapshot/, p. 11 (accessed 11 October 2012).

2 Jesus speaks of serving him when we serve others in Matthew 25:31–46: 'I was hungry and you gave me something to eat' etc.

Chapter 8

[1] Authors' translation. See the report from the conference: *'De Arme Kant van Nederland: feiten, meningen en het vervolg'* ('The Poor Side of The Netherlands: Facts, Opinions and Consequences'), Aalsmeer, Amsterdam: Uitgeverij Luiten (1988): p. 13.

[2] See www.armekant-eva.nl (accessed 12 October 2012). There are various studies that address the same movement: see R. Vlek, *'Inactieven in Actie: belangenstrijd en belangenbehartiging van uitkeringsgerechtigden in de Nederlandse politiek'* 1974–1994 ('Inactives in Action: Struggle and Advocacy of Welfare Beneficiaries in Dutch Politics 1974–1994'), Gronigen, The Netherlands: Wolters-Noordhoff, 1997); J.R. Beaumont, 'Socially Inclusive Governance? A Comparison of Local Antipoverty Strategies in the UK and The Netherlands', unpublished PhD thesis, Department of Geography, Durham University, UK (1999); J. Beaumont and H. Noordegraaf, 'Aid Under Protest: Churches Against Poverty in The Netherlands', Dialogue Series 11: *Faith-based Organisations and Poverty in the City*, Antwerp: UCSIA (2007): pp. 41–59.

[3] For more details on the restructuring of welfare in this period see N. Gilbert, *Transformation of the Welfare State: The Silent Surrender of Public Responsibility* (Oxford: Oxford University Press, 2004); C. Pierson, *Beyond the Welfare State? The New Political Economy of Welfare*, third edition (Cambridge: Polity Press, 2006); and P. De Beer and F. Koster, *Voor Elkaar of uit Elkaar? individualisering, globalisering en solidariteit (For Each Other or Broken Up? Individualisation, Globalization and Solidarity)* (Amsterdam: Amsterdam University Press, 2007).

[4] By 'new poverty' we mean poverty in the context of a wealthy country that is characterized primarily by social exclusion: the lack of the means to participate of full value in the 'normal' life of society in all dimensions, such as in social, cultural, education, housing, mobility, healthcare and so on. This type of poverty should be distinguished from poverty in the absolute sense, according to which people cannot fulfil basic needs. The term therefore holds some similarities with a relative conception of poverty.

[5] The narrative of 'workfare', the punitive system of labour market activation and responsibility, is commonplace for those familiar with the politics of welfare in the UK and North America. See P. Peck, *Workfare States* (New York: The Guiford Press, 2001). See also J.R. Beaumont,

'Workfare, Associationism and the "underclass" in the United States: Contrasting Faith-based Action on Urban Poverty in a Liberal Welfare Regime', in *European Churches Confronting Poverty: Social Action Against Social Exclusion* (eds. H. Noordegraaf and R. Volz; Bochum: SWI Verlag, 2004), pp. 249–78; A. Williams, 'Moralizing the Poor? Faith-based Organisations, Big Society and Contemporary Workfare Policy', in *Faith-based Organisations and Exclusion in European Cities* (eds. J. Beaumont and P. Cloke; Bristol: The Policy Press, 2012).

6 For a history of poverty and welfare in The Netherlands see L.F. Van Loo, *Arm in Nederland* 1815–1990 (*Poor in The Netherlands*) (Boom: Meppel, 1992); see also J.M. Roebroek and M. Hertogh, *De Beschavende Invloed des Tijds: twee eeuwen sociale politiek, verzorgingsstaat en sociale zekerheid in Nederland* (The Civilizing Influence of Time: Two Centuries of Social Policy, Welfare and Social Security in the Netherlands) ('s-Gravenhage: VUGA Uitgeverij, 1998).

7 There are many different churches in The Netherlands: the Roman Catholic Church and many Protestant churches of which the *Nederlandse Hervormde Kerk* (Dutch Reformed Church) was the largest one and the *Gereformeerde Kerken* (Reformed Churches) the second largest. These churches, along with the Evangelical Lutheran Church in the Netherlands, merged in 2004 to form a new church: the Protestant Church in The Netherlands. The Roman Catholic Church, Protestant churches already mentioned and also some other small churches are working together in the Council of Churches.

8 See www.stichtingclip.nl/ (accessed 12 October 2012). Foundation Client Perspective (CliP) was established in 2005 as the main body promoting participation from a client perspective in The Netherlands. CliP grew out of the Sjakuus Foundation, an association of national organizations representing welfare beneficiaries that was an active player in the anti-poverty movement during the 1980s. CliP operates within a multi-scale network of organizations today, housing the Secretariat of Het landelijk overleg c;ientenraden Sociale Zekereid (LocSZ) (National Consultation of Provincial Networks of Local Client Councils); it also carries out the secretariat for De Sociale Alliantie (Social Alliance). which is the national network for combating poverty and social exclusion.

9 The Council of Churches members are the main Protestant churches and the Roman Catholic Church. See A. Houtepen, H. Noordegraaf and M. Bosman-Huizinga, *Waakvlam van de Geest: 40 jaar Raad van*

Kerken in Nederland (Pilot of the Spirit: 40 years Council of Churches in The Netherlands) (Zoetermeer: Uitgeverij Meinema, 2008).

[10] See Beaumont, op cit. DISK is a national ecumenical (Catholic and Protestant) organization providing pastoral services for industrial workers, with branches in cities such as Rotterdam. In Rotterdam, where the Catholic Church predominates, DISK was especially active in the old, declining industries on the southern bank of the Maas River around Feijenoord. Working closely with the Christian trade union (CNV), largely Protestant, DISK developed a critical and radical social perspective on poverty, based on rights to jobs and welfare in industrial society. As with trade unionism, its importance has declined in parallel with the rise of post-industrialism in the wider society.

[11] See J. Wills, 'The Left, its Crisis and Rehabilitation', *Antipode*, 38: (2006): pp. 907–15; L. Jamoul and J. Wills, 'Faith in Politics', *Urban Studies*, 45 (10): (2008): pp. 2035–56; A. Herman, J. Beaumont, P. Cloke and A. Walliser, 'Spaces of Engagement in Postsecular Cities', in *Faith-based Organisations and Exclusion in European Cities* (eds. J. Beaumont and P. Cloke; Bristol: The Policy Press, 2012).

[12] See A.L. Molendijk, J. Beaumont and C. Jedan, eds., *Exploring the Postsecular: The Religious, the Political and the Urban* (Amsterdam: Brill, 2010); J. Beaumont and C. Baker, eds., *Postsecular Cities: Space, Theory and Practice* (London: Continuum, 2011); J. Beaumont and P. Cloke, eds., *Faith-based Organisations and Exclusion in European Cities* (Bristol: The Policy Press, 2012); P. Cloke and J. Beaumont, 'Geographies of Postsecular Rapprochement in the City', *Progress in Human Geography*, 37 (2012), pp. 27–51.

[13] See M. Augé, *A Sense for the Other* (trans. A. Jacobs; Stanford, CA: Stanford University Press, 1998); M.J. Sandel, *Justice: A Reader* (New York, NY: Oxford University Press, 2007); M.J. Sandel, *Justice: What's the Right Thing to Do?*, reprint edition (New York, NY: Farrar, Straus and Giroux, 2010).

[14] See A. Baart, *Een Theorie van de Presentie* (A Theory of Presence) (Utrecht: Boom Lemma Uitgevers, 2001).

[15] It is interesting that the European Union acknowledges that policies against poverty and social exclusion require three pillars: a guaranteed minimum income, paid employment for those who can work, and alternative activities for those unable to do so, including access to public services. This broad scope differs from the policies in member countries, including The Netherlands; in the latter the focus is much more on activation policies.

[16] See S. Chant, ed., *The International Handbook of Gender and Poverty: Concepts, Research, Policy* (Cheltenham: Edward Elgar Publishing, 2011; see also J. Brenner, 'Radical versus liberal approaches to the feminisation of poverty and comparable worth', *Gender & Society*, 1(4) (1987): pp. 447–65; S.M. Bianchi, 'Feminisation and Juvenilisation of Poverty: Trends, Relative Risks, Causes and Consequences', *Annual Reviews of Sociology*, 25 (1999): pp. 307–33; A. Sen, *Development as Freedom* (Oxford: Oxford University Press, 1999); A. Sen, 'Many Faces of Gender Inequality', *Frontline*, 18 (22): 2001, see: www.flonnet.com/fl1822/18220040.htm (accessed 6 September 2012); M. Buvinić, 'Women in Poverty: A New Global Underclass', *Foreign Policy*, 108 (1997): pp. 38–53.

[17] This situation has since changed: in 2008, 59 per cent of women aged 15 to 64 years were working (men 76 per cent). Most women are working part-time (20 to 30 hours a week).

[18] Werkgroep Arme Kant van Nederland/EVA, *Om Sociale Gerechtigheid* ('For Social Justice'), Jaarverslag 2001/2002 (Utrecht: Werkgroep de Arme Kant van Nederland/ EVA), p. 43.

[19] See http://www.socialealliantie.nl (accessed 4 September 2012). See also W.J. Nicholls and J.R. Beaumont, 'The Urbanisation of Justice Movements? Possibilities and Constraints for the City as a Space for Contentious Struggle', *Space & Polity*, 8 (2) (2004): pp. 119–36; J. Beaumont and H. Noordegraaf, 'Aid Under Protest: Churches Against Poverty in The Netherlands', Dialogue Series 11: *Faith-based Organisations and Poverty in the City* (Antwerp: UCSIA, 2007), pp.41–59.

[20] See Sociale Alliantie, *'Nederland Armoedevrij! met solidariteit & eigen kracht'* ('The Netherlands Free from Poverty! in solidarity and own strength') (2010): p. 7, see: http://www.socialealliantie.nl/Armoedevrij%5BWEB-A4%20 kleur%5D.pdf (accessed 5 September 2012).

[21] The notion of shadow state corporatism is more fully articulated in Nicholls and Beaumont, op cit, 'The Urbanisation of Justice Movements? Possibilities and Constraints for the City as a Space for Contentious Struggle', *Space & Polity*, 8 (2) (2004): pp. 119–36.

[22] Christians Against Poverty (CAP) in the UK use similar devices, see www.capuk.org/home/index.php (access 5 September 2012). Gaming can also be used as a means of getting the message across, e.g. within Fair Trade, see J. Pykett, P. Cloke, C. Barnett, N. Clarke and A. Malpass, 'Learning to be Global Citizens: the Rationalities of Fair-trade Education',

Environment and Planning D: Society and Space, 28 (3) (2010): pp. 487–508; see also P. Toynbee, *Hard Work: Life on Low Pay in Britain*, first edition (London: Bloomsbury Publishing PLC, 2003), where the author describes the realities of everyday life on the Clapham Park estate in Lambeth, south London where she lived while writing the book.

23 See K. Driessens and T. van Regenmortel, *Bind-Kracht in Armoede: leefwereld en hulpverlening* (Binding Strength in Poverty: Lifeworld and Assistance), (LannooCampus: Leuven, 2006); for the general literature on empowerment, see P. Friere, *Pedagogy of the Oppressed* (trans. M.B. Ramos; New York: Seabury Press, 1970); P. Florin and A. Wandersman, 'An introduction to Citizen Participation, Voluntary Organisations, and Community Development: Insights for Empowerment Through Research', *American Journal of Community Psychology*, 18 (1) (1990): pp. 41–54; I.M. Young, *Justice and the Politics of Difference* (Princeton, NJ: Princeton University Press, 1990); S. Kreisberg, 'Transforming Power: Domination, Empowerment, and Education' (Albany, NY: State University of New York Press, 1992); S. Lukes, *Power: A Radical View* (London: Macmillan Press Ltd., 1994); P. Wilson, 'Empowerment: Community Economic Development from the Inside Out', *Urban Studies*, 33 (4–5) (1996): pp. 617–30.

24 'Dress for Success' is a voluntary organization that helps jobseekers find clothing appropriate to the employment for which they apply. The current twelve 'stores' clothes are donated by businesses and individuals; all services, clothing and opinions on what to wear are free of charge. See www.dressforsuccess.nl (accessed 5 September 2012).

25 See www.armekant-eva.nl/projecten/vakantiegids.html (accessed 5 September 2012).

26 This insight came from research among local churches, see T. Nederland, P. De Bie and H. Noordegraaf, *De Kerk als Vangnet? een verslag van een onderzoek naar individuele financiële hulp door kerken* ('The Church as Safety Net? A Report of a Study on Individual Financial Assistance through Churches) (ed. E. Van der Panne; Utrecht: Arme Kant van Nederland-EVA & Kerk in Actie, 2002).

27 See the most recent publication on this issue: P. Bie et al. (eds), *Armoede en Rechtdoen: helpen onder protest in de praktijk* (Poverty and Doing Justice: Help Under Protest in Practice) (Utrecht: Arme Kant van Nederland & Kerk in Actie, 2010), see http://www.armekant-eva.nl/projecten/helpenonderprotest-2.html (accessed 4 September 2012). The report distinguishes between

four types of help under protest within social work of ministries: (1) strengthening people experiencing poverty in obtaining their rights; (2) stimulating church and wider societal awareness and recognition of poverty; (3) identifying and raising awareness of bottlenecks in local and regional public agencies, and (4) addressing national policy on poverty issues, as well as income policies.

[28] See M. Baltussen and J. van Workum, *De Rijke Kant van Nederland: armoede staat zelden op zichzelf* (The Rich Side of The Netherlands: Poverty is Rare in Itself), with a contribution by W. Albeda (Amsterdam: Van Gennp, 1998); see also H. Crijns et al. (ed), *Komen Rijken in de Hemel? over de verleiding van het geld* (Are the Rich Going to Heaven? On the Distraction of Money) (Gorinchem, Narratio: 2000).

[29] Werkgroep De Arme Kant van Nederland/EVA, '*Meer dan Voedsel Alleen: kerken, armoede en voedselbanken*' ('More Than Just Food: Churches, Poverty and Foodbanks'), Utrecht: Conference, 21 April, 2006, see http://www.armekant-eva.nl/projecten/meerdanvoedse-lalleen-conferentie.html (accessed 4 September 2012).

[30] This tension between aid and protest echoes a similar stance over debt and related problems at the *Church Action on Poverty* (CAP) in the UK, see http://niallcooper.wordpress.com/2012/08/31/picking-up-the-pieces-or-going-upstream-is-the-church-more-than-just-the-fourth-emergency-service/ (accessed 6 September 2012).

[31] See J. Raf, J. de Jong, R. van Nistelrooij, '*Armoede de Baas!? het perspectief van voedselbanken*' ('Poverty Rules!? The Perspective of Foodbanks'), Utrecht: Sociale Alliantie en Stichting CliëntenPerspectief (CliP) (2008). See http://www.armekant-eva.nl/projecten/armoedebaas.html (accessed 4 September 2012).

[32] See Kerk in Actie, '*Armoede in Nederland: onderzoek naar financiële hulpverlening door diaconieën van de Protestantse Kerk in Nederland*' ('Poverty in The Netherlands: Research into Financial Aid by Diaconal Institutions of the Protestant Church in the Netherlands'), Utrecht: Kerk in Actie (2005); Kerk in Actie, '*Armoede in Nederland: onderzoek naar financiële hulpverlening door diaconieën van de Protestantse Kerk in Nederland*' ('Poverty in The Netherlands: Research into Financial Aid by Diaconal Institutions of the Protestant Church in the Netherlands), Utrecht: Kerk in Actie (2006); Kerk in Actie, 'Armoede in Nederland: onderzoek naar hulpverlening door diaconieën, parochiële caritas instellingen en andere kerkelijke organisaties in Nederland' ('Poverty in The Netherlands: Research into Relief by Ministries, Local Charitable Institutions

and Other Religious Organizations in the Netherlands'), Utrecht: Kerk in Actie (2008); Kerk in Actie, 'Armoede in Nederland: onderzoek naar hulpverlening door diaconieën, parochiële caritas instellingen en andere kerkelijke organisaties in Nederland' ('Poverty in The Netherlands: Research into Relief by Ministries, Local Charitable Institutions and Other Religious Organizations in the Netherlands'), Utrecht: Kerk in Actie (2010): see www.kerkinactie.nl/site/uploadedDocs/PKNArmoedeinNederland2010herzien.pdf (accessed 4 September 2012).

33 Up until that point, Orthodox Protestant churches and evangelical churches did not cooperate with mainstream churches such as the Protestant Church in the Netherlands and the Roman Catholic Church. Theologically speaking, there are large differences, but there has been a growing interest in Christian social practice in the former churches, which has made working together on questions of poverty possible.

34 Kerk in Actie, op cit.; see also H. Noordegraaf, 'Diaconaat en verzorgingsstaat', in *Diaconie in Beweging: handboek diaconiewetenschap* (Ministry in Movement: Handbook of Ministry Studies) (eds. H. Crijns et al.; Kampen: Kok, 2011), pp. 271–93.

35 See H. Noordegraaf, *Migrantenkerken en armoede in Nederland: een verkennend onderzoek* (Migrant Churches and Poverty in The Netherlands: An Exploratory Study), (Utrecht: Kerk in Actie, 2010). See www.kerkinactie.nl/site/uploadedDocs/summarymigrantchurches.pdf (accessed 4 September 2012); see also N. Noordegraaf, (2012) 'Migrant Churches Confronting Poverty in the Netherlands', *Diaconia: Journal for the Study of Christian Social Practice*, 3 (1) (2012): pp. 66–87.

36 See P. Osendarp, J. Bos and H. Crijns, (First Aid with Debts) '*Eerste Hulp bij Schulden*' (Utrecht: Arme Kant van Nederland-EVA & Kerk in Actie, 2009). See http://www.armekant-eva.nl/projecten/ehbs-boek.html"www.armekant-eva.nl/projecten/ehbs-boek.html (accessed 4 September 2012).

Chapter 9

1 Jason Hackworth provides a critical account of the ideological and theological convergence between Protestant evangelical groups and neoliberal ideologues in the US context. He illustrates how faith-based welfare is seen to legitimatize neo-conservative notions of self-responsibility and Welfare State retrenchment. See J. Hackworth, *Faith-Based: Religious*

Neoliberalism and the Politics of Welfare (Athens, GA: University of Georgia Press, 2012). Also see J. Goode, 'Faith-based Organisations in Philadelphia: Neoliberal Ideology and the Decline of Political Activism', *Urban Anthropology* 35 (2–3) (2006): pp. 203–36.

2 For further work on discerning the powers, as they operate in the self, or in distant/proximate relationships with others, see C. Myers, *Binding the Strong Man: A Political Reading of Mark's Story of Jesus* (New York, Orbis, 2008). Myers draws on Walter Wink's (1984; 1986; 1992) proposition that the heart of oppressive systems is spiritual as well as material, and that to challenge the outer, political manifestations of unjust powers and structures, one needs to discern and resist their spiritual interiorities in the self. W. Wink, *Naming The Powers: Language of Power in the New Testament* (Fortress Press: Minneapolis, MA, 1984); W. Wink (1986) *Unmasking The Powers: The Invisible Powers That Determine Human Existence* (Fortress Press: Minneapolis, MA, 1986); W. Wink, *Engaging The Powers: Discernment and Resistance in a World of Domination* (Minneapolis, MA: Fortress Press, 1992).

3 P. Cloke and J. Beaumont, 'Geographies of Postsecular Rapprochement in the City', *Progress in Human Geography*, 37 (2012). pp. 27–51.

4 In Matthew 25, Jesus outlines the church's priority for caring for the poorest in society by suggesting there is translatability between loving your neighbour and loving God: 'I tell you the truth, whatever you did for one of the least of these brothers of mine, you did for me' (Matt. 25:40, NIV).

5 See P. Cloke, 'Exploring Boundaries of Professional/Personnel/Personal Practice and Action: Being and Becoming in Khayelitsha Township, Cape Town', in *Radical Theory/Critical Praxis: Making a Difference Beyond the Academy* (eds. D. Fuller and R. Kitchin; Gainesville, GA: Praxis Press, 2004), pp. 92–102.

6 On the differences regarding a sense for the other and a sense of the other, see: P. Cloke, 'Deliver us from Evil? Prospects for Living Ethically and Acting Politically in Human Geography', *Progress in Human Geography* 26 (5) (2002): pp. 587–604; and M. Augé, *A Sense for the Other* (trans. A. Jacobs; Stanford, CA: Stanford University Press, 1998).

7 M. Davelaar (1997). 'Grenspost KSA', in *50 jaar kerkelijk sociale arbeid in Rotterdam* (ed. H. Visser, Rotterdam: KSA), pp. 97–107.

8 Diaconal bodies are coordinating committees responsible for diaconal and social work within and outside its own church; its members are elected by the members of the local church.

⁹ On pillarization and de-pillarization in the Dutch context and its impact on FBOs, see J. Beaumont and C. Dias, 'Faith-based Organisations and Urban Social Justice in the Netherlands', *Tijdschrift voor economische en sociale geografie*, 99 (4) (2008): pp. 382–392.

¹⁰ Since arriving in the Netherlands in the 1560s, the theological teachings of John Calvin irreducibly shaped religious culture and informed the political elite. Neo-Calvinist Kuyper's influential idea of sphere sovereignty is accredited as initiating pillarization or denominational segregation in Dutch society; see Beaumont and Dias op cit. p. 367.

¹¹ KSA *Annual Report* 1964: 50 (Rotterdam: KSA).

¹² M. Davelaar, N. De Witte, H. Swinnen, and J.R. Beaumont (2009). 'FBOs and Social Exclusion in the Netherlands', in *Faith-based Organisations and Social Exclusion in European Cities, National context reports* (eds. D. Dierckx, J. Vranken and W. Kerstens; Leuven/Den Haag: Acco), p. 202.

¹³ KSA *Annual Report 1979–1980* (Rotterdam: KSA), pp. 3–4.

¹⁴ KSA *Annual Report 1979–1980*, op cit.

¹⁵ KSA *Annual Report 1979–1980*, p. 4.

¹⁶ On incarnational ministry in deprived communities, see Mike Pears' and Sam Thomas' chapters in this volume: M. Pears, *Urban Expression*; S. Thomas, *Re-engaging with the margins*. Also see A. Williams, *Practical Theology and Christian Responses to Drug Addiction* (this volume) on the different ways the idea of incarnational presence can be thought about in drug ministries.

¹⁷ KSA *Annual Report 1980–1981* (Rotterdam: KSA), p. 1.

¹⁸ KSA *Annual Report 1981–1982* (Rotterdam: KSA).

¹⁹ For further information on the details of the Pauluskerk, see J.R. Beaumont, 'Faith Action on Urban Social Issues', *Urban Studies*, 45 (10) (2008): pp. 2019–34; and see also M. Davelaar, op cit.; and M. Davelaar, 'Pauluskerk in *de problemen: Grenzen van het particulier initiatief'* *Tijdschrift Voor De Sociale Sector TSS*, 59(4), (2005): pp. 14–19.

²⁰ Guest worker programmes in the sixties and seventies brought migrants, mostly from southern Europe, Turkey and Morocco to fill specific work needs.

²¹ For a detailed discussion of theo-ethics, see P. Cloke, 'Theo-ethics and Radical Faith-based Praxis in the Postsecular City', in *Exploring the Postsecular: The Religious, the Political and the Urban* (eds. A. Molendijk, J. Beaumont and C. Jedan; Amsterdam: Brill, 2010), pp. 223–41.

²² Matthew 25:40, NIV.

[23] M. Castells, *The City and the Grassroots: A Cross-cultural Theory of Urban Social Movements* (London: Edward Arnold, 1983).

[24] Visser's reflections on Castells' theory of urban social movements are developed in detail in H. Visser, *Creativiteit, wegwijzing en dienstverlening: de rol van de kerk in de postindustriële stad* (Zoetermeer: Uitgeverij Boekencentrum, 2000).

[25] Beaumont, op cit.; Davelaar et al., op cit.

[26] Davelaar, op cit.

[27] H. Galesloot, and A. Harrewijn, *Burgerschap in de rafelrand: Over preventie van armoede en uitsluiting* (Amsterdam: Instituut voor Publiek and Politiek, 1999); and Davelaar et al., op cit; M. Davelaar, J, van den Toorn, N. De Witte, H. Swinnen, J.R. Beaumont and C. Kuiper (2011). *Faith-based organisations and Social Exclusion in the Netherlands*, http://www.verwey-jonker.nl/doc/participatie/3636_(s) Faith-based-Organisations-and-Social-Exclusion-in-European-Cities_ FINAL.pdf (accessed 1 September 2012).

[28] As above, op cit.

[29] As above, op cit.

[30] As above, op cit.

[31] Hans Visser openly says the most difficult aspect of his ministry was the lack of a Christian base within the supporters of the Pauluskerk, and the difficulty of working as a church with a majority of volunteers who are not Christian. For further information, see M. Rowles and B. Schell (2001) *A Human in Action: The Reverend Hans Visser of the Pauluskerk in Rotterdam* (2001), http://www.humanityinaction.org/knowledgebase/12-a-human-in-action-the-reverend-hans-visser-of-the-pauluskerk-in-rotterdam (accessed 1 September 2012).

[32] Between 1995 and 2007, the municipality was paying for part of the personnel in the church (security, nurses), as part of a wider harm reduction strategy aimed at the public health of drug users and local residents.

[33] Davelaar et al., op cit. p. 38.

[34] Interview with Hans Visser, 24 February 2005.

[35] Davelaar et al., op cit., p. 39.

[36] M. Davelaar and W. Kerstens, 'A Shelter from the Storm: Faith-based Organisations and Providing Relief for the Homeless', in *Faith-based Organisations and Exclusion in European Cities* (eds. J. Beaumont and P. Cloke; Bristol: The Policy Press, 2012), pp. 199–218. For further

241

research on the clearance and containment of marginal groups from prime city spaces in Rotterdam and elsewhere, see J. Uitermark, and J.W. Duyvendak, *Civilizing the City: Revanchist Urbanism in Rotterdam* (Amsterdam: Amsterdam School for Social Science Research, 2005); J. Uitermark, and J.W. Duyvendak, 'Civilizing the City: Populism and Revanchist Urbanism in Rotterdam', in *Urban Studies*, 45 (7) (2008): pp. 1485–1503.

37 Interview with Hanny de Kruijf, Society for Diaconal Social Work (KSA), 20 February 2009.

38 Davelaar et al., op cit., p. 217.

39 Davelaar et al., op cit.

40 For further work on the evolving service portfolios of FBOs that elude simple classification into neoliberal politics, see D. Conradson (2008) 'Expressions of Charity and Action towards Justice: Faith-based Welfare Provision in Urban New Zealand', in *Urban Studies* 45 (10) (2008): pp. 2117–41.

41 New Living Translation.

42 W. Brueggemann, *The Prophetic Imagination*, second edition (Minneapolis, MA: Fortress Press, 2001), Minneapolis MA.

43 Cloke, op cit.; Myers, op cit.

Chapter 10

1 Christina Bergqvist, *Equal Democracies? Gender and Politics in the Nordic Countries* (Oslo: Scandinavian University Press, 1999).

2 Lars-Erik Olsson, Marie Nordfeldt, Ola Larsson and Jeremy Kendall, 'Sweden:When Strong Sector Historical Roots Meet EU Policy Processes', in *Handbook on Third Sector Policy in Europe and Organised Civil Society* (ed. Jeremy Kendall; Cheltenham: Edward Elgar, 2009), pp. 159–83.

3 Ingemar Elander and Charlotte Fridolfsson, *Faith-based Organisations and Social Exclusion in Sweden* (Leuven/Den Haag: Acco, 2011).

4 Paul Cloke, Andrew Williams and Samuel Thomas, 'FBOs and Social Exclusion in the United Kingdom', in *Faith-based Organisations and Social Exclusion in European Cities. National Context Reports* (eds. Danielle Dierckx, Jan Vranken and Wendy Kerstens; Leuven/Den Haag: Acco, 2009), pp. 283–342.

5 Anette Kyhlström. Interview by Charlotte Fridolfsson, Hela Människan, Stockholm (The Whole Person/Healing the Person),

Endnotes

Stockholm, 20 March, 2009. Our translation. This note will not be repeated in the rest of the cases where we have translated interviews and citations from Swedish texts. Most of the interviews cited in the chapter were conducted by one of the authors, Charlotte Fridolfsson, during 2008–2010. For further information about this, see Elander and Fridolfsson, *Faith-based Organisations and Social Exclusion in Sweden*, appendix II.

6 Abdallah Salah (chairman of the Islamic Association in Stockholm; IFS). Interview by Charlotte Fridolfsson, Stockholm Mosque, 12 March 2009.

7 Eric Andersson. Interview by Charlotte Fridolfsson, Filadelfia, Stockholm, 5 May, 2010.

8 Andersson. Interview by Charlotte Fridolfsson.

9 Henrik Enarsson. Interview by Charlotte Fridolfsson, Göteborgs kyrkliga stadsmission, Göteborg, 18 March 2009.

10 Facts about the Church of Sweden
http://www.svenskakyrkan.se (accessed 16 October 2010).

11 Elisabeth Hjalmarsson. Interview by Charlotte Fridolfsson, Central Church Office, Uppsala 18 February 2009.

12 Sveriges kristna råd [Christian Council of Sweden] (2010) *Utsatthet – en brist på möjligheter. Diakonins månad 2010 lyfter fram fattigdom och social utestängning* (Vulnerability – Lack of Opportunities. The Month of Deacony 2010 Brings to the Fore Poverty and Social Exclusion)
http://www.skr.org/verksamheter/ekumenisk-diakonikyrka-samhalle/diakonins-manad/ (accessed 21 October 2012).

13 Sveriges kristna råd (2011) *Öppet brev från SKR:s styrelse till regeringen om de utförsäkrades situation* (Open letter from the Christian Council of Sweden governing board to the government regarding the situation of people who have been expelled from the insurance system), press release 11 March 2010
http://www.skr.org/nyheter/nodvandiga-andringar-i-sjukforsakringssystemet-vidare-arbete-lokalt-och-nationellt/
http://www.skr.org/nyheter/nodvandiga-andringar-i-sjukforsakringssystemet-vidare-arbete-lokalt-och-nationellt/ (accessed 21 October 2012).

14 Elander and Fridolfsson, *Faith-based Organisations and Social Exclusion in Sweden*, pp. 46–53.

15 See for example David Ley, 'The Immigrant Church as an Urban Service Hub', *Urban Studies* 45 (10) (2008): pp. 2057–74.

243

[16] Abdallah Salah, FACIT cross evaluation interview. The Islamic Association in Stockholm, Stockholm Mosque, 14 September, 2009.

[17] Abdallah Salah. Interview by Charlotte Fridolfsson, Stockholm Mosque, 12 March 2009.

[18] Mostafa Kharraki. Interview by Charlotte Fridolfsson. The United Islamic Congregations in Sweden, Stockholm, 29 January, 2009.

[19] Abdul Rashid, Mohamed. Interview by Charlotte Fridolfsson. *Islamiska förbundet i Göteborg* (The Islamic Association in Göteborg), 12 May 2009.

[20] Named after the Muslim scientist/philosopher based in Cordoba, Spain, during the twelfth century. The name is derived from the word 'Ibn' meaning son and 'Rushd' which means reason. The information on Ibn Rushd, including the quote, is taken from: http://www.ibnrushd.se/index.php?s=start (accessed 16 October 2012).

[21] The so-called Cartoon Crisis in Denmark started on 30 September 2005 when the newspaper *Jyllands Posten* published a blasphemous picture of Mohammed. As for the following debates and conflicts, intimately related to the culture and ideology of 'Danishness' (*danskhet*), in *Faith-based Organisations and Social Exclusion in Denmark* (Larissa Bachora, Ingemar Elander and Charlotte Fridolfsson; Leuven/Den Haag: Acco, 2011), pp. 8–9 and passim. See also Catarina Kinnvall and Paul Nesbitt-Larking, *The Political Psychology of Globalization* (Oxford: Oxford University Press, 2011), pp. 141–46.

[22] Abdallah Salah. Interview by Charlotte Fridolfsson, Stockholm Mosque, 12 March 2009.

[23] The empirical basis for the story briefly told here are articles and interviews published in the wake of the Easter Call process in spring 2005, in David Qviström, ed., *Välgrundad fruktan. Om asyl, amnesti och rätten till trygghet* (Well-motivated Fear. On Asylum, Amnesty and the Right to Security) (Örebro: Cordia, 2005).

[24] *Livskraft* (magazine published by the Social Mission), Bättre kunskap krävs för bra asylbeslut (Better knowledge needed for better decisions in asylum matters), no. 3, 2006.

[25] Following the homepage of the Easter Call 157,251 people, sixty-four secular organizations, the twenty-five member churches of the Christian Council of Sweden, and three observers signed the call that was delivered to the government on 16 May, 2005. *Påskuppropet* (The Easter Call), Christian Council of Sweden, 2005 http://www.skr.org/nyheter/157-251-skrev-under-paskuppropet/ (accessed 21 October 2012).

Endnotes

[26] Qviström, *Välgrundad fruktan*, p. 100. Jämtland and Värmland are two of twenty-four geographical provinces, or shires (landskap) in Sweden.

[27] Qviström, *Välgrundad fruktan*, p. 233. In March 2011, six years after the Easter Call, the Christian Council of Sweden launched another Easter Call, by sending an open letter to the government regarding the situation of people who have been expelled from the insurance system, raising demands for a quick revision of the rules in order to save individuals and households from 'economic and social destruction'. See above note 13.

[28] Kerstin Billinger. Interview by Charlotte Fridolfsson. Church of Sweden Parish, Skärholmen (Svenska kyrkan Skärholmens församling), 1 April, 2009.

[29] *Det förenar religionerna* ('That's what unites the religions'), *Nerikes Allehanda*, 23 September 2010.

[30] Marika Markovits. Interview by Charlotte Fridolfsson, Stockholm City Mission (Stockholms stadsmission), 15 April 2009.

[31] Västra Skrävlinge Församling, 2010. *Församlingsblad* No. 2 (Newsletter from the Västra Skrävlinge Parish, Malmö).

[32] Ann Lidgren. Interview. Church of Sweden, Malmö (Svenska kyrkan Möllevången-Sofielunds församling [Church of Sweden, Möllevången-Sofielund Parish]), 2 April 2009.

[33] *Örebro Kommuns interreligiösa/interkulturella råd* ('Örebro inter-religious/inter-culural committee'), Information sheet, 18 June 2009. Similar boards have been established or are on its way in Göteborg, Linköping, Malmö and other towns and cities.

[34] *ETC Örebro*, 2010, *Örebrokvinnor tar mer makt* (Örebro Women Seize More Power), 14 February.

[35] Leif Dahlin. Interview by Charlotte Fridolfsson, Church of Sweden, Göteborg. April 2009. Cf. Qviström, pp. 97–103.

[36] The blog message is no longer available at the Internet, but a written copy is kept by the authors.

[37] *Hon är årets idrottsledare* (She is the sports leader of the year), Nerikes Allehanda, 6 August 2010, p. 9.

[38] The story of the Romanian family was reported in a number of articles in the regional newspaper Nerikes Allehanda, some of them announced on the front page with striking photos and headlines such as 'Here's the beggars' hut', 'A dwelling of cardboard pieces', and 'Help from a church saves the beggars' (*Nerikes Allehanda* 11,14,15,19,22,26 November 2011).

Endnotes

39 *Nerikes Allehanda*, 14 November 2011.
40 For a detailed discussion of theo-ethics, see P. Cloke, 'Theo-ethics and Radical Faith-based Praxis in the Postsecular City', in *Exploring the Postsecular: The Religious, the Political and the Urban* (eds. A. Molendijk, J. Beaumont and C. Jedan; Amsterdam: Brill, 2010), pp. 223–41.
41 Ninna Edgardh, A Gendered Perspective on Welfare and Religion in Europe, in *Welfare and Religion in 21st Century Europe*, vol. 2: *Gendered, Religious and Social Change* (Anders Bäckström, Grace Davie, Ninna Edgardh and Per Pettersson; Ashgate, Farnham, Surrey: Ashgate, 2011), pp. 61–106.
42 There is a strong tendency in Sweden that big, international prof-it-making companies are taking over parts of social welfare (schools, social, elderly and healthcare), basically financed by tax money. Due to the combination of 'selling out' public welfare and conspicuous mismanagement, this has been strongly criticized by parties to the left of the liberal-conservative government coalition in Sweden. Ingemar Elander, Maarten Davelaar and Andrés Walliser, 'FBOs, Urban Governance and Welfare State Retrenchment', in *Faith-based Organizations and Welfare in European Cities* (eds. Paul Cloke and Justin Beaumont; Bristol: Policy Press, 2012).
43 Örjan Wallin. Interview by Charlotte Fridolfsson, Hela Människan, Stockholm (The Whole Person/Healing the Person), 20 March 2009.

Chapter 11

1 K.H. Boeßenecker, *Spitzenverbände der Freien Wohlfahrtspflege: Eine Einführung in Organisationsstrukturen und Handlungsfelder der deutschen Wohlfahrtsverbände* vol. 1 (Aufl. Weinheim, München: Juventa-Verl, 2005), p. 237.
2 K.H. Boeßenecker, *Spitzenverbände der Freien Wohlfahrtspflege; also see G. Hollweg and M. Franke, 50 Jahre Parität: Die Geschichte des Paritätischen Wohlfahrtsverbandes, Landesverband Berlin* (e.V. Frankfurt am Main: Paritätische Verlagsgesellschaft, 2000), p. 12.
3 R. Landwehr, 'Zur Geschichte der jüdischen Wohlfahrtspflege in Deutschland', in *Jüdisches Leben: Berliner Topografien* vol. 4 (eds. A. Ehmann, L. Heid, N. Kampe, R. Landwehr, W. Dreßen and A. Friedlander; Berlin: Verl. Ästhetik und Kommunikation, 1985), pp. 44–52.

4 *'Zentralwohlfahrtsstelle der Juden in Deutschland', Über uns – Geschichte* http://www.zwst.org/cms/documents/107/de_DE/ueber_ uns-geschichte.pdf (accessed 22 October 2012).

5 *'Zentralwohlfahrtsstelle der Juden in Deutschland'.*

6 For further information: Landwehr, op cit., p. 46; also see C. Sachße and F. Tennstedt, *Geschichte der Armenfürsorge in Deutschland* (Aufl. Stuttgart: Kohlhammer, 1980), p. 233.

7 As above.

8 Boeßenecker, op cit., p. 238.

9 Boeßenecker, op cit., p. 238.

10 Boeßenecker, op cit., pp. 239–40; Hollweg and Franke, op cit., p. 21; Landwehr, op cit., p. 51; also see H. Steppe, '... *den Kranken zum Troste und dem Judenthum zur Ehre ...' Zur Geschichte der jüdischen Krankenpflege in Deutschland* (Frankfurt am Main: Mabuse-Verl, 1997), p. 175.

11 B. Scheller, *'Zedeka im neuen Gewand. Neugründung und Neuorientierung der Zentralwohlfahrtsstelle der Juden in Deutschland nach 1945'*, in *Zedaka: Jüdische Sozialarbeit im Wandel der Zeit: 75 Jahre Zentralwohlfahrtsstelle der Juden in Deutschland 1917–1992* (eds. G. Heuberger and P. Spiegel; Frankfurt am Main: *Zentralwohlfahrtsstelle der Juden in Deutschland*, 1992), pp. 142–57; also see *'Zentralwohlfahrtsstelle der Juden in Deutschland', Selbstdarstellung* http://zwst.org/de/zwst-ueber-uns/selbstdarstellung/ (accessed 21 February 2011).

12 J. Friedrichs and J. Klöckner, 'Faith-based Organisations and Social Exclusion in Germany', in *Faith-based Organisations and Social Exclusion in European Cities: National Context Reports* (eds. D. Dierckx, J. Vranken and W. Kerstens; Leuven: Acco, 2009), pp. 69–135. Also see Scheller, op cit.; *Zentralwohlfahrtsstelle der Juden in Deutschland*, op cit.

13 P. Kirchner, *'Jüdische Wohlfahrtspflege in der DDR: 1945–1990'*, in *Zedaka: Jüdische Sozialarbeit im Wandel der Zeit. 75 Jahre Zentralwohlfahrtsstelle der Juden in Deutschland 1917–1992* (eds. G. Heuberger and P. Spiegel; Frankfurt am Main: *Zentralwohlfahrtsstelle der Juden in Deutschland*, 1992), pp. 158–61. Also see *Zentralwohlfahrtsstelle der Juden in Deutschland* (2010), *'Mitgliederstatistik der jüdischen Gemeinden und Landesverbände in Deutschland für das Jahr 2009 (Auszug)'*.

14 As above.

15 Bundesamt für Migration und Flüchtlinge, *Migrationsbericht 2009* (Nürnberg: Bundesamt für Migration und Flüchtlinge, 2011), p. 103.

16 Data from 2001, more recent data not available.

17 See above.

18 Boeßenecker, op cit., p. 250; '*Zentralwohlfahrtsstelle der Juden in Deutschland, Mitgliederstatistik der jüdischen Gemeinden und Landesverbände in Deutschland für das Jahr 2009 (Auszug)*'.

19 Zentralwohlfahrtsstelle der Juden in Deutschland, (2011a) '"*Zedaka*" – *Das Leitbild der Zentralwohlfahrtsstelle der Juden in Deutschland*' (ZWST) http://www.zwst.org/cms/documents/110/de_DE/Zedaka-Leitbild.pdf (accessed 4 August 2011).

20 Zentralwohlfahrtsstelle der Juden in Deutschland, (2011c) *Über uns – Geschichte*, and (2011b) *Selbstdarstellung* http://www.zwst.org/cms/documents/107/de_DE/ueber_uns-geschichte.pdf (accessed 22 October 2012).

21 J. Friedrichs and J. Klöckner, *Faith-based Organisations and Social Exclusion in Germany*, vol. 2 (Leuven: Acco, 2011).

22 Data in this table is taken from: Statistisches Bundesamt, *Bevölkerung und Erwerbstätigkeit*. Fachserie 1. Reihe 2. Wiesbaden; *Zentralwohlfahrtsstelle der Juden in Deutschland*, 2010) *Mitgliederstatistik der jüdischen Gemeinden und Landesverbände in Deutschland für das Jahr 2009* op cit.; *Bundesamt für Migration und Flüchtlinge* (2009) *Ausländerzahlen 2009*. Nürnberg: Bundesamt für Migration und Flüchtlinge; and Bundesamt für Migration und Flüchtlinge (2011) *Migrationsbericht 2009*, op cit.

23 Friedrichs and Klöckner, 'Faith-based Organisations and Social Exclusion in Germany', op cit.

24 D. Ley, The Immigrant Church as an Urban Service Hub, *Urban Studies*, 45: (2008): pp. 2057–74.

25 Friedrichs and Klöckner, 'Faith-based Organisations and Social Exclusion in Germany', op cit.

26 Friedrichs and Klöckner, 'Faith-based Organisations and Social Exclusion in Germany', op cit.

27 Interview with Dr Michael Bader, 7 October 2008.

28 *Ministerpräsidentenkonferenz, Beschluss zur Aufnahme jüdischer Emigrantinnen und Emigranten aus der ehemaligen UdSSR*, 1991.

29 Interview with Dr Bader.

30 As above.

31 As above.

32 As above.

33 As above.

34 As above.

[35] As above.

[36] *Jüdische Liberale Gemeinde Köln Gescher LaMassoret e.V.* (2006) Grundsätze   http://www.gescherlamassoret.de/grundsatz.html (accessed 4 August 2011); *Union progressiver Juden in Deutschland e.V.* (2011) 35 *Grundsätze* http://www.liberale-juden.de/uber-uns/35-grundsatze/ (accessed 4 August 2011).

[37] Interview with Dr Bader.

[38] *Jüdische Liberale Gemeinde Köln Gescher LaMassoret e.V. (2006) op cit.; Union progressiver Juden in Deutschland e.V.* (2011), op cit.

[39] *Bundesamt für Migration und Flüchtlinge* (2011), op cit., p. 101.

[40] Interview with Dr Bader.

[41] As above.

Hospitality and Community after Christendom

Andrew Francis

Andrew Francis re-examines Jesus' intentions, the wider biblical material, and congregational practices of sharing Communion as well as drawing on radical church history to
demonstrate that hospitality and community are essential to
the church's nature, well-being and mission.

'Reading this book is like enjoying a stimulating conversation over a meal with the author. Andrew's style bursts with
anecdotes from his life experience of meal-sharing and com-
munity-building. He knows what he is talking about. With
Jesus as host and exemplar, Christian community becomes
prophetic practice.' – **Eleanor Kreider, writer, musician and
Mennonite educator.** *Co-author, Worship and Mission
After Christendom*

978-1-84227-747-8